Giving legal advice

an adviser's handbook

Elaine Heslop has practised as a solicitor in a London law centre and a university law clinic. She has provided education and training for a wide audience including law students, lawyers, advisers in the not-for-profit sector and HR professionals. She is also published in employment law and practice. She is currently involved in the launch of a new employment law dispute resolution charity providing legal advice for employees.

Available as an ebook at www.lag.org.uk/ebooks

Giving legal advice

an adviser's handbook

SECOND EDITION

Elaine Heslop

 Legal Action Group
2014

This second edition published in Great Britain 2014
by LAG Education and Service Trust Limited
3rd floor, Universal House, 88–94 Wentworth Street, London E1 7SA
www.lag.org.uk

First edition 2007 (published as *The Adviser's Toolkit: giving legal advice*)

British Library Cataloguing in Publication Data
a CIP catalogue record for this book is available from the British Library.

Crown copyright material is produced with the permission of the
Controller of HMSO and the Queen's Printer for Scotland.

This book has been produced using Forest Stewardship
Council (FSC) certified paper. The wood used to produce
FSC certified products with a 'Mixed Sources' label comes
from FSC certified well-managed forests, controlled sources
and/or recycled material.

Print ISBN   978 1 908407 43 6
ebook ISBN   978 1 908407 44 3

Typeset by Regent Typesetting, London
Printed in Great Britain by Hobbs the Printers, Totton, Hampshire

Preface

When this book was first published in 2007 it sought to fill a gap for a variety of individuals giving advice in many different contexts by providing guidance on the core skills of giving legal advice. At that time there were various features of legal advice provision which complemented the aims of the book. The National Occupational Standards, skills standards in employment, had developed a suite of standards in relation to legal advice. Legal advice was being offered by practising lawyers both as part of their day to day work and as advisers providing a free advice service in their local communities. Other typical advisers were the paid advisers and trained volunteers working side by side in law centres and citizens advice bureaux, students under supervision in university law clinics, as well as volunteers and community workers in charities and community centres.

Whilst all of these activities are still taking place, in some respects the emphasis has shifted. Many community-based organisations have seen a reduction in funding and resources, and perhaps to partially compensate for this, there has been a growth in free (or 'pro bono') advice clinics in many parts of the country. Fewer would-be solicitors and barristers are progressing to the stage of vocational training, and numbers enrolling for the professional stage of their education are currently declining. The map of lawyers' professional education and training is under scrutiny by their professional standards bodies, with some universities taking initiatives to offer combined academic and professional training degrees. Fewer higher education institutes offer courses in social welfare law or the generic skills of legal advice work than when the first edition was written, with a shift in emphasis towards the more traditional areas of law and practice, including qualification courses for legal executives and paralegals. The growth of paralegals in the legal services field perhaps reflects the high fees to be paid for legal professional education in addition to those incurred at university, or the competition for training contracts or pupillage. University law clinics are also increasing in number, posing difficult questions about their role, whether it should be as legal advice centres, centres of academic excellence, or of employability or a combination of all three.

In looking at the developing picture of who is giving legal advice the recent substantial reduction of legal aid must be taken into account. Many advice resources have been affected by this and are no longer able to provide the comprehensive legal advice service they believe their clients are entitled to. Innovative ways are being explored to meet that challenge but the gap left by the loss of legal aid with the consequent inability of many to access legal services is unlikely to be filled in the foreseeable future, with many individuals now having to navigate their way around the legal system unaided in their attempts to achieve a just outcome to their legal problem.

Readers may be encouraged by the recent publication of The Low Commission Report[1] which looks at the impact of reductions in government funding for legal advice services, in addition to addressing the more fundamental question of how money can be saved and advice provision managed and resourced in ways other than 'death by a thousand cuts'. Encouraging case studies are supplied highlighting cost-effective and innovative advice services. A project run by Age UK in Kensington and Chelsea[2] which has brought health carers and advisers together in order to save money and increase health care and advice in their local community typifies these excellent initiatives.

This second edition aims to provide support and guidance to this array of advisers who continue to engage in the vital function of advice provision in order to give as many individuals as possible access to justice. I am also conscious of the group of individuals usually referred to as litigants in person who need as much help and guidance as possible if they are to have the confidence to self-manage their claims or cases in the legal system,and in this edition there are two additional chapters designed specifically for this audience.

By way of outline, I have endeavoured to follow, as before, a pattern of the typical stages in the advice giving process, offering pointers and suggestions along the way as to best practice and effective advice giving. As before there is also at the start an outline of some typical community advice organisations, outlines of some of the training and education resources available for various skills levels of

---

1   Report of The Low Commission on the future of advice and legal support: Tackling the advice deficit – a strategy for access to advice and legal support on social welfare law in England and Wales, Legal Action Group, January 2014.

2   Low Commission Report, chapter 5.

adviser, and throughout, reference to some of the current National Occupational Standards in Legal Advice to underpin the guidance offered.

The content of this edition has been considerably revised to provide an up to date and relevant approach to giving legal advice. Much of it is based on my own experience in law centres and a university law clinic as a solicitor practitioner, as well as being underpinned by solicitors' professional conduct guidance. I have focussed my message largely on areas of social welfare law, including small claims in the civil courts. Where the law is referred to it is done by way of illustrative examples; any errors or omissions in that respect are entirely my own. I have however been able to obtain the kind permission of The Bar Council to reproduce from their handbook for the self-represented litigant, *A Guide to Representing Yourself in Court*, an outline of the law and procedure for some of the key areas of social welfare law, which I hope will be of use equally to the adviser and the litigant in person. My thanks are due to them as well as to Legal Action Group for their unstinting guidance in producing this second edition, to my colleagues at Kent Law Clinic, to the University of Kent who afforded me the opportunity to write this further edition, and to friends, colleagues and family for their encouragement throughout.

Elaine Heslop
February 2014

Contents

Advice frameworks

CHAPTER 1

Advice agencies

1.1   Legal advice: what does it mean?

You are probably reading this book because you have embarked on a process of thinking about the best way to deliver advice within your organisation or are already in the business of giving advice, either as your main function in the workplace, or as part of your job. You may be reading it because you are interested in a career or a job as an adviser, or perhaps because you are trying to navigate your way through a legal problem of your own and you are looking for some guidance to help you resolve it.

The process of giving and receiving advice is familiar in a number of contexts. It may be offered by or provided to family or friends as a form of guidance or support. Alternatively we may look to a skilled professional for advice, consulting a doctor for advice about our health or an accountant for financial advice. As with these other professionals the legal adviser has acquired a body of specialist knowledge. This relates not only to knowing what the law says and means in a number of contexts, but also how it impacts on people's lives, and how they can use it to effect change or achieve a just outcome to a dispute.

The provision of legal advice involves imparting that knowledge to the lay person in a meaningful way, as well as assisting them to utilise the law and legal procedures to achieve their desired outcome. The activity will vary from explaining to someone what their legal rights are, to advice provided as part of assisting them to resolve a legal dispute. As part of that process the legal adviser will exercise a number of other skills. They will listen and counsel, process detailed information, relate well to a variety of individuals and act as an advocate, guide and champion for their client.

This book will aim to provide you with guidance to the key elements and processes of advice-giving, much of which is based on the methods which lawyers are trained to use when providing legal advice and services. The aim is to demystify as many of these processes as possible at the same time as highlighting both the professional and practical aspects of advice-giving. Even though law and legal processes underpin most advice-giving, in order to follow the key steps and skills outlined in this book it will not be necessary to know a great deal of law. Where the law has been outlined it is done solely as a way of illustrating how advice-giving works in practice. The type of legal examples provided focus mainly on areas of law traditionally known as social welfare law, where rights and benefits are at stake for many people in our communities.

1.2 Who is giving advice: lawyers and community organisations

First it might helpful to see what the 'map' of advice is. What are the various ways in which legal or legal-related advice can be delivered? There are a number of options available for those who want to obtain legal advice. We will start by looking at perhaps the best known routes to obtaining this, first the traditional lawyers' practices where advice is usually paid for, and second the community-based legal advice services where it is usually free.

Solicitors' practices and barristers' chambers

Lawyers, both solicitors and barristers, give legal advice to their clients as part of their services, exercising the professional skills which they have acquired through both training and practical experience.

Most people will regard contacting a solicitor as being the traditional route to obtaining legal advice. The most common model of a solicitors' practice is still that of a firm (a legal partnership) or a solicitor running a firm alone as a sole practitioner, both usually referred to as a 'high street practice'. They will usually provide legal services in areas of law which are likely to affect people at some time in their lives such as will-making, conveyancing or civil disputes. Their services are likely to be provided on a fee-paying basis. They usually operate from an office in or near the centre of a town or suburb. A commercial or corporate client is more likely to consult a larger urban (or 'City') practice. Furthermore, solicitors may now also provide legal services in tandem with commercial businesses, under what is known as an alternative business structure (ABS). More information concerning the differing structures in which solicitors can operate can be obtained by looking at the profession's regulatory body, the Solicitors Regulation Authority (SRA).[1] Whatever context they practice in, solicitors will be bound by regulations overseen by the SRA in terms of management and professional conduct and ethics.

By tradition, solicitors work closely with barristers in providing legal advice and services to a client. If more specialised advice is required for a client on a particular legal matter or if the solicitor's client wishes to instruct a legal advocate to represent them in court,

---

1 www.sra.org.uk. The SRA is the regulatory body for solicitors and mention will be made of it from time to time. It should be distinguished from the Law Society which is the solicitors' professional body.

the solicitor will refer that aspect of the client's case to a barrister who practises in chambers. This is the usual business structure of a barrister's practice. A group or 'set' of self-employed barristers will operate from their chambers carrying out their main functions of giving legal advice, drafting legal documents and acting as advocates in court. Barristers may also be employed by organisations acting as their 'in-house' barrister (or 'counsel') providing advice and legal representation for that organisation. Barristers have also seen changes in how they can provide advice and representation to the public. A fairly recent and more flexible approach to how they can provide legal services is their Direct Access scheme. Under this scheme they are able, in certain cases, to take on a client's case directly (but only in order to represent that client in a court or other hearing) instead of the traditional route of the client paying first to see a solicitor and then being referred through that solicitor to a barrister whom the client will also need to pay. As with solicitors, barristers have their own regulatory body, the Bar Standards Board.[2]

Community advice organisations

Community advice organisations provide a legal advice service which is usually free, to low income clients. These advice organisations usually focus on the provision of advice in the areas of social welfare rights and law. Traditionally these areas of law encompass advice in relation to obtaining state benefits or dealing with debts (welfare benefits or debt advice), resolving immigration problems or advising on rights for asylum seekers (asylum and immigration law), employment rights (employment law), consumer-related problems (consumer law) or housing problems (housing or landlord and tenant law).

The most common models of the community advice organisation are community law centres[3] and citizens advice bureaux.[4] Each will provide legal advice services in relation to some or all of the areas of law outlined above, with some differences between how they each provide their services. Citizens advice bureaux usually specialise more in the provision of welfare benefits and debt advice and do not always offer legal representation. Law centres will usually provide

---

2   See: www.barstandardsboard.org.uk.

3   See the Law Centres Network which is the law centres' national organisation providing links for the public to getting access to a law centre as well as providing advice and issuing publications and policies on the work of the law centre movement in the UK: www.lawcentres.org.uk.

4   See: www.citizensadvice.org.uk.

legal representation as well as advice; they often employ both practising solicitors and barristers. Law centres will also look to pursue legal cases which have policy implications of benefit to the wider community as well as the individual client. They tend to focus their advice services on the party in a legal relationship who they perceive as less empowered, for example the employee or tenant. Citizens advice bureaux will provide advice services to employer or employee, landlord or tenant alike, but like the law centre will focus the provision of their advice services on the low-income client. Other examples of local community organisations offering advice with a significant legal element include racial equality units or tenancy or housing advice centres.

All these organisations are likely to operate as charities and may employ practising lawyers as well as other legal advisers. Solicitors and barristers working in these organisations will also be regulated by their relevant regulatory body. Although some charities employing solicitors may now charge clients for the work they do in addition to providing a free service, and any fees paid or other income received is used to provide the charitable legal advice service. They will describe themselves as operating in the not-for-profit sector of legal advice provision.

Pro bono advice and representation

Pro bono ('for the public good') has always been a tradition in the legal profession and is an integral part of free community legal advice services. As an adjunct to providing their legal services to fee paying clients, individuals in solicitors' firms and barristers' chambers will give free legal advice to clients who cannot afford to pay. Newer members of the professions will be encouraged to see this as part of their work as practising lawyers and will welcome the variety of work pro bono advice offers them. They will never assume that the lower income client's case is less legally relevant or less meritorious; in fact, quite often the reverse view is likely to be taken. There are many examples also of high profile legal cases being conducted by senior counsel (barristers) for little or no fee in order to achieve justice for a client with little means.

Free or pro bono legal advice or legal services can be offered either as part of the lawyer's legal practice or outside working hours in one form or another in a community setting, perhaps under the auspices of a community advice organisation such as a law centre. There are also well-established organisations emanating from the Bar who will take referrals to carry out free representation in courts or tribunals.

These are the Free Representation Unit[5] and the Bar Pro Bono Unit.[6] Each of these organisations will only take referrals from their member organisations who have paid a subscription to be able to refer their existing clients to them for legal representation. These are, however, only two examples of the numerous ways in which the legal profession provides unpaid legal services for the community which are aimed at being as flexible and accessible for the public as resources will allow.

1.3   Models of advice agencies

We will now look at two models of community legal services described above to see how they operate on a day-to-day basis. The first is a community advice organisation, a real citizens advice bureau (but given a fictitious title), located in the centre of a busy thoroughfare in an English town. It stands as a template for how Citizens Advice provides advice services to local communities throughout the UK. The second is Law-Works, a national pro bono organisation, with its head office in the heart of the legal centre in London, which harnesses the pool of solicitors and barristers willing to provide free legal advice in their local communities throughout the UK to provide support, links and training as well as other free legal projects to further the provision of pro bono advice.

A community advice organisation: Citizens Advice

Casterbridge is a real place but its name has been changed. It is a medium-sized city in England with a population of around 45,000. The council's population, which includes the wider area around the city, is three times that size. There are relatively high levels of employment there, based around hospitals, national businesses and two local universities. The Citizens Advice Bureau here ('the CAB') was set up in the late 1930s and has undergone many structural changes in that time but has always provided a free legal advice service to the local community. Due mainly to funding cuts, two satellite bureaux in neighbouring towns have merged under the umbrella of a district CAB known as the Casterbridge CAB which now has one Board of Trustees. The present manager, supervised and supported by the board, is responsible for providing and administering an advice service in those two towns and their local catchment area as well as in Casterbridge. This largely takes the form of providing what is known as an outreach advice service in those towns. In addition there are a number of

---

5   See: www.thefru.org.uk.
6   See: www.barprobono.org.uk.

partnership initiatives running with bureaux in the various catchment areas covered by the CAB where specialist advice is provided, for example to the over-50s, in areas relevant to their legal requirements.

Due to the increased demand caused by a combination of cuts to local advice services, closures of local solicitors' firms and the economic setbacks causing unemployment and reduced access to housing and benefits, the CAB has worked hard to provide a service which aims to reach as many people as possible. Advice is given during opening hours on a 'drop-in' basis. The caller will either be given some brief general information (which may be in the form of a referral to a more appropriate service) or they will be referred to a generalist adviser or a specialist in the bureau for a further appointment. Where it would be of assistance, the inquirer will be given an information leaflet which has been drawn from Citizens Advice's open website (which any member of the public can also access).[7] This drop-in service is known as the Gateway service (and bears no relation to the recently established Telephone Gateway which is part of the publicly funded legal aid scheme).[8]

The Gateway service is run by a team of volunteers, called Gateway Assessors, all of whom have obtained training in their bureau and whose advice to the caller is supervised by a qualified supervisor as it takes place.[9] Advice and information can be offered in relation to housing problems such as tenancy rights or disputes, entitlement to obtain or to appeal against the refusal of state benefits, relationship breakdowns, unfair dismissal or other employment rights and consumer complaints (many of which are referred to the local branch of Citizens Advice's national Consumer Service Direct which is around 20 miles away). Around 30 per cent of enquiries out of an annual total of 3,000 relate to benefits and 20 per cent relate to debt. This demonstrates the ongoing need for this type of advice and assistance even in an area of relatively high employment like Casterbridge.

Casterbridge CAB is fortunate enough not only to be staffed by experienced volunteers but also trained and qualified advisers who can take on cases and represent their clients in relation, for example, to benefit appeals or employment tribunal claims. They will be able to take on some of the cases referred from the Gateway sessions if they have the capacity to do so. Across the district now served by

---

7 See: www.adviceguide.org.uk. See also section 19.5 for more on this facility.

8 Under the recently overhauled legal aid scheme, for certain types of cases and claims the only route to getting legal aid advice is by calling an organisation approved as part of the Telephone Gateway service. This is required for cases involving debt, special educational needs and discrimination. More information on this can be obtained on the Ministry of Justice (MoJ) website at www.justice.gov.uk/legal-aid.

9 See chapter 2 for more detail on the type of training and education available for staff and volunteers in citizens advice bureaux.

Casterbridge CAB there are 50 staff, many of who are trained Citizens
Advice volunteers.

The Manager of Casterbridge CAB not only manages the staff but
also the whole service provision of the district CAB. She oversees
training (although there is a training manager employed there as
well), recruitment and selection, quality of advice service and, most
important of all, funding. She also leads the way with a number of
social policy issues which are a part of the service and ethos of the
CAB. This might include the development of projects in the locality
in tandem with other advice agencies to assist in the reduction of
homelessness by, for example, setting up joint initiatives with the
local council. Recently the bureau became involved in a local project
to develop other ways of giving advice, for example via Skype, in
partnership with other agencies and in a bid to reach as many people
as possible seeking free legal advice.

Like many community advice organisations, funding is a constant
feature of the business and service delivery planning and provision
of Casterbridge CAB. Recently, like many free advice agencies, the
CAB lost its legal aid contract which was a source of funding (and
indeed pride) due to changes in legal aid.[10] Funding still continues
to be provided by the local authority and also more recently by The
Big Lottery Fund. The bureau is also in receipt of grants for smaller
projects, such as the prevention of homelessness. However, the
manager and the Board of Trustees have to ensure that these funding
streams, which usually have not only a limited shelf life but are given
for a specific purpose, are kept under review and the service is adapted
accordingly. The Casterbridge Trustee Board are all local volunteers
but their membership reflects a very high level of experience in terms
of law, finance, equality issues and business expertise.

The bureau, like all citizens advice bureaux, is part of the national
organisation Citizens Advice[11] which provides training and support for
all bureaux staff and managers. They design the information sheets
and other materials used in the bureaux, keep the information on
the advice website up to date, carry out audits of bureaux including
audits of the quality of advice provided. All bureaux also provide
feedback to the Head Office about their campaigning and social policy
work, for example how the introduction and limitations of recent
welfare reform has affected their local client base. Citizens Advice
is a well-recognised cornerstone of free legal advice in the UK, and
numerous people over many years have been saved, for example
from bankruptcy, homelessness or dismissal, by being placed in the
capable hands of a local adviser in one of their bureaux.

---

10   See further section 2.5 on what legal aid is and how it is currently being
     provided for by the government.
11   See: www.citizensadvice.org.uk.

A pro bono support service – LawWorks

Another and different model of how people can access free legal advice is provided by the national organisation LawWorks which has its offices in London. Its core service is to provide access to free legal advice for as many individuals as possible using a range of different options. The organisation began life as the Solicitors Pro Bono Group. Community advice organisations, such as law centres, had (and still have) a tradition of running free open advice sessions for the local community in addition to providing free representation to their own clients. The advisers at these advice sessions were usually local solicitors and in London often came from the City firms. In 1997 this service was channelled into the Solicitors Pro Bono Group. A system was established whereby the lawyer volunteer advisers and the advice organisations could be put in touch with each other and where training could be provided by the Pro Bono Group for the volunteer advisers in areas of social welfare law. Furthermore the service provided for referrals where an advice organisation which was part of the Pro Bono Group had a client whose legal problem did not end with the open advice session. A panel of solicitors (usually London-based) would see if a lawyer volunteer could assist the client further by, for example, representing them in court.

This initiative has grown and developed into LawWorks, where it continues largely in this form but now has developed other aspects of its services, enabling as many people as possible to access free legal advice. LawWorks is a charity, providing a national legal advice and support service. It obtains funding primarily from membership fees (it is a membership organisation) as well as from grants and donations from various other sources including the Law Society, and a number of solicitors' firms.

The organisation shares premises with the Bar Pro Bono Unit and five other legal charities committed to accessing justice and providing legal advice and assistance, all housed in the National Pro Bono Centre in Chancery Lane, London.[12] There are a relatively small number of paid staff running the organisation, with the services provided by LawWorks underpinned by volunteers. At one level these will be law students gaining work experience in terms of administrative support and legal research work carried out in the office and at another, experienced lawyers offering their services in order to review applications and assist or represent clients in legal disputes. The LawWorks Roll of Honour shows the commitment and

---

12 See: www.nationalprobonocentre.org.uk/.

success of many lawyers who have offered their services pro bono and achieved justice for individual clients.[13]

The main activity of LawWorks is still to offer membership to its 'clinics' (a membership organisation providing a legal advice service) and to support the work of the clinics. The national membership and service is constantly developing, with recent initiatives, for example in Wales, to extend the geographical spread of advice networks. LawWorks clinics provide around 40,000 advice sessions a year, with LawWorks identifying and placing volunteer advisers in the clinics for their advice sessions and continuing to provide free training for the volunteer advisers in areas of social welfare law. The greatest demand for legal advice overall in a LawWorks clinic advice session relates to debt and welfare benefits, employment law, housing law and contract and/or consumer queries.[14] Member organisations can still refer a more complex problem to LawWorks to request further legal advice and casework assistance for their client to be provided by a panel member of LawWorks' volunteer lawyers.

Individuals may also now approach LawWorks directly to ask for pro bono advice and assistance on a legal matter. The application form looks at the person's financial situation and any other options they may have for getting advice (such as house insurance), as well as asking questions about the merits of the case. The applications are carefully scrutinised and not everyone receives assistance as many do not fulfil the criteria to qualify. If an application is accepted the client will be put in touch with a LawWorks volunteer lawyer who will take the case on for no fee.

There are additional initiatives which LawWorks has set up recently, all aimed at providing free advice and legal advice to as many people or organisations as possible. These include an advice service for small organisations who may need help setting up as a legal entity or with understanding how data protection law impacts on their service delivery. There is also an internet advice service where short passages of advice can be offered to member advice organisations to help in their work of advising clients.

The organisation runs an information telephone line staffed by volunteers who give callers guidance as to where they can obtain advice and assistance. (This is an example of the 'signposting'

---

13   See, for example, the page provided by one of the pro bono organisations housed in the Centre, CILEX: http://cilexprobono.wordpress.com/category/roll-of-honour/.

14   In the *Law Society Gazette* of 15 July 2013 it was reported that requests for help and advice to LawWorks had gone up by almost a third in the period 2012–2013. LawWorks stated that they thought this was due to the 'desperate state' of frontline services, namely a severe lessening in the provision of free advice due to the closure and cuts in funding of many local advice agencies as well as the impact of substantial reduction in legal aid in that period (see chapter 2).

approach to providing advice which we will look at below.) Another project, Voices for Short Lives, involves supporting families of children with serious medical conditions.

The work of LawWorks is likely to be of even greater importance in the coming years as cuts to legal aid and funding for free advice organisations continue to make an impact on how low income people can find their way into the provision of free legal advice and assistance. The commitment and dedication of all those who give up their time and volunteer to support the provision of pro bono advice in this country is encapsulated in this organisation and in the vision of those who run and support it.

Staff in advice agencies

As we have seen, these two types of organisation are likely to share similar patterns of staffing. As well as legal advisers or lawyers, there will also be receptionists and administrators, some of who will be volunteers.

Of these, perhaps volunteers deserve particular mention. Volunteers have formed a vital part of the process of running advice services for many years. Many organisations actively recruit volunteers and some run a specific programme of work and training for the volunteers they take on. In some cases the time the volunteer will spend with the organisation may be limited, either because the organisation encourages short placements only, or because the individual, possibly as a student, is looking for work experience on a short-term basis. In other cases a volunteer may stay for a longer period of time working alongside paid staff, and be given specific tasks to do or areas of work to cover. For many students, voluntary experience can help with their career progression into law or advice work.

Although the presence of volunteers is a necessary and effective aspect of the provision of legal advice services, their high profile in many community advice settings does to an extent reflect the lack of resources which many agencies have: they are needed in order to keep the services running. Another explanation for their presence is that the caring and giving nature of advice work will always attract people who are willing to volunteer to give up their time to become involved.

1.4   Other advice services

In addition to the better known routes to obtaining legal and legally-related advice outlined above, there is a rich tapestry of other advice agencies and services available to the public, many of which are still free or largely free but all of whose services, where they are provided to the public, are in considerable demand. They may be staffed by legally qualified volunteers or paid lawyers, advisers or other volunteers. Not every type of service is outlined here but hopefully as broad a spectrum as possible has been provided to show the range of options available.

Signposting and information services

Some organisations provide a service to the public in terms of advising and assisting them to obtain more information, access to a service or benefit, or advice about their rights or remedies. Not all of these organisations will regard themselves as giving advice or legal advice but see what they do as providing information or 'signposting'. An example of such a service would be a reception area in a local authority office, or a local library. The inquirer may be provided with information which identifies the nature of the problem or concern they have in a legal or administrative framework and be referred to an appropriate service for a resolution of that problem. In some agencies the process is more sophisticated, and will require a knowledgeable analysis of facts provided in order to identify both problem and referral sources. As we saw earlier it is a key part of the service offered by both citizens advice bureaux and LawWorks.

Advice services for special interest groups

Other organisations, some of which are national, serve to represent the interests of a specific section of the population, such as women, older people or people with disabilities.

The organisation will usually provide legal advice to callers or clients representing their target group as well as providing general information and advice about policies or related services for that group. It may also have experienced, and usually legally qualified, advisers or case workers who can in some circumstances assist individuals to pursue legal claims.

An example of such an organisation is Rights of Women[15] (ROW) which advises women on legal issues such as domestic violence and family rights. Advice is given through their telephone advice service by volunteer women lawyers. ROW also seeks to influence government policy on rights affecting women in society and provides guidance and publications on these issues.

These organisations do not usually run on a membership basis but provide advice either on a particular legal topic or to benefit a specific group of individuals. Trade unions, who are referred to in more detail in chapter 2, are an example of national, member-based organisations who provide free advice and representation on workplace issue and disputes for their paid-up members.

Online advice

It is increasingly common for individuals to seek advice online. Some national advice agencies provide advice and local referrals via their websites. Various examples of websites providing advice and information are referred to when we look at research resources in section 19.5. Here we will pick out some websites which may be of value to the public looking for basic advice or where to find legal advice resources.

The main function of AdviceUK is to support community advice organisations but their website is packed with useful and user friendly advice on a variety of legal topics.[16] The website also pinpoints local organisations throughout the UK offering advice in their local communities. Other useful websites include those of the Equality and Human Rights Commission (EHRC)[17] in relation to equality issues and ACAS (in relation to employment queries).[18] The government also supports a number of websites where useful information and advice on resources, services and legal topics can be obtained.[19]

---

15 See: www.rightsofwomen.org.uk.

16 See: www.adviceuk.org.uk.

17 See: www.equalityhumanrights.com.

18 The Advisory, Conciliation and Arbitration Service: www.acas.org.uk. Its main function is to conciliate in employment disputes but its website has much that is useful by way of advice and guidance for both employers and employees in this area of law.

19 Reference has already been made to the MoJ website in which information can be found about the court and tribunal system and how it operates, as well as fees, legal aid and other practical aspects of using the justice system – see www.justice.gov.uk. The government site www.gov.uk provides information

Law clinics

Many universities are now running law clinics as part of their under-graduate law programmes. The model of a law clinic will vary from one university to another, but the overall aim is to provide what is usually called clinical legal education to their students. Students, supervised and supported by legally qualified practitioners and/or lecturers, will be given the opportunity to work with clients on resolving their cases. Some law clinics will arrange for students to provide representation for a client in a tribunal, such as a benefit tribunal or an employment tribunal where it is not necessary to be legally-qualified to represent clients. Clients in the community around the university will be offered advice, either by the solicitors or barristers employed in the law clinic and/or by local volunteer lawyers. Students will sit in on or prepare for these sessions and may be required to write up notes or letters following the advice sessions.

The service to the community is free but can often be limited to the capacity the law clinic will have, not only in terms of numbers of cases, but in terms of blending the process of advice with that of supervision and the academic process for the student of learning, researching and engaging with the relevant law which the university will be prioritising. This model of a law clinic closely resembles Kent Law Clinic in the University of Kent[20] but it will vary from one university to another.

Innocence Projects

Innocence Projects are not strictly part of the map of legal advice in the UK, but nevertheless, an overview of what they do (and do not do) is worth a mention. The best known Innocence Project is based at the University of Bristol where Innocence Network UK was set up in 2004.[21] There are currently 24 university law schools who are members of the organisation. As with law clinics, the work begins with an academic process. Students volunteer to carry out research into the legal issues surrounding particular cases whereby a convicted prisoner asserts their innocence of the crime. This research may include forensic research and can involve making prison visits to the person maintaining their innocence. Those involved in running these

about many aspects of government activity which can prove useful when researching current procedures or recent changes.

20 See: www.kent.ac.uk/law/clinic.

21 See: www.innocencenetwork.org.uk/.

projects do not give legal advice but they do gather information and go over the facts, trial and conviction and the evidence put before the jury in order to see if the verdict can be challenged. They will then usually refer their findings to the Criminal Cases Review Commission which is the government body set up to review any unsafe criminal convictions.[22]

Although it is possible for the commission to look at cases of any convicted individuals asserting their innocence, the Project feels that it is an alien and challenging process and so has established the network to provide this support. They do not give advice or offer what they describe as legal aid and so for that reason are not strictly a part of the map of advice. However their work has been enormously effective in ensuring that miscarriages of justice are corrected and they have been associated with many high profile cases where convictions have been overturned. It is important also to note that all the work they do is pro bono.

Court advice desks

High Court

The concept of a court advice desk is well established in the UK and these operate throughout the court system, both civil and criminal. In the Royal Courts of Justice (RCJ), the building in London where the High Court[23] is housed, can be found the RCJ Personal Support Unit (PSU).[24] This is perhaps the best known example of a court-based advice service. The PSU can assist a litigant in person to navigate their way around the court system in pursuing or defending a case. Volunteers, who are not in the main legally trained, will be able to go into court hearings with litigants in person and offer them support and guidance as to the process they are undergoing. The PSU not only has a base in the RCJ in London but also operates in other major cities, namely Birmingham, Cardiff, Leeds, Liverpool and Manchester. The RCJ also houses its own citizens advice bureau.[25] This CAB also offers advice in the areas of law covered by a typical CAB, as in the model described in section 1.3 above.

22 See: www.justice.gov.uk/about/criminal-cases-review-commission.
23 See chapter 18 for an explanation of the court system and structure in England and Wales.
24 See: http://thepsu.org.
25 See: www.rcjadvice.org.uk/civil-law/. The High Court is in the Strand, London WC2.

County court

In addition, many county courts (the local civil court centres) run advice desks in relation to housing or mortgage possession cases. These courts will 'list' on one day or one morning, all hearings of cases being brought by landlords or mortgagees seeking to repossess a property due to rent arrears (or other tenancy breaches) or mortgage arrears. In some of these courts there will be present a qualified solicitor or experienced adviser, possibly drawn from a rota, who can offer advice prior to the start of the list of hearings. The adviser can also go into court or the judge's chambers with the tenant or mortgagee and make representations on their behalf, as to the amount owed or any offers to pay off the debt. These advice desks are set up by arrangement with the court's resident judges. Although the service offered is literally at the door of the court it can often result in defendants being given an opportunity to defend a claim properly or avoid immediate loss of their homes.

Magistrates' court

Defendants who are charged with a criminal offence and required to attend the magistrates' court (which is where all criminal cases begin) may take advantage of the services of the duty solicitor on the day they attend court if they have not had advice from a solicitor before. They may only take advantage of this service on one occasion and won't be able to use it if the offence is one which does not carry a sentence of imprisonment and they have been bailed (released on certain conditions) to attend the court by the police. As with the civil court housing advice desk system, the aim is to assist an individual with no previous recourse to legal advice. There is also a duty solicitor advice scheme operating in the police stations for some types of matters where individuals have been charged with a criminal offence, and a telephone advice service from practising criminal solicitors' offices to the police stations for other matters. Solicitors who take part in these advice schemes have been authorised to do so under the MoJ's legal aid scheme.

ELAAS

Another useful but perhaps lesser known court-based service is the Employment Law Appeal Advice Scheme (ELAAS). In some circumstances it is possible to appeal from a decision made in an employment tribunal following a workplace dispute. These appeals require fairly sophisticated knowledge of the relevant law as well as the procedures in the Employment Appeal Tribunal (which for England and Wales sits in London only). Those who are brave enough to do so unrepresented can sometimes be assisted by this service, which is operated by experienced and qualified barristers. Individuals cannot access the scheme directly but if they are unrepresented the appeal court may be able to direct them to a barrister who is part of the scheme.

CHAPTER 2

Funding legal advice and paying for advice

2.1   How advice work is funded: introduction

As we shall see later in this chapter, obtaining legal advice from a solicitor or barrister will more often than not involve paying them for their services. We will look into how that works, as well as the now rather rare circumstances in which they will be able to provide assistance under the legal aid scheme. Many of the community advice organisations referred to in the first chapter provide their services for free and will have obtained funding in order to do so. Any income obtained by way of grants, or fees paid by their clients, will be used solely to continue the charitable work of that not-for-profit organisation. We will look at some of the sources of that funding and the various ways it is likely to be used to support advice and legal advice services. Overall, apart from the process of paying privately for legal advice, funding for legal or related advice is likely to come from one of the following sources, which we will examine below:

- central or local government;
- charities or grant-giving organisations;
- educational or professional institutions and trade unions;
- legal aid;
- project funding.

2.2   Central and local government funding

Central government funding

It is rare nowadays for central government to provide direct funding to an organisation for the provision of free legal advice. As we shall see below, the government does provide funding for legal aid but now at a much reduced level. There are some examples of government supporting local communities with funding which can be streamed into community advice or similar services. Two examples of this relate to income raised from the National Lottery, and funding provided by the Department for Communities and Local Government (DCLG).

A percentage (around 40 per cent) of the income yielded by the sale of tickets to the government-sponsored National Lottery is set aside for charitable purposes. This fund is known as the Big Lottery Fund. The fund gives grant to projects with charitable purposes or aims. Examples might include giving funds to a women's aid project or to an organisation working to support local community groups.[1]

The DCLG[2] has a wide brief, including the provision of financial support to local communities. Local authorities have received funding to provide services to assist their homeless population with a better route into permanent housing or to provide vulnerable individuals with housing support. Initiatives like this will mean that local authorities can provide help in the form of advice as to the statutory services they are required by law to provide. The department will also provide smaller project funding, an example in 2013 being a project to provide skills and mentoring to social housing tenants to enable them to use computers and online services more fully.

Local government funding

Traditionally local government has not only provided a welfare-based service for its local community but has also provided financial support for local community groups to provide free advice themselves. Both these sources of funding are now less plentiful than they used to be due to recent cutbacks in the provision of funding from central to local government. Councils may also prioritise community funding in differing ways. One council may decide to close public libraries to meet its growing care bill; another may decide to preserve libraries and cut back on funding community groups. These varying approaches may sometime be connected to the political 'colour' of the council concerned.

Nevertheless there is still some local government direct funding to support advice work. We saw in section 1.3 that the bulk of the funding provided to the citizens advice bureau in that city was from the local authority, and this is fairly typical throughout the UK. Local authorities still continue to support law centres financially, although there have been some notable casualties recently with closures of community law centres due to local authority funding cuts.[3]

---

1 The Advice Partnership of East Kent (APEK) receives funds from the Big Lottery Fund to support a growing network of advice and legal advice agencies in East Kent and to encourage and provide local projects such as the provision of training or interagency referral systems. See: www.apek.org.uk.

2 See: www.gov.uk/government/organisations/department-for-communities-and-local-government.

3 In 2013 Birmingham Law Centre lost its local authority grant and was forced to close its doors. Charitable funding enabled the Birmingham Community Law Centre to start up later in the same year.

In addition, local authorities will themselves provide advice and support services to their local communities out of their own resources. Typical areas where this free advice is available relate to:

- private tenants' rights;
- consumer rights for businesses arising out of trading standards enforcement;[4]
- welfare benefits advice;
- advice on local authority community or social care provision;
- education advice or information arising out of education welfare services.

Local authorities' websites are the best way of finding out what advice services or web-based advice they have on offer.

2.3   Charities or grant-giving organisations

Any glance at the letterhead or website of an organisation which gives free advice or legal advice is likely to disclose that it has external funders. As well as a mention of central or local government grants or funding there will be the logos of charitable foundations set up for what is known in law as a 'charitable purpose'. The best known of these charitable purposes are those of advancing education and eliminating poverty. These are two of the charitable purposes laid down by the Charities Act 2011 which lists 13 aims or purposes all or some of which an organisation should have and must promote for the public benefit in order to be registered as a charity.[5] Many not-for-profit organisations themselves register as charities and are also able to apply for and qualify for charitable funding. The list of organisations who provide charitable funding is long and varies considerably in size and level of funds and charitable purpose from one organisation to another. Most of these grant-giving bodies have been set up as trusts as a result of gifts or donations either in a person's lifetime or in their will, with specific criteria built in to the gift as to who may benefit from grants or funding and the purposes to which the funding can be allocated.

---

4 Consumer Direct, an advice service for private consumers, is now part of Citizens Advice, with centres around the UK offering consumer advice, as well as a website. See www.adviceguide.org.uk/england/consumer or the Citizens Advice consumer helpline on 08454 04 05 06.

5 The Charity Commission oversees all charities which register with it: www.charitycommission.gov.uk.

A non-exhaustive list of charitable grant-giving foundations can be found on the website of the Association of Charitable Foundations[6] which lists over three-and-a-half thousand UK-based charities.

2.4 Educational or professional institutions and trade unions

In the higher education sector universities usually support welfare advice services through their student unions. They will often employ student welfare advisers, who can provide free advice on relevant matters such as housing, consumer and financial problems. The funding for this service is usually provided by a mixture of fund raising activities promoted by the union and a grant from the university. Many UK student unions now have charitable status.

A number of professional organisations also offer free advice for their members in matters relating to professional practice and conduct. Examples are the British Medical Association for doctors and the Law Society for solicitors. The Law Society also has a charitable arm which provides financial support for legal projects. It supports a number of legal projects abroad as well as the Royal Court of Justice's Personal Support Unit referred to in chapter 1 which specialises in working with litigants in person.

Trade unions are another example of membership organisations who provide free advice and representation for their members on a range of work-related matters. Union membership in the UK was on the decline for a number of years but recently has seen something of a comeback with a rise in membership reported in the year 2012. A government report indicates that around 6.5 million employees in the UK were trade union members in 2012 which is an increase of nearly 60,000 from the previous year (but about half the number of 13 million who were members in 2009). The biggest rise has been in private sector employment.[7]

Members can obtain information and advice on their union's website and can seek assistance from a shop steward on work-related issues as diverse as family-related leave, health and safety at work, or disciplinary or grievance procedures. Unions can also represent their existing paid-up members to pursue claims in employment tribunals

---

6 See: www.acf.org.uk.
7 Department for Business Innovation and Skills: *Trade Union Membership 2012: Statistical Bulletin* 2013.

although this will depend on resources available and the merits of the case. Most workplaces who do support trade unions will tend to support a union relevant to that area of work. For builders this will be UCATT, for the railway and other transport workers it will be RMT and for the Royal Mail it will be CWU. The umbrella organisation which supports all trade unions is the Trades Union Congress.[8]

2.5   Legal aid

Perhaps the best known form of public funding for legal advice services is legal aid, the provision of financial support for legal advice and representation. Since 1949, there has been a government-funded system of assisting with the payment for legal services provided by solicitors and barristers to low-income clients, then and now described as legal aid (although for a while it was known as public funding). Some features of how it operates will be discussed below. Its purpose is to provide financial support for certain types of legal claims or procedures on a means-tested basis. The government organisation which administered this system was called the Legal Aid Board for a number of years. It then became the Legal Services Commission and in 2013 was taken over by the Ministry of Justice (MoJ) and became the Legal Aid Agency (LAA).[9]

The system which operated meant that a client on low income (with the income of the household also being taken into account) could go and see a solicitor and their case would be conducted under the legal aid scheme if the area of law was one where legal aid was available. They would then be advised and represented by the solicitor in their case, and would pay less than the market price for the legal service provided. Their contribution to the legal aid fund to pay the solicitors' fees for the case would be assessed according to their means and they would pay this off on a monthly basis for as long as the case lasted.

---

8   See: www.tuc.org.uk. The other unions referred to above are, respectively, the Union of Construction Allied Trades and Technicians (ucatt.org.uk), the Rail Maritime and Transport Workers Union (rmt.org.uk) and the Communication Workers Union (cwu.org.uk).

9   The MoJ took over the operation of legal aid in 2013 and its website provides some basic information for the public as to how to apply. If you look at the 'provider' link you can also see a list of the legal advice areas where legal aid is now available and whether it is supplied in person or by telephone under the gateway system referred to in chapter 1. See www.justice.gov.uk/legal-aid. However, it remains the case that legal aid can only be granted to the client of a solicitor or legal adviser who is recognised as a supplier of legal aid by the MoJ.

Some clients would not be required to contribute to the fund at all if their assessable income fell below a certain threshold.

The solicitor could be working in private practice or in an organisation such as a law centre in the not-for-profit advice sector. In conducting the case under the client's legal aid certificate, the solicitor would be required to monitor the work being done and the costs of the case, and regularly provide reports to the Legal Aid Board (or its later equivalent). As part of conducting the client's case the solicitor would also be able, if required, to use the services of a barrister also working under the legal aid scheme, to obtain a legal opinion or to represent the client in court. All clients, whether required or not to make a contribution to the fund would receive exactly the same service, with regular reviews of the conduct of the case being provided to the Legal Aid Board by the solicitor. Where the legally-aided client's case involved a court hearing to resolve it, once it was concluded a number of things might happen in relation to the costs aspect of the case:

- A client who won the case may recover costs from the losing party and thus the legal aid fund could be reimbursed.
- A client who won the case and recovered certain types of compensation or property (such as a legal right over the matrimonial home) would be required to enter into an arrangement with the Legal Aid Board to reimburse the money paid out to them out of this acquisition.
- A client who lost the case would normally not have to pay the winner's legal costs as the issuing of the legal aid certificate 'protected' them from such an outcome as, self-evidently, it demonstrated that they were regarded as having very limited means.
- The solicitor who had set up the legal aid certificate for that client would be able to claim a payment themselves from the Legal Aid Board for the work done where the board had not been repaid by the client or by the losing party.

If the area of law was one that did not require access to a court or tribunal, the solicitor could provide contribution-based or free advice to the client as appropriate and then claim their payment from the Legal Aid Board.

It will be seen already, therefore, that legal aid did not add up to a pot of money to provide 'free legal advice' which many people believed it to be. It was subject to rigid means testing and a number of arrangements designed to repay the fund. It is also worth noting that the hourly rates of payment which solicitors and barristers could claim from the legal aid fund were considerably lower than the rates normally charged to a private-paying client. The solicitor was therefore often underwriting their legal aid work with private paid work, although a number of criminal legal firms (and some firms who only did civil work) would subsist entirely on legal aid income. Nevertheless, legal aid has sometimes been portrayed in some quarters as 'a free ride' for both the clients and the lawyers, which is somewhat wide of the mark.

Recently, legal aid has been subject to considerable change and a significant reduction in government funding available, and in many respects the original system has altered beyond recognition. The two most significant changes in terms of civil cases are a large-scale reduction in the areas where legal aid can be applied for and a reduction in the number of solicitors' firms or not-for-profit organisations who are now contracted to supply legal aid work. Firms or lawyers practising criminal law are likely to specialise in that area alone and as a result more likely to rely on legal aid to fund their services. They too have seen a significant reduction both in rates of pay out of the fund and in the ways in which their clients can obtain free advice if facing a criminal charge. How clients get access to the legal aid scheme has also changed, with some provision only now being offered by telephone in both civil and criminal areas of law. In recent years many solicitors have been forced to turn away from legal aid work, either because the rate and timing of payments has been unprofitable, or because the administration of the legal aid contracts has grown in complexity.

A more detailed exposition of how legal aid currently operates is beyond the scope of this book, but it is worth mentioning the most recent legislation underpinning the provision of legal aid, the Legal Aid, Sentencing and Punishment of Offenders Act (LASPO) 2012, which brought in a number of changes to both the criminal justice and the legal aid systems. Further regulations have added to and refined these changes.

2.6   Project funding

It is quite common for an advice or community organisation to obtain funding in order to run a particular project involving the provision of advice. This forms part of the mix of funding which community advice organisations seek to attract in order to provide as comprehensive a service as possible. Legal organisations such as the Law Society and community funds such as the Big Lottery Fund both support project funding in the legal services sector. The project run by LawWorks, 'Voices for Short Lives', which provides legal help and support for children with serious medical conditions and which we touched on in chapter 1, is an example of this approach to funding advice work.

The project-based approach tends to be the preferred option for a funder prepared to support a legal advice service and it is furthermore now relatively rare for such a service to receive all its funding from one source. Funding for projects involving the provision of legal advice is likely to be short-term and can be attached to a post-holder in the organisation who will see that project through. This can lead to instability in the organisation and may make it harder to decide if a new post should be made fixed-term or permanent. Expectations created in the community served by the creation and development of the project will have been raised as a result of the activity and it may not always be possible to replace that funding once it runs out or to continue with that area of work.

2.7   Private funding of advice

The most traditional form of funding for legal advice comes from the client's pocket. Most solicitors charge an hourly rate for advice and legal representation and this rate will vary according to the location, the work being undertaken and the experience of the solicitor being consulted. Barristers' fees for legal opinions and advice and court appearances are charged on a different basis and are traditionally also paid by their client to the solicitor and then passed on to the barrister through their clerk. There are now changes to this traditional system on the horizon. As well as the barrister now being able to see and charge a client directly under their Direct Access scheme outlined in chapter 1, there are moves afoot at the time of writing to allow barristers to partner non-lawyers and to provide a business service which is charged though the business they are operating within. This system has been operating as a model of a solicitors' practice since early 2012 as the alternative business structure.

We also saw above that not-for-profit advice agencies rely on external funding to operate their services. As a result of some changes reflected in LASPO 2012 in the context of legal aid, it is now possible for solicitors employed in a charitable not-for-profit organisation to charge clients for their services. The money charged is usually at less than a commercial rate and the service still likely to be underwritten by charitable funding. Nevertheless it does mean that such an organisation, perhaps with far less (or possibly no) legal aid income coming in than prior to the implementation of LASPO 2012 can support itself better financially with these contributions and continue to provide a free funded service in part. Time will tell whether, for many of these organisations, this hybrid approach to providing affordable or free advice to low income clients in areas where legal aid is now being pared back will have the effect of supplementing the diminishing legal aid budget.

CHAPTER 3

Studying, qualifying and becoming an adviser

3.1   Studying and the routes into advice work

Some readers of this book will be using it as a background to study-ing advice skills; others may already be practitioners. This chapter is aimed both at those who may want to train and work as advisers and at those who are interested in qualifying as a legally-trained adviser with the various options and levels on offer. It provides an overview of those various options and how education, training or qualification can be obtained in this sector of the job market.

Want to qualify as an adviser?

Many people think of qualifying to give legal advice in the context of training to be a qualified lawyer (solicitor or barrister) or perhaps a legal executive. In each of these areas of study there is an element of both academic and practical training in order to qualify. Separate to that route there are also some (but not many) courses of study in the higher education sector which are not career-linked. All these routes and courses involve not inconsiderable cost. Furthermore, in terms of qualifying as a lawyer, the process of getting on to the ladder of the practical stage of training and thereafter obtaining paid work can be highly competitive.

It is still possible to obtain paid advice work in the not-for-profit sector without degree level or formal qualifications. Life skills and experience can be a great asset when moving into this area of work. However, even there, either as an adviser or a volunteer, some form of training or courses already undertaken in advice-giving skills is likely to be expected when applying, or as part of job development once in post. We saw for example in chapter 1 that volunteers called Gateway Assessors in citizens advice bureaux who have face-to-face contact with the public undertake internal training in their bureaux, and as we shall see later, there are other qualifications that bureaux staff can obtain in advice-related skills.

The various training or qualification options are still quite flexible as routes into advice work, although it is true to say that in the not-for-profit advice sector there are fewer paid job opportunities than there used to be. We will examine these various options below. We will also look at the growing army of paralegals, who they are, where they work and what their options and aspirations are.

Finally we will look at volunteers, both those who are largely untrained or not legally qualified and who work in the advice field, and those who are trained and usually qualified legal practitioners, who give free advice as volunteers usually as part of a pro bono initiative they provide outside their day-time job or as arranged through their employment.

3.2 Qualifying as a lawyer

For many, the experience of working in an advice setting, perhaps as a volunteer or a case worker, whets their appetite and they plan ultimately to qualify as a lawyer. Others will volunteer as law students as part of developing their CVs and gaining relevant experience for when they qualify.

A practising and qualified lawyer has a number of options as to how and where they decide to practice. As well as the more traditional models of practice we looked at in the previous chapter there are qualified lawyers in paid jobs in the not-for-profit sector where they will usually specialise in social welfare law, such as housing, employment or welfare benefits, acting for low-income client groups. Others may practise in a more commercial setting acting as their employer's solicitor or in-house counsel in various business institutions or being employed in local government or a charitable or professional organisation. However, for all qualified lawyers the route to qualification is the same, although more tailored approaches to the practical element of training for solicitors specialising in certain types of practice have recently emerged, which we will touch on below.

Solicitor or barrister?

If the decision is to become a lawyer, the choice needs to be made as to whether to qualify as a solicitor or barrister. Each is a qualified lawyer. It would not be possible here to do full justice to the functions of each branch of the legal profession but a summary outline is offered. Traditionally the main difference was that barristers' functions were largely in the arena of conducting court cases, and providing expert legal advice and opinions, with solicitors preparing for court claims with the client, as well as advising and assisting in the legal areas which do not involve court cases, such as the execution of wills or the buying or selling of property. These distinctions are now becoming more blurred, with each branch of the legal profession being allowed to extend the way in which they can offer legal services. Solicitors, for example, can apply for rights of audience (the right to address the court and conduct the client's case) in the higher courts, such as the High Court,[1] which is a relatively new development. There are also changes afoot for how barristers may practice.[2] More can be learned about these developments and the functions of each branch of the profession from their professional bodies. Solicitors' training and qualification requirements are prescribed by the Education and Training Section of the Solicitors Regulation Authority (SRA). Barristers' routes to qualification are set down by the Bar Standards Board (BSB).[3]

Educational qualifications: solicitor

Before embarking on any process of qualification as a solicitor, enquiries should be made as to what type of educational qualification will be needed. It is not necessary to have a law degree, as non-law degree students can take a postgraduate conversion course: the Common Professional Examination (CPE) or the Graduate Diploma in Law (GDL). If a law degree is the preferred option, care should be taken to ensure that it is at the right level. The Law Society (the solicitors' professional body) sets out which undergraduate law topics count towards what is known as a 'qualifying degree' and has a link to universities that offer these degree courses.[4] In addition, if someone does not have a university degree or, for example, has educational qualifications which include a study of law, they may be able to count these towards becoming a qualified solicitor. If, for example, they are a qualified legal executive there is a route to qualifying as a solicitor but this is quite lengthy and is also outlined on the Law Society's 'Routes to qualifying' page of its website.

Educational qualifications: barrister

The BSB requires entrants to its profession to have either a law degree at a minimum level of a lower second or a university degree in a different subject together with the postgraduate conversion course, the

1 See chapter 18 for an outline of the court structure in England and Wales.
2 At the time of writing the Bar Standards Board intends to launch its new Handbook in early 2014. This extends the way in which barristers will be able to practice, including being able to go into business with non-barristers and to have the ability to 'conduct litigation'. This is an extension of the Direct Access scheme and means that barristers can now be directly instructed by a client at all stages of litigation and not just for representation to which the Direct Access scheme is limited.
3 See: www.sra.org.uk and www.barstandardsboard.org.uk.
4 See: www.lawsociety.org.uk/careers/becoming-a-solicitor/routes-to-qualifying/.

CPE or the GDL.[5] As with the solicitors' academic stage of qualifying, a law qualifying degree must contain certain core topics for it to count as valid at the academic stage.

Vocational or training stage

Once the degree or postgraduate conversion course has been completed the student will then be required to do a postgraduate practice course either to train as a solicitor (the Legal Practice Course (LPC)) or as a barrister (the Bar Professional Training Course (BPTC)).

Following that, a period of training in practice needs to be undertaken. For solicitors it will mean obtaining a training contract with a firm of solicitors (or a local authority or law centre) for a period of two years under the overall supervision of a solicitor authorised by the SRA to take on a trainee. The two years can be completed on a part-time basis and in certain circumstances relevant legal experience gained elsewhere can be counted towards that two-year period. Training contracts can now be offered as part of a package of post graduate vocational training in some of the more commercial large firms and some local authorities have formed consortiums in which training contracts are offered.

The present government has been encouraging apprenticeships in a number of areas of employment and the solicitors' profession is now developing legal apprenticeships[6] which are being offered by some firms and other providers of legal services and which do not require any higher education qualifications but can be a preliminary step on the route to qualifying.

A trainee barrister, before they commence the BPTC, will need to be taken on by one of the four Inns of Court. These Inns are in essence societies of which a practising barrister is required to be a member. They are Gray's Inn, Inner Temple, Lincoln's Inn and Middle Temple. While they are studying for the BPTC, trainee barristers will need to attend their Inn for 12 qualifying sessions. These used to be known as 'dining' since the trainee barrister would be required to eat a dinner in their Inn on each of these occasions. These sessions now take the form of various educational and collegiate activities, which may or may not be accompanied by dining.

Once the barrister has completed the BPTC they will seek to become a pupil in a barristers' chambers (or another authorised

---

5 See: www.barstandardsboard.org.uk/qualifying-as-a-barrister/academic-stage/.
6 For more on these, see section 3.4 below.

training environment such as a government department) where they will be required to be trained for 12 months. In the first six months they will be observing barristers in practice and researching the law and practice, and in the second six months they will be able to appear as advocates in certain courts. Most pupillages operate within a barristers' chambers, which is a group of self-employed barristers who work out of their offices obtaining their work through the assistance of their clerks. Competition for a pupillage is extremely fierce with less than a quarter of applicants being taken on. The training periods for both solicitors and barristers are paid but at relatively low levels. The SRA fixes an annual minimum salary for trainee solicitors but this has been frozen since August 2012. Barristers' minimum pupillage pay is low by today's standards and below the minimum wage which a worker or employee would be entitled to, although many chambers pay at a higher rate. There is also no guarantee of work at the end of these training periods in either branch of the legal profession although there is statistically more likelihood of a trainee solicitor being taken on by their firm or legal practice on qualifying.[7]

The SRA in conjunction with both the BSB and the Institute of Legal Executives recently carried out an extensive review of legal education and training which was published in July 2013.[8] The aim was to examine current training procedures in the legal profession and make proposals for future developments. One of the key recommendations which emerged was to suggest better recognition for paralegals, whom we will be discussing below. Another was to encourage the use of legal apprenticeships for school leavers as the first step on the road to qualifying, which a number of solicitors' firms, the Crown Prosecution Service and some legal education institutes now offer.[9]

7   Nevertheless, recent research carried out through Freedom of Information requests at some universities offering the LPC course shows on average that only around 20 per cent of their graduates have gone on to obtain training contracts. See: www.lawgazette.co.uk/news/lpc-students-struggle-to-get-training-deals/5039451.art.

8   See: http://letr.org.uk/the-report/executive-summary/executive-summary-english/index.html.

9   A good introduction to these very varied programmes is available at: www.lawgazette.co.uk/72105.article.

3.3   Legal executives and paralegals

Legal executives

The third type of qualified legal practitioner is the legal executive. These individuals, after gaining qualifications recognised by their professional body, the Chartered Institute of Legal Executives (CILEX),[10] can also qualify as solicitors if they wish to do so. Most, however, choose to practise as legal executives in a variety of legal settings and form the third branch of the legal profession. As with solicitors and barristers, there are two stages of qualifying, the academic and the vocational. The most advanced qualification that can be obtained is that of a chartered legal executive. However, there are legal executives who can practice as either associate or graduate legal executives as long as they have completed the relevant diploma courses as laid down by CILEX. As with training to become a solicitor or barrister, qualifications as a legal executive at the various levels require work-based supervision and training with either a solicitor, barrister or in national or local government, or under the supervision of a company in-house lawyer for a period of time. It used to be the case that five years' training was required in order to become a fellow of CILEX. This period was reduced to three years in June 2013. In addition CILEX has recently introduced a new training scheme whereby students who hold A-levels or equivalent can study for a law degree in addition to obtaining legal executive qualifications.

Legal executives now have considerable scope for how and where they can practise. They may qualify as solicitors and a CILEX Fellow need not now enter into a training contract. Chartered legal executives can also enter into partnership with solicitors.

Paralegals

The role and title of a 'paralegal' requires more careful analysis, as unlike the three traditional branches of the legal profession, their status is less well prescribed. A number of legal service providers employ non-qualified legal staff and refer to them as paralegals. There is a growing band of such individuals in the legal sector. Many of them will be law graduates who have not as yet been able to get on to the ladder of obtaining a training contract or pupillage. They will usually be employed by a firm of solicitors (rather than in a barristers'

---

10 See: www.cilex.org.uk.

chambers), and under supervision will carry out much of the office work a solicitor does, including seeing clients. The Crown Prosecution Service also employs paralegals to do preparation work for criminal prosecutions. They will not, however, be allowed to appear in the courts as they are regarded as unqualified lawyers.

Paralegals have their own association, the National Association of Licensed Paralegals[11] which offers support to this group of employees in the legal sector and provides information about their work options. The association also offers licensed status to paralegals. As well as pointing its members to various certificate and diploma courses described as vocational paralegal qualifications, the association offers a London-based graduate paralegal diploma course.[12] In doing this the association is following a growing tendency to provide education or training specifically geared to paralegals as we will see later. The SRA, in its legal education and training review referred to earlier, highlights the uncertain status of paralegals in the professional legal world and recommends exploring parallel routes for paralegals to qualify as lawyers. Time will tell whether this group of legal advisers and employees will be given this option.

3.4   Qualifications and courses in advice work

Degree level courses

Quite separate from the traditional routes into qualifying as a lawyer and practising as such, it is possible to study for advice skills which hopefully will provide an entry into practising as an adviser in the traditional areas of social welfare law. For anyone interested in obtaining a degree in advice work the options are very limited. At the University of Staffordshire there is a well-established degree course in Social Welfare Law and Advice Practice. A student can aim for either a BA Honours or an LLB (Bachelor of Laws) in this subject. There is also the option to take a BA through distance learning. The modules on the course include practical work experience in local citizens advice bureaux. The university has also developed an MA in the same topic which was launched in 2013.

---

11   See: www.nationalparalegals.co.uk.
12   A Level 7 (Postgraduate) Diploma in Paralegal Practice.

In addition there are some institutions which offer foundation degrees[13] linked to advice or legal advice skills. In the past these tended to focus more generically on education in advice work; now they tend to be aimed at providing stepping stones to legal executive or paralegal qualifications. Foundation degrees in Paralegal Studies are offered by the University of South Wales in Glamorgan, Peterborough Regional College and Newcastle College (who run their course in conjunction with the National Association of Licensed Paralegals). Furthermore, these courses tend to offer a somewhat mainstream mix of legal topics in order to provide a reliable base for traditional legal practice areas as well as providing CILEX qualifications as part of the course. Options to study social welfare law topics are less evident when looking at these course outlines. The Foundation Degree in Law and Business Studies offered at Truro and Penwith College in Cornwall does however offer an interesting package, including modules on legal research and writing skills, family law and employment law.[14]

Short courses

For those in work or thinking of applying to volunteer or to become a paid adviser in the not-for-profit sector there are some excellent short courses available in topics relating to social welfare law and related advice skills. AdviceUK, which we briefly referred to in chapter 1, runs a number of short courses in various aspects of advice work and at various levels within the Qualifications and Credit Framework (QCF, replacing the earlier model of a National Vocational Qualification or NVQ). For example, they offer a ten-day course in 'Learning to Advise' as part of the QCF which is a stepping-stone to further credits in legal advice.

A number of short course providers of advice-related topics (including Citizens Advice and AdviceUK) have tailored the content of their courses around the National Occupational Standards recognised by Skills for Justice, discussed in more detail below. Skills for Justice is one of a number of 'suites' relating to the vocational training provided in various workplace sectors. A group of national advice agencies have developed a portfolio of qualifications in advice work

---

13 A two-year degree course. Foundation degrees can also provide for progression for further study and the credits necessary to obtain an honours degree.

14 See: www.truro-penwith.ac.uk/ft/fdsc-law/.

under the QCF in conjunction with the Sector Skills Council Skills for Justice.

Within a citizens advice bureau the volunteers (usually Gateway Assessors) can take a Level 2 Certificate in 'Supporting legal advice provision', and advisers carrying out generalist or case work advice can do a Level 3 QCF course in either 'Providing legal advice' or 'Providing initial legal information and advice'. The advantage of these qualifications is that they are nationally recognised and the units in the modules have credit values which can incrementally build up the adviser's qualifications. Furthermore, Citizens Advice have seen value reflected in better staff retention rates, enhanced skills in the bureaux and in leverage when making funding applications. We saw earlier that some solicitors and other regulated legal services providers have begun to offer advanced apprenticeships in legal advice. Citizens Advice have in 2013 developed a legal advice apprenticeship which has been approved by the National Apprenticeship Service and which they intend to add to the growing range of qualifications their staff can pursue for the benefit of the pro bono advice sector of which they form a significant part.

Standards: the National Occupational Standards

The development of the National Occupational Standards (NOS) in legal advice came about in 2006. They are recognised as part of the national framework of occupational standards. Nationally recognised occupational standards mean that employers and educational institutions can work together to ensure that more areas of work and employment are recognised by reference to skills and learning needed to work within that sector, and standards can be set down and followed by employers and educational institutions within the relevant skills sector.

The NOS in Legal Advice are to be found in full on the Skills for Justice section of the Skills Sector Council. They were updated in 2009 and a further review was initiated in 2013 to take into account the changes to legal aid and welfare benefits reform. Organisations and educational institutions offering courses and qualifications in the legal advice field will now often refer to the NOS in legal advice as the approved benchmark against which advice skills will be taught and practised. These standards have also formed the backbone of much of the approach of this book. Some of the standards are reproduced in appendix D in order to give a flavour of some of the advice skills they prescribe, and those in particular will underpin a number of topics looked at in future chapters.

3.5 Paid advice work

Apart from the professional qualification routes into paid employment as a legal adviser there are routes into being employed as a paid but not legally qualified practitioner as we have seen. Apart from the growing army of paralegals many of whom have legal qualifications, there are others who work as paid but not legally qualified advisers in many parts of the legal services sector. Not all employers in the advice sector will look for paper qualifications. Some may regard previous experience as sufficient. They may look for experience as a volunteer in the advice sector or work experience in a similar field, such as social or community care, or in a local authority as an adviser or administrator.

It is likely to be difficult to predict the type of qualification which an employer may prefer out of the options discussed above. In deciding on the most appropriate course of study to take, it may be advisable to scan job advertisements over a period of time to see what qualifications or experience employers are looking for when advertising jobs in the advice field. Some may specify a QCF level of qualification, some may specify degree level or above. Degrees in related topics such as social care or business studies may well be regarded as appropriate. In addition, having the experience of volunteering in an advice organisation will usually enhance a job application.

Some advisers working in the not-for-profit legal advice sector have worked in similar settings in local authorities, others in central government departments such as the Crown Prosecution Service or as court clerks or administrators. Others may have worked as paralegals for solicitors, or may have experience of giving advice but in the commercial or private sector. Many jobs in finance, such as insurance or building societies, have information and advice aspects to them. The advice sector will always seek to ensure that job applicants can show a commitment to the type of client they serve, that they are aware of equal opportunities and of the work done within the advice sector generally to promote justice for all. Any relevant experience which shows that commitment will be of benefit. Experience is often built up by an adviser moving around in that field, perhaps moving from a local to a national organisation or from advice to policy work. This is partly because there is a fairly limited career structure in the advice field with most people earning and working at similar levels in most organisations. It is also because many people like that working environment and choose to stay in it.

Advice centres and their ethos

Those who do work in a not-for-profit advice agency are likely to find that the ethos of the organisation is one of inclusiveness. Staff are usually valued highly and efforts are made when recruiting staff and volunteers to ensure that the workforce is as diverse as possible. Many community organisations which serve clients in a mixed ethnic community will endeavour to ensure that the staff-mix reflects the diversity of the local community in one way or another.

Staff may work for less pay than in other sectors but are likely to have relatively generous terms and conditions of service relating to holidays, family-friendly leave or flexible working. Pay structures are usually fairly rigid with little capacity for progression up a given pay scale or opportunity to benefit from regular pay rises. Pay will always be a part of the equation in ensuring that the funding provided is sufficient to meet all the needs of the organisation.

It can often be the case that an adviser, within limits laid down by good practice or funding restrictions, will have relative freedom to organise and shape the work that they do to the time and resources they have available to do it. Mention will be made of this in chapter 8 when looking at external influences which might be brought to bear on the adviser/client relationship.

Although advice organisations need to be professional in relation to the important service they provide to clients, many are, within that framework, relatively relaxed about dress codes or working structures. They are likely to support family-friendly approaches to working as well as teamwork and an open exchange of information and training in order to develop staff and services. A positive and supportive working environment will usually reflect back on to the clients, who will thereby not feel intimidated in approaching the agency and seeking its help.

3.6   Becoming a volunteer

Volunteering in an advice organisation or even a legal practice is a useful way of building up relevant experience to work in the advice sector, as well as a way of testing out commitment to this type of work.

Legal practices are more likely to offer a period of structured and unpaid 'work experience' (or in the case of barristers' chambers 'mini pupillages') aimed at law students hoping to qualify as lawyers.

Advice agencies will usually accept volunteers but may look for experience or qualifications or vary as to the work experience provided. LawWorks whom we discussed in chapter 1 has a steady turnover of law undergraduates and graduates (in law and other subjects) volunteering to do tasks, many of which will involve engaging with the law and/or members of the public. Most citizens advice bureaux will welcome volunteers from any background to do basic administrative work for short periods of time. Once an individual is accepted as a citizens advice volunteer where they will be engaging with the law and the public, they will be required to undertake the volunteer training programme outlined earlier which will provide the skills and competencies necessary to advise on the bureau's rota under supervision.

Another route is to apply to become a volunteer in any local or community organisation. This might include charity shops, community cafes or drop-in centres, church or other religious community activities, or any national organisation which has a shop or community centre or information centre. Some of this work may not be advice-based, but will provide experience of working with and for individuals using community services and may well involve observing or using a number of skills related to or similar to advice-giving. All volunteering is unpaid although it is often possible to claim some travelling or subsistence expenses.

3.7 Volunteer advisers: pro bono activities

A different approach to being a volunteer emanates from the services provided by qualified lawyers. Mention was made in chapter 1 of the programme of law clinics which is run by LawWorks. These clinics can be run anywhere in the UK. They are attended by solicitors or barristers who wish to offer pro bono services to their local community. The sessions are set up by a host organisation such as a law centre or university law clinic. The organisation will usually require the adviser to be a qualified lawyer to comply with the terms of its own insurance arrangements for the provision of legal advice to the public. Clients are then booked in by the host organisation and a group of volunteers will attend to give advice, usually in the evenings. Advice slots will be allocated with each volunteer seeing a few clients and allocating a time slot to each advice session. There is usually liaison between the host organisation and the adviser on the forthcoming queries booked into the advice session as well as follow-up on the content of the advice given. Most of these advice sessions are 'one-off' with the client outlining their story and then brief legal advice being given to the client by the adviser. Some form of written record will be made by the adviser and in some of these systems the adviser will follow up the oral advice with a letter of advice.

Even where advice sessions are not a part of the LawWorks network of clinics they will follow the same pattern. There are many lawyers providing pro bono legal advice throughout the country, usually in the evenings, in local community halls and centres or on the premises of an advice agency in order to support clients who do not qualify for free advice with a legal firm and/or who have legal problems which deeply affect their quality of life such as housing or family-related matters.

The number of qualified lawyers offering these free advice sessions is considerable and the assistance they give to clients is of great benefit. However, it is worth noting that they cannot replace the full legal service offered to either a legally aided or a private paying client as time is not on their side. They are doing this work as an unpaid adjunct to what is often a very busy daily practice. However, they can identify problems for a client, provide brief advice, and in many cases point them in the right direction as a litigant in person, perhaps towards the small claims court or an employment tribunal.

Sometimes the areas of law these volunteers are asked to advise on are not those regarded as traditional practice areas but are usually the areas of law practised by the host centre or clinic, which has identified from an enquiry the possibility of a short advice session being able to offer a total or partial resolution for that enquirer.

In other cases the host organisation will have had enquiries relating to areas of law they do not practise and so will be extending their scope by offering the advice sessions in these additional areas of law. There is no particular pattern of exactly how pro bono legal advice works but it is for many a haven where they are able to obtain the free and expert services of an experienced lawyer to begin to address or resolve their legal problem or even in some cases to identify the lack of any possible legal claim or resolution.

For the less experienced (perhaps newly qualified) pro bono legal volunteer it is to be hoped that some of the tips and tactics offered in the next chapters in relation to advice-giving may be of some value in this aspect of their work.

Core adviser skills

4.1   Introduction

Before we discuss in detail the various processes of advice-giving we will look at some of the attributes and requirements underpinning those processes. Part of being an adviser is to be aware not only of the key steps and strategies involved in giving advice but also some of the generic skills involved and an awareness of how they need to present themselves to their clients in order to provide a professional and rounded service.

4.2   Knowledge of the topic

Hopefully it will be self-evident that an adviser will know their subject area well in order to engage in the process of advice-giving. Those who have qualified as lawyers or have taken courses in advice work will quickly realise that they need to keep that knowledge active. In chapter 19 we will see how to conduct legal research and keep reference systems so that updates are readily accessible. In addition it will be important to keep abreast of changes in the law. One of the features of being a legal adviser which for some can be a source of despair and for others a source of challenge and interest, is the awareness that our legal system never stands still. Changes in the law come about frequently, not only in relation to what exactly the law says but in relation to judgments or decisions which clarify and interpret the law. No matter how advanced or detailed an adviser's knowledge is on any given area of law, they will always be keeping an eye on changes, amendments and updates.

At this stage it will be helpful to note that as continuous activity an adviser will ensure that they continue to research the law actively, rather than hoping that each time a relevant change comes along they will be able to grasp at it. They will have access to suitable resources to enable them to research their clients' legal problems. As we shall discuss further in chapter 19, if they are using textbooks or handbooks or even online reference systems they will ensure that these are up to date and/or be the latest editions: advice based on law or procedures which are out of date will be of little practical use.

4.3   Preparation and planning to give advice

Even where the adviser is well armed with a good body of knowledge concerning their subject area, they will still need to apply themselves to the specific topic which presents itself for advice. Initial instructions taken by a receptionist or volunteer in a legal or legal advice office are likely to be fact-based, not necessarily with all the relevant facts gathered at that stage. Prior to seeing or talking to the client, the adviser will be looking at any information they have received, starting to focus on the possible legal issues raised, and carrying out some preliminary research. An example of a telephone memo taken by a receptionist might be:

> Ms A rang in for advice in relation to a new sofa she bought. She says that the seats are sagging already even though the salesman in the shop said that they were good for bad backs. She wants to know what her rights are.

In this example, even prior to seeing the client, the adviser (who has some knowledge of consumers' legal rights), will be researching the following aspects of these instructions:

- Time limits – when an item was bought and the impact that might have on the buyer's rights.
- How the item was paid for and what the law says about rights for consumers in terms of methods of payment for goods.
- Who sold the item and their liability for any defects.
- Whether the client was persuaded to buy the item as a result of what the salesman told her.
- What the law says about statements about the quality of goods.
- What the law says about remedies and rights for defective goods bought.
- How remedies are effected – what court or jurisdiction deals with such claims.

So it will be seen that even given a brief set of facts the adviser will have the ability to test out their knowledge of the subject in advance by carrying out research. Some of that research will be aimed at checking and consolidating their knowledge of that area of law. They will at the same time be checking to see what the law currently says about each of these issues, including any recent case-law.[1] This will assist

---

1   We will look at case-law in more detail particularly in section 19.4. This is the description used in the legal world for 'judge-made' law, where a judge has

in making further enquiries of their client in a face-to-face meeting, in relation to the facts of their particular case and how, if at all, these might lead to a legal resolution. They will make notes of their preliminary research so that these can be added to and, if necessary, further research carried out once the client's story unfolds.

4.4   Independence and impartiality

These two concepts are really more about ethics than practice. They are familiar to a trained lawyer as they are part of their training and their ongoing obligations as professional practitioners. However, they are principles which should underpin the adviser's approach to their work, relating to how they conduct themselves with their own clients when advising or conducting case work and in relation to how they behave and present themselves to opponents or the public generally as the client's adviser.

What is meant by impartiality?

To be impartial means to treat all parties equally and fairly.[2] In the world of legal advice it is a term used to describe both an unbiased and even-handed approach not only to the conduct of each client's case but also to the provision of a legal advice service which aims to serve all comers in an even-handed manner. In relation to the first aspect, the adviser will ensure that they have no involvement in a case or with a client which might prevent them, or be seen to be preventing them, from acting in an objective manner for the client. An example of an involvement might mean being closely related to the client or having an interest in the outcome of a client's case whereby they might be able to gain some sort of benefit or advantage.

Equal opportunities

The second aspect is usually translated into an organisation committed to providing an accessible and inclusive service to the public. For public sector organisations this will be underpinned by a legal obligation

---

decided on a legal dispute and provided a decision for the parties in dispute as well as guidance on how the law should be interpreted.

2   'The quality or state of not being prejudiced towards or against any particular side or party/not prejudiced towards or against any particular side.' See: www.collinsdictionary.com/dictionary/english/impartiality.

to promote equality and diversity.[3] Advice-giving organisations will adopt equal opportunities policies and procedures in the provision of their services which are compliant with equality legislation.

Furthermore, the organisation's equal opportunities policy is likely to embrace a consideration not only of who makes up the local community, ensuring that all sections of that community obtain equal access to the organisation's services, but also awareness that the more 'hidden' members of the community should have equal access to their legal service. These individuals may include the housebound, those with mobility limitations or those who may not be able to communicate without interpreting services.

Maintaining impartiality with a difficult client

As we will see later, clients will present themselves to advisers in different ways and some can be more demanding of an adviser's time and patience. They may express unhappiness with an opponent or even their own adviser. Should this occur the adviser will seek to preserve their impartiality bearing in mind the strain a client is likely to be under dealing with the difficulties inherent in their case. In some rare instances a client's language or expressed views may border on the intemperate or inappropriate, in which circumstances the adviser will seek to remind the client of the need to communicate appropriately bearing in mind the ethos of the adviser's organisation in relation to tolerance and diversity. They will also reiterate for the client their own impartiality and willingness to do whatever they can to relieve for the client the stress and anxiety they face in dealing with their legal problem. If a client is acting in a difficult manner it will not inevitably mean that the relationship between adviser and client has irretrievably broken down. An adviser will always consider very carefully whether that has happened, a situation we will return to in section 5.5.

---

3 See for example Equality Act (EqA) 2010 s149, which in summary requires a public sector authority to promote equality and diversity, foster good relations between those who share 'protected characteristics' (such as age, race, religion, sex, sexual orientation, disability – see EqA 2010 s4) and those who do not, and to avoid discrimination in the provision of its services. Advice agencies are not 'public authorities' within the meaning of the EqA 2010, unless they are a branch of, say, a local authority. However, many not-for-profit advice agencies nevertheless do adopt a clear ethos of equality and diversity in the provision of their services.

Two clients with conflicting interests

Another allied but slightly different angle to the question of what might impact on an adviser's impartiality arises where they might have a conflict of interest. This is one of the elements of solicitors' professional conduct, but one which is known about and adopted by anyone giving legal advice. It can arise where an organisation or an individual adviser is placed in the position of having to advise two clients who have an opposing interest in the same matter, such as divorce proceedings or a landlord and tenant dispute. The adviser is unable to advise them both since there would be a conflict for them in terms of conducting each client's case with no appearance of bias and impartiality.[4] The adviser and their organisation will have systems in place whereby they make checks when a new client is entered into the system in order to find out whether the organisation or adviser is already advising another client who has an opposing interest in the same matter. If the second client is taken on unwittingly and the conflict discovered, the adviser will have to decline to advise that second client. They will explain what is meant by the conflict of interest that has arisen and ask the newer client to go elsewhere to seek independent advice.

Independence

An adviser, or the organisation they work for, should be free to act independently for their clients. This means that they must be free from any outside influence which seeks to affect the way in which the service is offered and/or to whom it is offered.

An example of where this might occur would be where an advice agency receives funding from a local housing association, or one of the association's staff sits on the agency's management committee or trustee board. The agency's advisers may be approached by a tenant of the association for advice. Where this does arise it may be prudent to inform a client of the position but to assure them of the adviser's independence and that as a professional adviser their primary obligation is to their client. The questions the adviser will ask themselves are whether there is any close connection between them and an opponent of their client and if there is, can they distance themselves from it in

---

4   Note that solicitors can in some specialised circumstances act for two clients where there may be or appears to be a conflict. Here we only set out the general principle which guides an adviser to avoid a conflict.

order to advise a client. They will be assisted in this latter process by their obligations of confidentiality.

4.5 Client confidentiality

A further ethical principle but one which underpins much of the adviser's work on a day-to-day basis is the duty to keep a client's affairs confidential. Any information which is given to the adviser by the client should not be disclosed by the adviser without the client's permission. A client can be assured of this at all times, including where there may be the appearance of a lack of independence on the part of an adviser due to the type of situation outlined above. The basic position is that most of the information the client passes on to the adviser and all of the advice given to the client is subject to a strict veil of confidentiality which the adviser is bound by. This concept is also embedded in solicitors' professional conduct rules but will be practised by others who offer advice and legal advice in whatever setting.

Not all information will need to be kept confidential as there will be some aspects of the client's story which will inevitably need to be passed on to third parties in order to assist in outlining the client's position or progressing their case. For convenience therefore we can talk about 'kinds' or 'types' of information to distinguish between what could be passed on and what should not be passed on by an adviser to the outside world. These kinds of information can be outlined as follows:

1) Facts of the client's case: what happened to them.
2) How the client may have suffered loss or hurt as a result of what a third party has done or failed to do and what the loss or hurt entails for that client.
3) Personal information about the client, their medical, financial or family details.
4) The advice which the adviser gives to the client.
5) What steps the client wishes the adviser to take based on the advice given to the client by the adviser.

Which of these five types of information are confidential?

1) **Facts:** The adviser may be authorised by their client to disclose facts to an outsider as relayed to them by their client in order to clarify with that party what exactly happened or what their client is saying happened to them. This often happens where there is a dispute as to what the true facts of a situation are.

2) **Losses:** The adviser will in all probability need to relay to an opponent what their client's losses are or how they felt about what happened to them where the client is making a claim for losses or compensation.

3) **Personal information about the client:** On the face of it this information is highly sensitive. However, there may be circumstances where it would be appropriate, with the client's consent, for an adviser to disclose it to a third party. This might be for the purposes of giving substance to a claim for an injury (medical information) or to support a claim for benefits or an offer to pay off rent arrears. There are also some circumstances in which such information will be required to be disclosed. A benefit appeal tribunal will expect full disclosure of an appellant's financial affairs in order to reach the correct decision as to their entitlement to benefit. A civil court will require medical evidence to be disclosed where injuries are alleged to have occurred and claims for compensation being made.

4) **Advice and client privilege:** The adviser has no obligation to disclose to any third party the advice they give to their client, or the discussions surrounding that advice-giving. The adviser should not only explain this to their client but also let the client know that the client has no obligation to tell anyone what their adviser advised them or what discussions took place around the adviser giving the client advice. This is known in legal circles as client privilege or privileged information and for a lawyer it means they have no obligation to tell anyone (including a court of law) what passed between them and their client as part of the process of offering advice. There are, however, often debates about which information is truly privileged in law, and there are occasions when a summary of the advice given to a client may usefully be offered to an outsider (with the client's permission) in order to clarify the client's stance or what actions the adviser or client mean to take to resolve the client's problem.

5) **Further instructions to the adviser:** As indicated above, these are likely to arise out of the advice relayed to the client. The client's further instructions can, in appropriate instances and with the client's consent, be relayed elsewhere. If, for example, the adviser says that a client has a good chance of recovering money, and a sum is discussed, that sum can be relayed to a third party having arisen in the context of the client giving instructions to their adviser to accept that sum if offered.

Because client confidentiality is so important, advisers will always follow up interviews with written confirmation of instructions, advice and next steps and require the client to confirm all these matters and to check drafts of letters to be sent to third parties. We will look at this as part of the process of taking instructions in chapter 7 and advice skills in Part 3. In relation to what is confidential and what should be disclosed to a third party, the rule of thumb is that the closer the communication is to the heart of the client's case, the more likely it is that the adviser will judge it to be subject to the duty of confidentiality.

4.6 Listening and counselling

Listening: supportive and focused

A client may find it upsetting to outline the problem they need advice on. They may be surprised to find that their adviser will require them to talk about it in considerable detail, not only at the outset but on an ongoing basis, which may be a painful process. They may also react emotionally to advice or other information given or display symptoms of stress arising out of the circumstances of the legal problem they require advice on. There may also be other aspects of the client's life which underlie the problem they have come to see their adviser about, such as family or financial worries. An adviser who is dealing with one aspect of the client's life may find that they will need to adopt a sensitive and supportive approach to others, giving their client the confidence to discuss these matters where they form part of the whole picture the client needs to present. Advisers will develop strategies for offering such support by, for example, adopting a listening stance which is sympathetic and patient and provides a safe and trusting environment where the client will feel able to speak freely and frankly.

Counselling and offering encouragement

Legal advisers may also find themselves engaged in the process of counselling their clients as their cases progress and at their conclusion. This activity is likely to relate to supporting the client through the problem which they bring to their adviser as well as suggesting practical solutions or ways forward for the client. Counselling is a specialised field of expertise and there is no assumption made in referring to this activity that an individual engaged in advice work has or should have the necessary skills of a trained counsellor, although part of their function may involve them in offering encouragement and support from time to time.

For example, at the conclusion of a client's case, the client may not only seek to know the legal significance of an outcome or a decision but how it might have an impact on them and others. Many clients come for advice because they want to see justice done, as well as obtaining an outcome that is beneficial for them. The adviser is likely to find that they are counselling their client at this stage, reflecting with them on the process they have gone through and its positive and negative outcomes. This will involve encouraging the client to take a realistic view of how the process has changed them and may be able to change others. At the end of the advice process the adviser will know when to 'draw the line' and when they will cease to provide advice, even though they may offer encouragement to their clients in their future plans and actions.

4.7   Displaying confidence in the client's case

This might not appear to require any explanation given that the legal adviser acts as a champion for their clients, putting their case to a court or opponent, or defending the client's rights. Nevertheless it is not uncommon for an adviser to find that clients will approach them with an apparently incredible set of facts or ones which are entirely contradictory. They may describe a situation which is the polar opposite of information the adviser may have received from the client's opponent. In spite of this, the adviser will express confidence in the client's case. As we will see later, part of the process of taking instructions will involve testing out the client's case and ensuring that it is consistent and fits in with the way in which the adviser hopes to achieve a positive result for the client. Even where there are gaps and the adviser has personal doubts as to how the evidence or the case will stand up, they will avoid adopting a critical or judgmental stance. This will allow them to probe for as much detail as they need to put the case at its best and offer realistic advice (which of course may be negative as well as positive).

It is, however, important to distinguish between testing out the case, displaying confidence in the case and a situation where either the client admits to being untruthful or discloses information which puts them and their adviser into legal jeopardy. An adviser with an untruthful client is likely to be entitled to withdraw from being their adviser as the client would be either asking the adviser to present an untruthful picture in order to ameliorate the client's position or would be putting the adviser in a position where they could no longer have confidence in their client. There are also a number of situations which advisers must be wary of where a client might admit to fraud, mishandling of funds or other possible criminal offences. Most legal advisers are strictly bound by money-laundering rules and are also required to avoid any situation where they can be seen to be aiding someone in the commission of an offence. Where either of these two situations arises, the adviser will need to not only take steps to remove themselves from the client relationship but may have an obligation to report criminal wrongdoing to the relevant authorities, an obligation which overrides their duty of confidentiality.[5] Fortunately these situations are rare and this aspect of the adviser's work will usually be demonstrated by a firm and unwavering commitment to and confidence in the client's case in all its aspects, both obvious and obscure.

4.8 Providing advice – appropriate and client-focused

This aspect of the adviser's work follows on from all we have covered in this chapter about the core skills of the adviser. The legal adviser will be seen to be a legal expert, well-prepared and researched for the task in hand, an individual exercising an unbiased and independent stance in order to provide the best advice for their client. They are good listeners, can offer basic counselling to support their client through the difficulties caused by their legal problems. They will ensure that the client's affairs are kept confidential and will ensure that the advice they give is appropriate for that client in order for the client to process the advice and if necessary act upon it.

In this era of standard letters and templates, there is an inherent danger that the process of giving advice can be obscured. Clients are sent client care letters, letters about fees, costs and the organisation's structure and letters about how to complain. While this is necessary and useful information, at the forefront of the relationship must be the provision of advice. For a new adviser this can be quite a daunting process. Even though they will have carefully prepared for an

---

5   Rule 4 of the Solicitors Code of Conduct 2007 also deals with the difficult balance a solicitor may sometimes need to exercise in terms of what information to disclose where there may be a legal obligation to disclose or the possibility of a criminal offence having been committed or the wellbeing of others, such as children, may be at risk. See rules 4.9–4.19.

interview in advance, including researching the relevant law, they will have to face the point in that process where they are asked to advise – will I win my case or achieve what I want to achieve by way of an outcome? There are, of course, many variables to be built in to advice provided in response to this question, but nevertheless this is at the heart of the advice-giving process and is a skill which develops over time. There is nothing wrong with telling a client that part or indeed all of the advice needs to be relayed later once the adviser has further considered all the relevant aspects of the case. Nevertheless, there is nothing more satisfying for the adviser, once they are ready to advise, than identifying for the client the relevant facts of their case, how the law impacts on those facts, and the best way in which the law can be utilised in order to achieve a just outcome. There is a sample advice letter in appendix A which has been written as part of the process of an imagined case set out there which will hopefully be a useful template to show how legal advice can be delivered to the new client.

PART 2

The adviser/client relationship

CHAPTER 5

The adviser and their client

5.1   The definition of a 'client'

Seeks advice and assistance using specialist resources

The word 'client' is now used much more widely than it used to be. It was once the case that only professional advisers, such as lawyers, architects or accountants had clients, while other organisations might have 'callers' or 'customers'. Nowadays it is quite common for anyone who provides a service for another individual or group of individuals to describe that group as their 'clients'. Examples might include the description of the relationship between a business and its external contractors, or a service provider such as a hairdresser.

In the legal advice field the word 'client' has a specific meaning. A potential client will approach a legal advice organisation because it describes itself as offering advice or information in respect of a particular field of legal knowledge, which will assist the client in effecting change or resolving a problem they have in that area.

The individual seeking to become a client will require an adviser to take from them part of the burden of the unresolved problem. They will expect the adviser to meet their expectations as an expert or someone with acquired knowledge which will be used to resolve the client's problem. They will also place their trust in the adviser in terms of expecting the adviser to act as their champion, and achieve the desired outcome for the client, using their skills and knowledge in the process. They will expect the adviser to be non-judgmental and impartial in relation to what the client tells them. They will also form the assumption that the trust they place in the adviser will include a commitment by their adviser not to tell others what passes between the client and the adviser.

5.2   Enquiries, matters, problems and cases

Before looking at models of the adviser/client relationship in more detail, it may be helpful to clarify some different terms used to describe what it is the individual is bringing to an organisation when seeking its help. Depending on the complexity or type of legal query, it may be given one of a number of descriptions by a legal agency, although when dealing with each of these queries it can be the case that the term 'client' is used to describe the person making the approach.

Enquiries

Many organisations where substantive legal advice is given will also provide a service for the general public making an 'enquiry'. The nature of such an enquiry may be to find out what help or assistance might be available for them in that organisation or elsewhere. It may simply be a request to specify the type of problem that they have. It may be to ask for information and guidance as to what their options are for taking a particular enquiry further. For example, an individual may come to an organisation and say that they have left their violent partner. They may be given information about the different services they might want to use in that situation, such as those of the police, a refuge or a lawyer. They may be referred to a solicitor for advice. These enquiries are usually dealt with in the context of providing a signposting service which we will look at below.

Matters

The type of enquiry the client has will often be referred to as a 'matter'. This gives it a context, such as the client's 'housing matter' or 'welfare benefits matter'. This way of describing the subject matter of clients' cases has been used by solicitors' firms for many years and it does seem to be a useful way of 'pigeon-holing' different types of cases.

Problems

Within the framework of the type of matter they bring to the adviser the client will be seeking a resolution of some sort. Within the context of the housing matter they may be seeking help because they are facing eviction, or within the context of their welfare benefits matter they may have been refused a benefit.

The *fact* of their impending eviction or lack of the benefit will be referred to as a 'problem'. The word 'problem' in the context of advice-giving is sometimes replaced by other words such as 'issue' on the basis that calling something a problem perhaps denotes fault on the part of the person with the problem. However, the word 'issue' in a legal context usually means something which needs to be resolved between two opposing parties, for example whether or not a landlord has the legal right to evict a tenant in a specific set of circumstances (that right is declared to be 'in issue'). Furthermore, in its current everyday meaning of 'query' or 'concern' the word may not always carry with it the seriousness of an unresolved legal problem which the client is carrying the burden of and is looking for expert help to resolve, and so the word problem will be used for preference.

Cases

Once the problem has been formulated and it has been agreed that the burden of it will be shared by the adviser, it will be referred to by the adviser as a 'case'. As we shall see later,[1] sometimes what the client wants others to accept (eg, that they have a legal entitlement not to be evicted or to the welfare benefit they have applied for) will be referred to as the client's 'case'. The adviser will be dealing with that as part of advising their client as well as referring to the client's case as being the totality of the client's problem and its need for a resolution. Where advisers have a number of clients they are advising and assisting they will refer to that as their 'caseload'. The adviser may offer advice only, in order to enable the client to resolve their case themselves, or the adviser may take certain limited steps to resolve a client's case, depending on the nature of the service they are offering. Alternatively, they may 'take on' a client's case. There are various models of an adviser/client relationship in the advice sector as we shall see in the next section.

5.3   Models of the adviser/client relationship

It is important for both the adviser and the client to reach a clear understanding of the point at which an individual actually *becomes* a client. Under each of the models described below, organisations may refer to those that they assist as 'clients'. There are distinctions, however, between advisers who provide specialist information, those who give information and advice relevant to the facts of the client's case, and those who take from the client the burden of conducting their case, and who may also act as an advocate for their client with a third party. Different types of advice agencies will adopt a different approach in the advice service they offer. In all models however, the adviser/client relationship will have the hallmarks of offering expert advice in a confidential setting. Some examples of the various approaches to forming or describing an adviser/client relationship which arise in the legal services sector are outlined below.

---

1   See section 14.1.

Giving information or signposting

An individual may come to an organisation with all the expectations outlined above as to what they would like an organisation to achieve for them but may benefit from or be initially offered only some preliminary information and advice. It may be explained to them that this is not the organisation best suited to their needs and they will then be given some 'signposting' information and directed to another type of service.[2] The organisation may provide a signposting service which involves analysing the nature of the legal problem for the enquirer. The gateway assessor service in a citizens advice bureau referred to in previous chapters can include supplying an analysis of the nature of an individual's legal problem as well as suggesting a route for them to obtain further assistance and advice where necessary, either at that bureau or at another agency better suited to meeting their needs.

A signposting service will quite commonly be provided as an adjunct to that of the provision of legal advice or representation, both in solicitors' offices and community advice agencies. In providing the service the organisation will deal with the individual's expectations by providing useful information and guidance which not only identifies the nature of their legal problem but provides them with an appropriate route to resolving it. As we saw above, this process will often be described as dealing with an enquiry. However, some organisations in providing this service may describe the enquirer as a client and may keep records of these enquiries even though they do not take on any further responsibility for progressing the client's legal problem.

Giving advice but not taking on a case for the client

In the advice sector, advisers may work on more than one level in terms of the advice service they offer. One approach is to offer advice to callers or people who come to drop-in sessions or via email advice services. An individual may tell the adviser in some detail what their problem is and in return will obtain legal advice. This process has many of the hallmarks of the adviser/client relationship and even where the advice is 'one-off' the individual will usually be referred to as a client.

When providing this type of service the adviser is fulfilling the client's expectations to the extent that the advice given will be specialist and relevant to the client's legal problem and will be provided

---

2 See section 1.2.

in confidence. The adviser's role will be limited to the provision of advice even though further steps may need to be taken to resolve the client's problem. Advice will be provided in person, by email or over the telephone and in some instances also recorded in writing for the client. Some of these advice services will also help clients to write letters or may even write a letter on behalf of a client to an outside person or agency. Whatever the preliminary steps are, they will not involve the adviser 'taking on' the client's case, a process we will look at next. In section 3.7 we saw an example of this model of the adviser/client relationship when a legal volunteer takes part in an evening advice session or a LawWorks clinic. Later in section 10. 5 we will see an example of that process operating in practice.

Taking on a case: advice and representation

Where the adviser agrees to take steps on behalf of a client and to share the burden of the client's problem, they will usually refer to this as 'taking on the client's case'. This includes giving advice in the way outlined in the previous paragraph, but taking on more for the client, sharing the burden of the client's case and pursuing all necessary steps to resolve it on behalf of the client. It will also involve the adviser informing any other parties with an interest in the client's case that they are the client's adviser and/or representative and that communication to and from the client can be made through them. The actions they may take on behalf of the client may extend to offering to represent a client in a court or tribunal in which case it may also be referred to as providing 'advice and representation'. Where representation is not part of the service offered, other substantial steps will nevertheless be taken to resolve the client's case. In any event a file will be opened, letters or emails written and telephone calls made on the client's behalf which are likely to involve setting out the client's case, and attempting to negotiate or resolve the case for the client. This model of the adviser/client relationship where the adviser steps into the shoes of the client and conducts their case for them is the one most commonly found in a solicitor's practice or law centre.

As we will see later, the formation of that relationship is contractual. It will be recorded in writing, with details provided as to how the two parties have agreed that the relationship will be conducted. The adviser will write the client a letter recording the creation of the adviser/client relationship, what its terms are and how it will be conducted by both parties. This is usually referred to as a 'client care letter' and an example of such a letter is in appendix A.

Specialist advice and support

We saw in chapter 2 an example of a national organisation, AdviceUK which provides information and support to other advice agencies. Another model of this type of advice-giving arises where a local advice agency which employs legal specialists in a particular field, such as immigration law, provides information or advice to other agencies in the locality assisting with a different aspect of a client's legal problem. An example of this localised support is the provision by immigration legal advisers within Kent Law Clinic of specialist advice (channelled through a local advice partnership called the Advice Partnership of East Kent referred to in chapter 2) to other agencies dealing with various aspects of support provided to refugees and asylum seekers. This is just one example of this model of the provision of advice or exchange of information at community level. In no case, however, will one organisation be described as a client of the other. The entire process will be aimed at providing as comprehensive an approach as possible to meeting the needs of various client groups in that locality or community.

5.4   Key elements of the adviser/client relationship

Introduction: in the nature of a contract

The list of expectations which a client will bring to the adviser/client relationship were listed in section 5.1 above. From the adviser's perspective, the formation of the relationship will involve them in meeting these expectations as well as ensuring that the adviser/client relationship is professional and binding, Once the adviser and the client are in agreement that the adviser will offer assistance, they will have entered into a contract in which there are obligations on both sides. Even if the client is not paying money to their adviser for the service they provide, the arrangement will still be in the nature of a contract with expectations as to how it will be performed by each party.

Where the adviser is taking on the case for the client, they will take an active part in its resolution. They will give the problem a name, a legal context, analyse it in terms of how best it can be resolved, and plan with the client how to resolve it. The adviser cannot take ownership of the problem away from the client, although some clients will initially hope that their adviser can do just that by taking it over and dealing with all aspects of it. It is crucial that the burden is shared, with the adviser shouldering the responsibility of analysis, advice and taking steps towards resolution. The client will need to understand the analysis, act on the advice and take an active part in the resolution.

Adviser's primary functions

In taking on a client's case, the process of giving advice and taking steps to resolve a client's legal problem will involve the adviser engaging in the following activities.

Taking and following instructions

The client will be asked by the adviser to tell them their story, in other words, all they are able to say and recall about what happened to them and what they think they need help in resolving. This process of telling the adviser their story is known as the client instructing the adviser or giving instructions to the adviser. Furthermore a client will also ask their adviser to take certain steps on their behalf (such as writing a letter to another person or organisation). This is also known as giving instructions. The adviser will then be following the client's instructions. We will look at these two processes in more detail in the next chapter.

Advising the client

Once the adviser is satisfied that they have understood the client's problem they will offer them advice, usually in the following pattern:

- explaining what the relevant law is;
- analysing the client's problem by giving it a legal context;
- advising on the most effective way of resolving the problem in terms of using the law which will also involve taking practical steps;
- advising on a course of action which the client can take themselves to resolve the problem; or
- advising on a course of action which the adviser is prepared to take on behalf of the client to resolve the problem.

More detail as to how this process operates will emerge as we progress and particularly in chapter 10, as part of giving and recording advice.

Taking steps to resolve the problem on the client's behalf

Following on from the advice given, the adviser may be authorised to take certain steps on the client's behalf. These may include writing letters or emails, speaking to agencies, landlords, employers, or solicitors representing others. Many outside agencies will expect an adviser to produce written authorisation from the client to speak and act on their behalf to them. In the context of conducting court proceedings, a solicitor will refer to themselves as 'going on the record'. In other words, they are making a statement to the court that they are the authorised representative of that client for the purpose of the conduct of that case. In the civil courts a solicitor will be required to file a formal notice with the court to place themselves 'on the record' as being that client's qualified legal representative.

Acting in the client's best interests

The adviser will seek to resolve the client's problem in a way that is most helpful to them. For example, a client may have a credit card debt and be advised to take out a loan to pay it off. If they then disclose to their adviser that have other existing debts, this may not necessarily be the solution which is in their best interests as it will add to their burden of debt. The adviser may therefore move on to advise on other options such as consolidating all the client's debts.

Having trust and confidence in the client

As well as the adviser requiring the client to provide full and frank disclosure of all matters relevant to their legal problem, the adviser will also contribute to the element of mutual trust and confidence inherent in the relationship. The client should be able to assume that their adviser will treat them with respect, will offer their services in the manner and at the times promised and will act responsibly and professionally in dealing with the matters which the client has entrusted to them. The adviser will also display confidence in the client's case, maintaining an open approach to whatever position the client adopts in relation to their legal problem. An adviser is fully entitled to put a client's story or case to the test to ensure it is accurate and watertight, but will do so without jumping to conclusions, showing a judgmental attitude or displaying incredulity or disbelief in what the client tells them.

Keeping the client's matters confidential

We saw in the previous chapter that knowing how and when to preserve client confidentiality is a key skill for the legal adviser. The client is entitled to be confident that what passes between them and their adviser will not be repeated except in the limited circumstances referred to there. Furthermore, within an organisation there will be procedures in place about file and information sharing which we will look at in chapter 12 as part of case management.

5.5   Ending the adviser/client relationship

Although this book focuses on the skills inherent in building up and developing a successful adviser/client relationship, it may be helpful to be aware of the traditional routes which lead to the termination of that relationship. These are where:

- the adviser has resolved the problem and the client agrees that no further action need be taken;
- the adviser loses contact with the client and can no longer take their instructions;
- the client decides to stop instructing the adviser or changes to another adviser; or
- the adviser is no longer able to continue to advise or advocate for the client due to a breakdown in the adviser/client relationship.

With the exception of the first of these situations, in each case the relationship will be terminated prior to the adviser resolving the case. The various ways in which cases are resolved with adviser input will be examined in Parts 4 and 5 on case progression and case resolution.

Losing contact with the client

Where an adviser cannot conclude because of a lack of client contact, the adviser will ensure that the termination and the reasons for it are recorded in writing. Reminders will be written seeking further instruction and checks made of the client's contact details to ensure that they are accurately recorded. A letter concluding the case will confirm the lack of contact. Recording this state of affairs will also be a form of protection for the adviser in the unlikely event of the client complaining that the adviser has sought to terminate the relationship prematurely or inappropriately.

Change of adviser

If there is a change to another adviser, the new adviser will contact the existing adviser with the client's authority to request the release of any copy papers or information which the existing adviser may have collected to date in relation to the matter which they are dealing with for that client. Obtaining the client's authority will usually involve the client signing a form in which they are requesting their existing adviser to hand their papers over to the new adviser. Referrals to another adviser are also discussed in section 13.5.

Breakdown in adviser/client relationship

If a client states that they are unhappy with their adviser, every effort should be made to explore the problem and resolve it. If necessary, the adviser's complaints procedures should be used to assist. If the client nevertheless indicates that they no longer wish to use the adviser's services, the adviser will record this in a letter to the client. This record will also refer to any complaints procedure followed to try to resolve the problem.

Alternatively the adviser may have reached a point where they do not feel able to continue to advise or assist their client. This will arise where the adviser has decided that trust and confidence between the adviser and the client has broken down. This mutual relationship of 'trust and confidence' is a cornerstone of the adviser/client relationship as we have already seen.

The breakdown of trust could arise in a number of different ways. A client may:

- become abusive or unco-operative;
- fail to give their adviser key information or accept their advice;
- deliberately withhold or falsify information; or
- complain in terms of showing a lack of confidence in their adviser.

These situations are thankfully rare but nevertheless will give rise to a need for the adviser to terminate the relationship. This will be done after careful consideration and in writing, setting out the reasons for the termination.

Finally, it should be noted that the legal limitation period for claims for breach of contract is six years. In other words the courts will be able to entertain claims based on a contract or part of a contract at any time within that limitation period starting from the date the contract was originally formed. For this reason, organisations that are insured to provide legal advice will be expected to keep a copy of a client's file for at least six years following the conclusion of the case should any such claim be raised by an ex-client.

The client

6.1   Features of a client – general

There are some general features in terms of how a client relates to the adviser which the adviser will be looking for to assist them in the smooth running of the client's case. Not all clients will find it easy to adapt to that process and some will require particular attention as we will see. Furthermore, as will be discussed in chapter 8, there are likely to be a number of external pressures and influences brought to bear on the adviser/client relationship. In spite of such factors, every effort will be made to accommodate each client, with what will invariably will be their differing ways of relating to an adviser.

The ideal client

As a starting point we will look at the client who can relate to their adviser in ways which will assist the adviser in conducting their case effectively and within any time constraints imposed. Ideally such a client will:

- keep to pre-arranged appointments;
- answer the adviser's questions promptly and fully;
- provide information requested by the adviser in a timely and clear manner;
- give clear instructions about how they would like to progress their case;
- communicate effectively any agreement to actions to be taken to progress the case, both by the adviser and the client;
- take responsibility for certain aspects of their case if requested to by their adviser and see those tasks through;
- have available any relevant documentation which supports what they say about their case including any requested by their legal adviser;
- have that documentation arranged in a helpful or ordered fashion;
- be consistent in what they tell their adviser about their case or things that they have said or done in the past or that have happened to them; and
- when accepting legal advice from their adviser act consistently on it.

Advisers will reinforce those expectations when they meet or write to their clients as being the most efficacious way of working with them towards achieving a helpful outcome to the case.

Pressures on the client

Nevertheless, many clients do not or cannot conform to these expectations, and usually with good reason. The request for legal advice and assistance is likely to arise in the context of a highly stressful or upsetting situation which has affected the client. They may have other domestic or financial pressures to deal with, and the combination of these factors may lead to difficulties in keeping to the ideal format as outlined above in order to assist with the progress of their case.

Furthermore, once someone becomes a client they continue to shoulder the problem which is causing them to seek advice together with the anxiety of awaiting its outcome. They may also feel upset or angry about the attitude or behaviour of any opponent or decision-maker and nervous about giving evidence in a court or tribunal. All these concerns are likely, from time to time, to lead to lapses in clear thinking. Furthermore, not every client will find the legal advice given to them acceptable or palatable as it may differ from what they were expecting. For some clients the process of accepting advice and placing their trust in the skills of their adviser may be more gradual. The adviser will therefore need to be flexible in terms of how these concerns and expectations, and sometimes personal circumstances, might factor into how each client may relate to them. They will be able to accommodate clients' differences and maintain awareness of the pressures they are under, in order to achieve an equally efficient and effective outcome for each client.

6.2   Clients who are vulnerable

In addition to dealing with these understandable pressures brought about by the circumstances of their legal problem, some clients may also be vulnerable. Where this aspect of a client presents itself, the adviser may need to identify the source of the client's vulnerability or in any event accommodate that aspect of the client in terms of how they are able to relate to their adviser.

There are some types of legal claims which a client will have in which they claim that their current state of health, mental or physical, has arisen as result of a legal wrong. An example would be a client seeking damages for a road accident in which they have been injured, or compensation for an act of racial or sexual discrimination or harassment in the work place which has affected their mental health. Unless they lack 'capacity', which is a legal term we will discuss below, this aspect of the client will be one which the adviser will need to be sensitive to. The adviser should ask the client for any guidance on how they can best relate to their adviser in terms of keeping to appointments, the length and conduct of interviews, or how best to communicate advice to them. A client with this type of legal problem is likely to be advised to obtain medical evidence in the form of doctors' reports in order to support a claim. If the adviser has obtained such a report on behalf of the client, information concerning the client's medical condition provided in it may also be able to assist the adviser in how to best communicate with the client, as well as being of evidential value in supporting the client's case.

In addition there may be clients who are vulnerable but whose vulnerability is not the source of the legal problem they have brought to their adviser. Such a client may not necessarily describe themselves as vulnerable to their adviser. The adviser may, however, note that the client is finding it particularly difficult to order their thoughts, understand what is being explained to them or the advice which is being given. They may have difficulty in concentrating, recalling events or understanding documents. Advisers should be alert to this possibility and take extra time wherever possible to accommodate these features, as well as regularly checking with the client that they are engaging in the process of the conduct of their case.

Lacking capacity?

If difficulties in communication appear be quite substantial, the adviser may need to decide whether the client is or appears capable of making a decision. This has a more formal meaning. In considering what might be a lack of capacity to make decisions, advisers will be asking themselves the following questions :

- Is the client able to recognise and describe their problem/situation in order to seek assistance in resolving it?
- Can the client explain to the adviser (even with the help of friends, carers or others) what their problem is?
- Can the client properly understand the advice given to them – either face to face or by letter? If they are asked to confirm that they do understand and they do so, how does the adviser know this to be the case?
- Can the client take any necessary steps to progress the matter, eg, find documents, recall incidents and provide a statement?

- Is the client able to evaluate and understand the effects of taking the advice offered and are they capable of putting the advice given into effect?

If a client appears unable to comply with any of these requirements, it is possible that they may lack capacity. The steps above are those which form the 'test' of whether a client lacks capacity (which usually arises from their age or mental capacity). They are set out in a Court of Appeal decision giving guidance as to when a client may lack the capacity which would enable them to instruct an adviser and understand and act upon advice given.[1]

The legal presumption is, however, that everyone has capacity to give instructions and follow legal or other advice in relation to their affairs (which includes legal affairs). This presumption is provided for in the Mental Capacity Act (MCA) 2005 s1. The Act then goes on to state that the key test of capacity is whether or not a person is capable of making a decision.[2] In consequence of this, the adviser will not assume that the client lacks capacity unless they have formed a considered view that the client is unable to comply with this legal test. There will be instances where clients may have short-term illnesses, or unwell periods for those with long-term mental illnesses, or may have experienced life-changing events which cause them severe shocks or set-backs. These situations, however, are most unlikely to amount to a lack of capacity within the meaning of the MCA 2005. The adviser will therefore persevere with such aspects of a client's approach to them prior to considering whether they might lack capacity. Useful guidance is offered in a booklet issued by the Office of the Public Guardian (OPG) as to when a client may or may not have capacity to attend to their affairs (including legal affairs).[3] The Public

1 *Martin Masterman-Lister v (1) Brutton & Co; and (2) Jewell & Home Counties Dairies* [2002] EWCA Civ 1889.
2 See MCA 2005 s2: People who lack capacity:
   (1) For the purposes of this Act, a person lacks capacity in relation to a matter if at the material time he is unable to make a decision for himself in relation to the matter because of an impairment of, or a disturbance in the functioning of, the mind or brain.
   (2) It does not matter whether the impairment or disturbance is permanent or temporary.
   (3) A lack of capacity cannot be established merely by reference to –
      (a) a person's age or appearance, or
      (b) a condition of his, or an aspect of his behaviour, which might lead others to make unjustified assumptions about his capacity.
3 See OPG 604 *Making decisions: a guide for advice workers*. See also the link to it on the Ministry of Justice website at www.justice.gov.uk/protecting-the-vulnerable/mental-capacity-act.

Guardian was appointed under the MCA 2005 to provide further safe-guards for those lacking capacity in circumstances where others have been appointed to make their decisions for them, some of which we will examine below.

Lasting power of attorney

Occasionally an adviser may be approached by someone who states that they are an attorney for another person. In these circumstances it is likely that the client has created a lasting power of attorney (LPA) which they must have taken an active part in creating prior to their loss of capacity.[4]

An LPA will grant someone else, often a close family member, the power to make decisions on that person's behalf. The need to take such a step may arise where a person is becoming very elderly or is diagnosed as being in the early stages of a medical condition which will mean that they are likely to lose capacity. Prior to 2007 these powers were called enduring powers of attorney (EPA) and so an adviser may find they are approached by a client's attorney acting under one of these. The MCA 2005 lays down the requirements for a valid power of attorney, and if an adviser is approached by someone describing themselves as an attorney who is authorised to make deci-sions in relation to the conduct of another's person's affairs, it would be prudent to check for proof that a valid LPA has been created. Both an LPA and an EPA must be approved and registered by the Public Guardian and so the simplest way to check that they are valid would be to search the register of the Public Guardian's office.[5]

Court of Protection and the Official Solicitor

This court is also described in terms of its functions under the MCA 2005 and has powers to make orders in relation to the conduct of legal or other affairs for a person lacking capacity. For example, the court can appoint a deputy to deal with a person's affairs.[6]

Where someone is a child (see below) or lacks capacity within the meaning of the MCA 2005, the Official Solicitor, an individual appointed by the government to oversee and advise on various public

---

4 See MCA 2005 s9.

5 See: www.gov.uk/find-someones-attorney-or-deputy Form OPG100.

6 MCA 2005 s18 outlines what is meant by these and includes dealing with property, contracts, debts, trusteeships and the conduct of legal proceedings.

legal functions of the government, can appoint someone (usually a solicitor in a firm of solicitors) to represent that person in court proceedings where it is clear that there is no one able or willing to represent them. An adult with a disability which means they lack capacity is called a protected party. The legal adviser appointed is called a litigation friend.[7]

There are some decisions nevertheless which should not be made by another person on behalf of someone who lacks capacity. These include decisions concerning marriage, divorce, sexual relations and voting which are referred to in section 27 of the MCA 2005.[8] If an adviser is instructed on any of these matters they must tread very carefully in relation to the obtaining of consents.

Advocates

Lay advocates, who assist vulnerable clients in getting through interviews or meetings, can also be of assistance to both the client and the adviser to enable the smooth process of an interview or the ongoing conduct of a case. An organisation like Voice Ability[9] has a national network of trained advocates to support such individuals in dealing with formal matters. In addition, the MCA 2005 provides for NHS Trusts to employ mental health advocates[10] to support clients who

---

7 See: www.justice.gov.uk/protecting-the-vulnerable/official-solicitor/other-civil-proceedings/litigation-friend.

8 Section 27: Family relationships etc:
   (1) Nothing in this Act permits a decision on any of the following matters to be made on behalf of a person –
   (a) consenting to marriage or a civil partnership,
   (b) consenting to have sexual relations,
   (c) consenting to a decree of divorce being granted on the basis of two years' separation,
   (d) consenting to a dissolution order being made in relation to a civil partnership on the basis of two years' separation,
   (e) consenting to a child's being placed for adoption by an adoption agency,
   (f) consenting to the making of an adoption order,
   (g) discharging parental responsibilities in matters not relating to a child's property,
   (h) giving a consent under the Human Fertilisation and Embryology Act 1990 (c 37),
   (i) giving a consent under the Human Fertilisation and Embryology Act 2008.

9 See: www.voiceability.org/.

10 Called Independent Mental Health Advocates (IMCA) in the MCA 2005 – see, eg, section 35.

lack mental capacity as outlined in the MCA 2005[11] where certain decisions are made about their lives, such as the provision of sheltered or local authority accommodation.

Enforced lack of ability to make decisions

It may be that the client has been placed in a position where they have been required to do something against their will. The client may be a woman who has entered into an arranged marriage or who is a domestic servant being abused by her employers and who is unable to leave. Alternatively, the client may be someone who has learning disabilities and who is being taken advantage of or held against their will. These are examples of situations the adviser may encounter where a decision has been made to deprive a client of their ability to make choices or the capacity to act freely in certain circumstances. In this context the client will be seeking a remedy which will include restoring their ability to act freely. This for the adviser is a specific legal process they will be engaging in for the client and bears no relation to the circumstances above describing a lack of capacity.

6.3   Reading and writing

There is some guidance which can be offered in respect of a client who is unable to read or write. Clients may not always admit to this initially, saying that they have poor eyesight, or have forgotten to bring an important document to an interview. If the adviser does identify this as being a barrier to communication for the client and the client is happy to agree ways of dealing with it, the adviser may canvass some or all of following approaches with the client to assist in the advice-giving process:

- If letters are sent to the client by the adviser, is there anyone that the client can call on for help in reading them?
- If there is no one, or if the client does not wish others to be aware of the confidential matters they are seeking advice on, is the client happy for the adviser themselves to read out to them the content of letters or documents either in person or by telephone?
- Would it assist if interviews or discussions between the adviser and client were recorded and sent to the client to complement letters which the adviser will send out setting out discussions and advice?

---

11   See MCA 2005 s16A onwards.

Signing documents

Where there is a requirement for a client to write or sign a formal document, such as a witness statement, as part of the conduct of their case, it will be permissible for such a document to be prepared by the adviser and then 'marked' by the client. The adviser or a legally qualified individual can then witness the client's mark. At the foot of the document the adviser will set out a short statement that the document is the client's in that it has been read out to them and that they understand it and are satisfied with the contents. The client can use the mark X if they are unable to write their name, and in order to validate the document fully, some other identifying reference can be added such as a National Insurance number. A witness statement prepared in this way can then be read out in court by someone other than the client or their adviser.

6.4   Children and young people

Legal rights and status

There may be circumstances in which an adviser is approached for advice by a child or young person. These might be young asylum-seekers, homeless persons or workers seeking to enforce their rights.

There are specific rules about the way in which child clients of varying ages are dealt with in the criminal system which are beyond the scope of this book. In the civil legal system the age to be aware of is the age of 18. This is when the client will be regarded in exactly the same way as any adult client. Below that age, however, there are certain features to be aware of. For example, young people under 18 (referred to in legal terms as 'minors'):

- Can enter into contracts to buy goods. However, unless the goods bought are regarded as 'necessaries' (items the minor needs to live, such as food or clothing) a contract with a minor is not enforceable. Where the goods are regarded as necessaries the minor is required to pay a 'reasonable price' for them.
- Can be employed and have specific legal rights at work.
- Cannot become owners of property in law. They can have a form of tenancy with a landlord which is called a 'beneficial tenancy', where they have a right to live in and use the property. Once they

reach the age of 18 they become legal tenants and are described as such on the tenancy agreement.

• Can claim asylum.

An adviser may be approached by a child or young person who is perhaps pregnant, vulnerable, homeless or has run up debts buying goods or using mobile phones or has a problem with a job. It may be that a parent, guardian or carer will be asking for assistance in resolving the situation. Consideration will need to be given as to whether the child or young person, or the parent, should be seen as the client. Thought should also be given to whether the child or young person can give instructions and understand and follow advice and can lawfully exercise the rights they are seeking to exercise. Once the adviser has satisfied themselves that they can continue to help a child or young person in their own right, they will be able to proceed to do so as with any other client.

Person with parental responsibility

Where there is a parent, carer or guardian, they are the person likely to have 'parental responsibility'. This person has the legal responsibility of looking after the welfare of the child. This is a 'duty' rather than a 'right' over the welfare of the child. The duty will extend to ensuring that they make decisions which are in the interests of the child or young person in terms of where they live, what religion they follow, which school they attend and whether they should receive medical treatment.

If an adviser is approached by the person with parental responsibility for advice and assistance in relation to legal matters concerning the child or young person, it will be prudent to ask them if the young person agrees to that form of action. In this context the concern is to ensure that the young person feels safe and consulted. There are also some areas of law, notably family law, where there is a clear obligation on a court to make decisions in which the welfare of the child is paramount. Depending, therefore, on what is being sought and whether the issue is one in which the child and the parent or guardian are united, a decision may need to be made by the adviser as to whether to see both together or separately. Where they are both united, for example in terms of a challenge to a school's decision to exclude a child, or not to give the child a school place, then both can be seen together without too much difficulty.

Advising the child or young person on their own

Where the adviser is approached by a young person or child alone, who says they are seeking legal advice, they will initially endeavour to establish if there is a person in their life with parental responsibility. Even where there is, it will be necessary to establish whether the child or young person is saying that they want to make certain decisions on their own. They may, for example, be seeking advice in respect of a decision made by the person who has parental responsibility for them. It can therefore be a question of balancing what decisions a child or young person will be able to make and in what context.

There are various rules about when legal decisions or consent can be given by young people in different contexts. As we saw earlier, they can lawfully enter into contracts to buy certain types of goods. In terms of agreeing to or refusing medical treatment, it is assumed that between the ages of 16 and 18 they are able to make their own decisions. This is known as being 'Gillick-competent' and arose as a result of a parent's challenge to her daughter being prescribed with the contraceptive pill without the mother's consent. Many health professionals will also regard persons younger than 16 as Gillick-competent as long as they are satisfied that the child or young person has the ability to engage in the process of making that decision.[12] There are also guidelines given in the context of family proceedings, such as divorce, and linked arrangements for the welfare of children,[13] which will involve consulting with the child and, where considered appropriate, ensuring that they have separate legal representation.

Once the adviser does decide to see the child or young person on their own, they will ensure that their client is able to give instructions and understand advice and act upon it. If the adviser finds that what they are being told by their child client (for example, the reasons they have missed school or left home) conflicts with what a parent or guardian has said to them separately or when with the child or young person, the adviser will need to focus on not only what the child client's wishes are, but also what is in the best interests of the child or young person and discuss that with them. Care should be taken where a child raises any question of abuse or criminal behaviour being perpetrated against them by an adult or carer in their lives as there will

12 *Gillick v West Norfolk and Wisbech Area Health Authority* [1985] 3 All ER 402, HL.

13 See, for example, Children Act 1989 s1, which requires professionals and courts to ensure that the welfare of the child is the 'paramount consideration' in deciding on an issue relating to that child.

be certain circumstances when the adviser will have a duty to report certain information to the relevant authorities. If such a likelihood seems possible, contact should be established, initially anonymising the child, with the local social services to discuss whether this information should be taken any further.[14]

6.5   Clients using a different language

There may be circumstances in which a client will be communicating with their legal adviser in their second language or one for whom spoken language forms a communication barrier, such as a deaf client.

Caution should be exercised in terms of assuming that a client using English as a second language can communicate effectively in that language, particularly given the complexities that can arise in being giving advice and guidance on legal matters. Clients will sometimes indicate that they are able to do so in order to avoid 'making a fuss' or because they may be forced to do so in other areas of life. In addition, they may not initially realise that they will need to give their adviser often detailed information and understand advice which can at times be somewhat technical. If an adviser has any concerns about their ability to communicate effectively with the client using English as a second language they should ask if the client would find it helpful to have the services of an interpreter.

Using an interpreter or translator

The government supplies court interpreting services. These services are provided in the criminal justice system both at police stations and at courts. The government also provides interpreters in civil and family law cases and those concerning domestic violence or the loss of liberty and where the individual would not be able to take part in court proceedings without an interpreter. The Ministry of Justice website provides guidance as to how and when this service is provided in the court system.[15]

Otherwise, it is possible to use a commercial service for either interpreting services (including the use of an interpreter for deaf

14 Note that the Coram Children's Legal Centre provides guidance on rights for young people and children: see www.childrenslegalcentre.com and appendix B for full contact details.

15 See: www.justice.gov.uk/courts/interpreter-guidance.

clients) or for the translation of documents. These services do come at a cost and with the substantial reduction of legal aid, central funding in the legal system to pay for either the government-sponsored service or a private commercial service has now all but disappeared.

Using an interpreter: procedure

Guidance can be obtained in the key skills from the Skills for Justice National Occupational Standard SFJ AB2 about how to communicate via an interpreter with a client who uses a different language.[16] Some suggestions for conducting interviews with clients using the services of an interpreter are set out below:

- Look directly at the client, not the interpreter, when speaking to them.
- Encourage the client to look at the adviser directly when replying to questions or providing information – their interview is with the adviser and not the interpreter.
- Tell the interpreter that it is important that he or she interprets what the client is saying and does not *explain* what he or she is saying. It is the adviser's role, not the interpreter's, to analyse and process the information provided by the client and to offer advice based on what they say.
- Look for signals from the client's expression in order to gauge that they are taking an active part in the process, that they understand what is being said and feel that what they say has been clearly relayed back to the adviser.
- Regularly check with the interpreter that they have clarified the stage the interview is at with the client, including summarised progress so far.
- Try to allow as much time as possible. As a guide, interviews are likely to take double the time when an interpreter is being used.
- Build in rest-periods or suggest having interviews in more than one segment at different times.

6.6 Strategies for dealing with clients' differences

In summary, the aim of the adviser is to be able to communicate effectively and efficiently with a client in order to progress their case and to keep the client on board throughout the process of giving advice and

16 See appendix D.

progressing the client's case. Clients' differences or requirements need to be identified in order to process their cases effectively.

A chart summarising the strategies for dealing with clients' differences as outlined in this chapter is set out opposite.

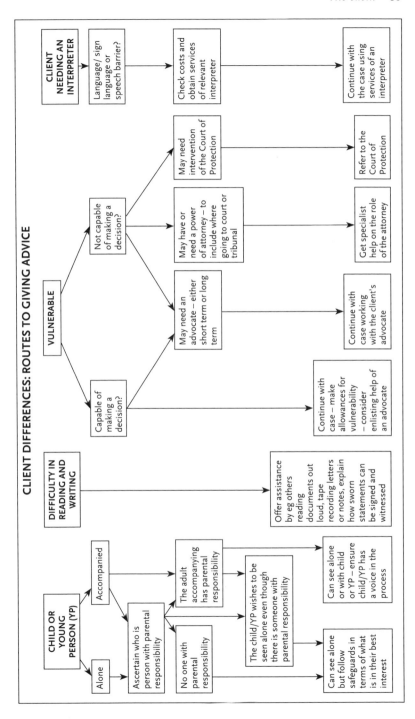

CLIENT DIFFERENCES: ROUTES TO GIVING ADVICE

CHILD OR YOUNG PERSON (YP)

Alone → Ascertain who is person with parental responsibility

Accompanied → Ascertain who is person with parental responsibility

The adult accompanying has parental responsibility

No one with parental responsibility

The child/YP wishes to be seen alone even though there is someone with parental responsibility

Can see alone or with child or YP – ensure child/YP has a voice in the process

Can see alone but follow safeguards in terms of what is in their best interest

DIFFICULTY IN READING AND WRITING

Offer assistance by eg others reading documents out loud, tape recording letters or notes, explain how sworn statements can be signed and witnessed

VULNERABLE

Capable of making a decision?

Not capable of making a decision?

May need an advocate – either short term or long term

May have or need a power of attorney – to include where going to court or tribunal

May need intervention of the Court of Protection

Continue with case – make allowances for vulnerability – consider enlisting help of an advocate

Continue with case working with the client's advocate

Get specialist help on the role of the attorney

Refer to the Court of Protection

CLIENT NEEDING AN INTERPRETER

Language/ sign language or speech barrier?

Check costs and obtain services of relevant interpreter

Continue with the case using services of an interpreter

CHAPTER 7

Taking instructions, identifying needs and moving a case forward

7.1   Introducing the client to the organisation

When an adviser first meets their client, and prior to embarking on the process of giving advice and resolving their legal problem, they will go through some preliminary stages with them. These are the building blocks necessary for the formation of an effective and binding adviser/client relationship. They will be relevant whether the adviser takes on the bulk of the task of resolving the case for their client or whether the adviser's role will be limited to advising without taking steps on behalf of the client.

The first stage is to ensure that the client is fully familiar with the organisation, how it functions, what service it provides and how and when they can gain access to it.

Services provided

New clients should be pointed in the direction of the organisation's full range of services, via websites or documentation such as letters or leaflets. They should be told what service the organisation will be able to provide for them, including how they will be able to use the service, its opening hours and physical access. In addition, clients should be alerted to other legal expertise within the organisation in case they need advice and assistance on more than one legal problem. Ancillary services, such as arranging for interpreters, home visits or the facility of instructing barristers or experts such as medical specialists, should also be made known to the client.

Complaints procedure

The client should also be told as part of their introduction to the organisation's services how the organisation's complaints procedure operates and the name of the person who will deal with the complaint including any appeal processes. Solicitors are guided by the Solicitors Regulation Authority (SRA)[1] to provide this information, and most legal advice organisations are likely to have a similar complaints procedure in place. A transparent complaints procedure is evidence of a willingness to listen to clients' concerns as well as of a fair and systematic approach to providing client services.

---

1   See SRA Code of Conduct 2011 Outcome O(1.9): www.sra.org.uk/Solicitors/ handbook /code.

Funding and costs

Where a client is paying their adviser for their legal advice, they should be informed both at the outset of the likely costs of conducting that matter and also kept up to date on a continuing basis with the likely projection of spending on their case. Solicitors are required to ensure that their fees are reasonable, to report to their clients on all expenditure and to provide them with regular updates and costs estimates.[2] This will include solicitors employed in law centres and other charities entitled to charge fees.[3]

If the service being provided is free and externally funded, it is likely that the funder will, like the paying client, be expecting to see value for money in its provision. For that reason, the time and resources an adviser may have to expend on any one case may not be as elastic as they would wish. There are also time limitations built in to the advice provided under legal aid funding. In such circumstances an adviser may only be able to allocate a certain number of hours to that client as well as being required to demonstrate to a funder at an early stage that a case has a reasonable prospect of success. Explaining funding arrangements to a client will help them to understand any possible limitations in relation to time or resources available to the adviser in assisting that client.

Furthermore, even where the advice provided is free, a legal advice agency is likely to require its clients to pay some of the costs involved in conducting their case. The adviser will explain to the client that these are likely to be what are known as 'disbursements', which typically are the fees paid by the organisation to an expert, such as a doctor (in order to obtain a medical report) or a barrister (for specialist legal advice or to appear in court) in order to assist the adviser in running the client's case.

Courts and tribunals have differing approaches to users paying fees and costs, and so, where legal proceedings are being contemplated, the relevant information for that venue will be provided for the client. If a claim is being contemplated in the civil courts for example, the adviser will explain that, as well as fees to be paid for taking part in the legal process, the legal costs of both parties at the end of a case are usually borne by the losing party.[4] In chapter 16 we revisit this topic in the context of conducting a court case. In addition in appendix A there

2 See outcome O(1.3) of the above Code.
3 See rule 4.16 of the Solicitors Practice Framework Rules 2011.
4 There are some exceptions to this 'rule of thumb', most notably in respect of small claims and personal injury cases.

is an example of a client care letter, which is the first letter a legal adviser should be writing to a new client and which contains some typical information about fees and costs.

7.2   Introducing the client to an adviser: roles and relationship

The adviser's obligations to the client

Confidentiality is, as we have seen, a cornerstone of the adviser/client relationship, as is the requirement of mutual trust and respect for each other's roles within that relationship. The adviser will outline for the client at an early stage these key elements of the relationship. They will explain that they will do their best to resolve the client's legal problems using their skills and expertise and will provide reliable legal advice on the merits of the client's case, including the provision of any negative or less optimistic advice where necessary. The adviser will tell the client that they will step into the spotlight in terms of directly engaging with other people who are involved with the client's case, will always endeavour to promote the client's case, and will work towards resolving it by not only providing advice but also by taking any necessary steps on behalf of the client to promote a realistic and acceptable outcome for the client.

The practical process

Having explained to the client what their function as adviser is, the adviser will also discuss the way in which they and the client are likely to work together from a practical perspective. They will tell the client that:

- The adviser and the client will meet at intervals in person to discuss progress, to review documents or letters sent and received, to allow the adviser to continue to advise the client and to plan next steps.
- The adviser will keep the client informed of all developments in relation to the client's case, for example, letters received or sent or offers to resolve or settle the client's case (for more on resolution see Part 5).
- The adviser will record for the client in writing the advice they provide.

- The adviser will keep the client informed in writing of any risks which exist or which might arise as the case develops; for example, a risk in relation to how well a client's story may stand up in court in the face of evidence provided by an opposing party.
- The client will keep the adviser informed of any developments which might have a bearing on their case, such as a change in family or financial circumstances.
- The adviser will keep all the client's affairs confidential.
- The adviser will at the same time expect the client to be open with the adviser about matters which are relevant to the conduct of their case.

The adviser will also give the client an estimate of how long they antici-pate it will take to complete the client's matter or case once they have taken it on. This time frame tends to be provided as an estimate, as there will be a number of external factors contributing to an adviser's conduct of a legal case. Courts or tribunals, for example, will decide when they can hear a claim or case and will impose timetables on the preparation of a case for a final hearing.[5]

Style of communication

In this era of relative social informality an adviser may be content with using a first name mode of address with their client. Some thought could be given to this to ensure that the relationship's professional footing is reflected in how people address each other. It may be appro-priate to use the more formal Mr or Mrs/Ms mode at the outset, with first names being adopted once the parties get to know each other better. The adviser should in any event ensure that the relationship is one in which the adviser is regarded as a professional and not a friend or a 'listening post'.

7.3   Identifying the client's needs

Needs relating to a resolution of the client's problem

An adviser will then embark on the process of identifying the client's needs in the context of the legal problem the adviser has been asked to deal with, as well as identifying an appropriate way of meeting those needs. Sometimes a client may attempt to 'lead' the adviser: 'this is

5 See section 8.5 for more on this topic.

my problem and this is how I want you to resolve it for me'. The adviser needs to take control and where necessary limit the client's expectations of what can be achieved, outlining also that the client will be required to play a focal role in that process. This will include the adviser explaining how, in their experience, matters like this are usually resolved, and factoring in a consideration of how the law operates in this sort of area.

For example, if a client has lost their job and tells their adviser that they want to recover a considerable amount of compensation from their ex-employer, their adviser will not only be engaging in the process of outlining for the client any legal claims they may have arising out of this situation, but also what the client's prospects of success in pursuing such claims might be and whether they might be awarded any compensation as part of any legal process as well as how much that might be. This advice might address some or all of that client's expressed needs.

7.4   Taking instructions

Initial instructions

Once these preliminary stages have been passed, the adviser will be embarking on the process of taking the client's instructions. This important process of taking instructions from a client has two meanings. The first relates to the adviser's requirements to listen to the client's story, and the second to ensuring that the adviser acts in accordance with the client's wishes.

We will look in more detail at the process of interviewing clients and advising them in chapters 9 and 10. Here, as an introduction to this topic, it is important to note that the adviser will, in taking initial instructions, be asking the client to outline their story and should be guiding the client through that story in a way which will allow the legal issues to emerge out of what the client is saying.

This is a process which requires some finesse as the client will not always be able to identify what is relevant and will not always tell their story in a logical sequence. The adviser may need to probe for more detail and/or filter out essential information from the client's instructions in order to take things forward.

Let us take the example of a client who comes to an adviser as a tenant with a rent arrears problem. The client may give the following information to the adviser by way of initial instructions:

- They have been unable to keep up their rent payments.
- They have some letters and other documents sent to them by their landlord about their rent arrears.
- They have financial problems and cannot make rent payments regularly.
- This situation is affecting them and their family adversely.

In order to develop these initial instructions and begin to process the client's legal problem it is likely that the adviser will need to know:

- The kind of legal tenancy the client has.
- The contents of any documents received by the tenant from the landlord, especially those which may be in the form of legal notices relating to the tenant's security.
- The exact rent arrears figure alleged by the landlord or accepted by the client (if known).
- Details of any payments recently made by the client to their landlord.
- Any particular circumstances, such as other payments owing, or formal debts or family illnesses, which have contributed to the client's inability to keep up with payments of rent.

An integral part of taking initial instructions, therefore, will be for the adviser to ask questions about all these matters in order to begin to formulate the legal nature of the client's problem. The client may not be able to answer all these questions, most notably they may not be able to identify the exact legal nature of their relationship with their landlord. With helpful guidance from the adviser, however, they ought to be able to provide sufficient detail so that the adviser is aware of their current legal status as a tenant, how that may be under threat and what formal or legal steps may have been taken already to recover rent arrears or bring the tenancy to an end. The adviser may also be able to obtain details of any personal circumstances contributing to the client's failure to keep up with rent payments which might mitigate in the client's favour when attempting to avoid eviction.

We saw earlier that advisers will usually have received and made note of some preliminary details prior to a first meeting with a client. In advance of that first meeting some advisers will write to their clients and tell them what information and documentation they are likely to want the client to provide. This will help the client to prepare for what for many is a stressful process where they first meet their legal adviser and will want to impress their story onto them and obtain assurances that the adviser can offer them some assistance.

Further instructions

At a later stage of their meeting, and once an adviser has heard the client's story and given the client legal advice on the nature of their problem and how it may be capable of resolution, the adviser will be asking the client to state what they wish them to do next. This process is also described as giving instructions, and can also be described as providing further instructions, since the client is asking their adviser to take certain steps on their behalf based on legal advice provided.

Another type of legal problem can be outlined to give an example of how this process might operate. The client may have outlined a problem they have encountered relating to a contract they entered into with a holiday company for a package holiday. Flight arrangements were altered and the accommodation provided was in a different place from that promised by the company, and was of an inferior standard. Having heard these details the adviser may have advised the client that they would be able to make a legal claim against the holiday company for their loss of the enjoyment of the holiday experience. Having received that legal advice (which would in real terms be more detailed and include advice on the risk and costs of pursuing a legal claim) the client may then request their adviser to write a letter to the company on their behalf seeking compensation. If that has not resolved the dispute they may ask the adviser to commence a claim in the small claims court if the adviser has advised that this would be an appropriate option. This process of continuing to give instructions will underpin the adviser/client relationship throughout its course, matched to the process of advice-giving.

7.5   Identifying and agreeing outcomes for the client

Identifying likely legal outcomes

An additional stage in the initial process of forming the adviser/client relationship is for the adviser to work with the client on identifying suitable outcomes and to reach agreement on the best way to reach those outcomes. An outcome for the client is a result which has been achieved by virtue of the adviser's intervention in the client's problem. In looking at examples of a client's stated needs above, it is possible to predict how the adviser is likely to assess the client's desired outcomes in terms of using the law to reach a resolution. These are likely to include obtaining money, such as a benefit or compensation, changing an aspect of their life, such as where they live or what their immigration status is, or achieving some form of just outcome as a result of pursuing claims in a court or tribunal.

Dealing with the client's required outcomes

An adviser will be familiar with the outcomes stated above as they are the anticipated outcomes which they know that the law can provide in the context of these types of problems. A client may be content to work towards these or they may express different priorities in terms of what they want the adviser to achieve for them. In those circumstances the adviser will be required to balance their own view of what remedy they will be able to achieve with what the client states they want to achieve. To give some examples relating to various types of legal query:

- **Employment:** A client may tell their adviser that they have suffered discrimination at work. The adviser is likely to advise that they have a good case to stay at work, pursue a grievance and/or a discrimination claim and seek compensation for that discrimination. The client's preferred outcome is just to leave the job and have no further contact with the employer. The adviser will have to balance this desired outcome with that of the client's expression of their sense of injustice and their wish to see their employer take responsibility for that treatment.

- **Debt:** The client may tell the adviser that they owe money to a number of different companies. The advice given is that an arrangement can be entered into with creditors in order to start to reduce the debt. The client states that their bank or building society accounts are in joint names and they do not wish their partner to be aware of their level of debt. The adviser will then have to balance the efficacy of entering into an arrangement with these creditors as against the client's wish for confidentiality.

- **Housing:** The client may say that they want their landlord to repair their rented property. The adviser will advise that the landlord should be written to and the landlord's legal obligations pointed out to him or her and also that the client can pursue the matter in court where an order will be made for the repairs to be carried out and compensation awarded to the client. The client does not wish the adviser to contact the landlord as they fear repercussions. The adviser will therefore need to balance this genuine concern with the client's legal right to require the landlord to keep the premises in repair.

In each of these scenarios what the client wants to achieve falls short or differs from the legal remedy or resolution the adviser with their experience can offer the client. As a result, the adviser is unlikely to be able to take any or all of the steps that would usually be taken in order to achieve the most effective or legally enforceable outcome for the client. The adviser will therefore look for ways to meet the client's preferred outcome, as well as advising the client of the more usual legal avenues they would be able to pursue.

What the adviser cannot do is to go beyond what the client wants. They will not be able to take any steps which differ from their client's instructions or which exceed those instructions. If, for example, a client states that they do not want letters to be written threatening legal action, the adviser will be bound by their instructions on that respect whatever limitations it imposes on the adviser's ability to achieve a more far-reaching outcome for that client.

7.6 Identifying next steps and agreeing the process of taking the case forward

Once the adviser has taken initial instructions ('heard the client's story') and identified with the client what their needs and desired outcomes are, the adviser will link the facts of the client's case, their knowledge of the law or regulatory procedures relevant to the client's problem, and their own capacity or that of the service within which they operate, in order to provide advice and reach an appropriate resolution for the client.

It may be useful to run the following checks at an early stage in order to assist in focusing on the most appropriate way of taking the client's case forward as well as reconciling the client's stated needs with both the client's desired outcome and one which is appropriate.

Preliminary checklist
- What is the client saying about what happened to them?
- What type of legal problem is this?
- Is this a problem which the adviser has the resources and expertise to address?
- What is the most effective and efficient way to reach a resolution in this case?
- Is this the resolution which the client wants to achieve?
- Does the client understand the process; has it been outlined for them sufficiently clearly?

- Is the client happy with advice on how to achieve that resolution?
- Is that route to resolution going to cause the client any difficulties, given what they might have said about their preferred outcomes?
- Is there an alternative way of resolving the case which matches better the client's desired outcome?
- Can this be effected?

The adviser will aim to reconcile any possible conflicts between their own tried and tested method of resolving the case and the clients' desired outcomes, and agree with the client as to how they will take the client's case forward for them.

Preliminary advice

In a first meeting with a client an adviser will offer to consider all that the client has told or shown them and will provide advice. The building blocks of a client interview are set out in chapter 9 and the process of giving advice is dealt with in more detail in chapter 10. They may provide some preliminary advice in that first interview with an advice letter written to the client thereafter which will contain full advice once the adviser has considered all the information or documentation provided to them by the client.

Next steps

The first meeting will also include an agreement of what the next steps are. In most cases this will be for the client to await an advice letter. Where it emerges that some immediate steps will need to be taken by the adviser on behalf of the client, such as the preparation of a court or tribunal hearing, they may be instructed to take that step straight away to minimise any risk for the client even though their detailed advice may be received by the client thereafter. The order in which things happen will depend on the nature of the legal query.

Agreeing the process of taking the case forward

At the conclusion of their first meeting as a practical process, the adviser and client will agree on how they will both work towards taking the case forward, whether by having further meetings, the adviser writing letters to opponents, or offering to embark on a court or tribunal case on a client's behalf. The adviser will impress upon the client, however, that even though a process may have been agreed it will require review on a regular basis as the matter develops and events unfold, particularly where influenced by the actions of a client's opponent. We will also see in the next chapter how external influences can impact on the adviser/client relationship and the agreed process of taking a client's case forward.

CHAPTER 8

External influences on the adviser/client relationship

8.1   Introduction

For a client, the adviser will be the sole person they have to advise and assist them in resolving their case. They will place the adviser at the centre of the case and expect them to deliver on the commitment they have made to initiate and/or assist in the process of resolving it. On the other hand, the adviser will have a number of clients and cases to deal with at any given time which will place additional demands on them as they process each client's case. The adviser will need to have a clear direction for each of their clients. They should also ensure that they build into each client relationship a consideration of the external factors which will influence that relationship, and take a realistic approach as to how they can best conduct the case for each client.

It is important for an adviser or would-be adviser to take on board the busy environment in which advice work is conducted and the pressure on them to deal with a number of competing demands on their time, and to ensure that a fair balance of time and resources is expended on each client. We will look later at good practice in relation to case management which will have built into it an awareness of the various factors which might impact on the smooth process of running each client's case in a timely manner. Here we will outline what some of these factors and external pressures might be.

8.2   Other demands on the adviser: time management systems

In working in an advice-giving environment the legal adviser is likely to have the following competing elements to deal with:

- calls on their time from other clients or other client-based tasks;
- calls on their time from the organisation they work in;
- rescheduled priorities as a result of developments in clients' cases; and
- the need to demonstrate value for money.

Other clients and use of case plans

An adviser will take a realistic view about the number of cases they are able to handle at any given time. Some advisers will have little say on this issue and may be required to meet targets by reference to numbers of cases being conducted or time spent on casework at any given time which are set either by the organisation or by their funders or both. Where the adviser is fortunate enough to have the freedom to choose how many cases they conduct, they will assess each new case to ensure they have sufficient time and resources to devote to it. They will bear in mind that client enquiries which appear to be simple at first sight can gather in complexity as more information is received and it is often a question of educated guesswork as to how long a case will in reality take to conclude or how many hours might be spent on each case.

Nevertheless, all advisers will be advising a number of clients at any one time and will therefore aim to manage their time so that each client receives the same level of service. Sometimes advisers can be drawn into spending more time with clients who contact them on a regular basis than with those who do not, although the latter may well be equally as deserving of the advisers' time. One way to ensure consistency of approach for each client would be for advisers to draw up individual case plans for their own reference. In doing so the adviser can plan at an early stage the likely progress of the case for each client and can refer to each case plan to ensure that consistent progress is being made.

A case plan can be set up for each of the adviser's cases in a format which they find helpful. There is rarely a requirement to have case plans in conducting legal casework unless part of an organisation's internal processes or as required under some high cost legal aid cases as a condition of funding.[1] Otherwise drawing up a case plan is simply a matter of good practice and a way of ordering progress on each client's case where it has become clear early on that a number of stages will need to be gone through in order to reach a resolution.

Below is an example of a simple case plan concerning a housing association tenant who has rent arrears. Note that detailed knowledge of the law relating to this type of problem would not be necessary to see the pattern of steps the adviser will plan to follow.

---

1 See the Civil Legal Aid (Procedure) Regulations 2012 SI No 3098 reg 6 which requires certain cases (including what are known as Very High Costs Cases) to be based on a case plan to be approved by the Legal Aid Agency in order for legal aid funding to be provided.

Case of Ms B: Rent arrears and claim for possession of property

Case plan

- Take initial instructions on whether arrears admitted and any reason given as to how and why they have arisen.
- Obtain client's documents from client and put into logical and sequential order – discuss significant documents with client.
- Obtain copies of landlord's documents received by the client and take client's instructions on these.
- Note and diarise any court appearances.
- Ensure steps taken comply with any court deadlines.
- Take witness statements from client and any supporting witnesses.
- Discuss with client the significance of any witness statements provided by landlord and advise accordingly.
- Advise client on next steps and merits of case.
- Attend court with client.
- Review case following any court appearances.
- Take any further follow-up action with client, including further advice on client's next steps.

The contents of this case plan are also likely to be discussed with and recorded for the client as the route to reaching a resolution for the client. It will be inherent in the plan that the adviser will continue to provide advice to their client at each of these stages. This type of case plan summary will hopefully assist in keeping each client's case on track and can be reviewed and revised as and when necessary.

Organisation-based tasks

An adviser will not be spending all their time working on clients' cases. They will have a number of competing demands on their time and resources and these should be realistically addressed. Advisers in a community advice organisation are likely also to be dealing with some or all of the following tasks:

- attending internal staff or team meetings and meeting with external agencies or community groups;
- taking part in telephone advice sessions;
- carrying out administrative tasks such as filing, typing;
- covering for other staff on sick leave, on visits or at courts or tribunals;
- attending training;
- writing reports or papers for funders or management bodies.

Advisers working in solicitors' legal practices usually have more time allocated to the conduct of case work (and will usually therefore have bigger caseloads than case workers in advice agencies) but will nevertheless have similar competing demands.

For any adviser, incoming emails can be a competitive demand on their time, and how and when they deal with these will ideally be systemised by, for example, setting up client or administrative folders or replying to emails in batches at specific times of the day.

Rescheduling priorities using a diary

An adviser will aim to balance time spent on client-focused work with other ancillary tasks, splitting working time into different types of activities, or allocating specific times of the day or week for client appointments. Some will use reminders in an electronic diary. Others will use a handwritten diary and will record and review daily tasks set and achieved. Diarising should make allowances for emergencies or unforeseen developments which are likely to arise, by rearranging less urgent tasks around that new development once it arises. A typical example would be of an unplanned court hearing set by a court during the conduct of a client's case. In any event, where cases will require the adviser to attend hearings on a regular basis they will operate a double-diary system to warn themselves that preparation will need to be carried out for the hearing some weeks or days ahead, a topic we return to in chapter 11. Having such a planned approach to all aspects of their work will assist an adviser in maintaining control of both anticipated developments on a case and unforeseen ones which will inevitably arise.

Value for money

As well as demonstrating to each of their clients an ability to progress their cases, advisers will also be exhibiting business sense in terms of service delivery. This will apply equally to work funded by the client or by grants or charitable donations. Advisers should be able to demonstrate to a client that they are efficient, well organised and ready to provide a competitive service. The provision of a well-planned and effective service should not therefore in reality be a distraction, although there may be activities to be carried out which are not directly related to case work for clients, such as report-writing or drawing up statistics. Furthermore, many legal services process client satisfaction surveys which add to the tasks surrounding advice work but which are nevertheless useful tools in demonstrating value for money. They may be used not only to show that the required outcomes linked to any external funding are being met, but also to assist in monitoring internally the quality of the service being provided.

8.3   Satellite problems: client's other advice needs

Where the adviser and client have an agreed plan of action to progress that client's case, a client may also bring into the equation other advice needs which are ancillary to the case but quite often important and necessary for the client to resolve. These will be satellite problems related to the main issue the adviser is instructed to deal with. For example, a client who has rent arrears may need a debt counsellor, or a client who has suffered discrimination may need medical help.

The adviser will therefore outline what advice and service they can offer and may need to refer the client elsewhere for advice in relation to any ancillary matters. We will look more at the process of referring in chapter 13. This process of referrals for different elements of a client's case or problem can be fragmenting and time-consuming both for the client and the adviser. On the positive side, once such a referral has been made, the adviser will aim for as much cohesion as possible. Where there are links between these various aspects of the client's legal problem the adviser will, with the client's consent, aim to maintain contact with the referred source in order to keep abreast of progress on that matter and to ensure as far as possible that the client's interrelated legal problem progresses in a helpful and unified fashion.

8.4   Satellite people: involvement of client's friends or family

Some clients will come to see an adviser accompanied by friends or family. This may be in order to help them to recall what they need to tell the adviser or to give them some confidence. Sometimes another individual may ring the adviser and speak to them on behalf of a client, or another person may answer when the adviser rings the client.

Maintaining client confidentiality

At a first interview, if a client comes along with someone else, the adviser will tell the client that they will expect a full and frank exchange of information to take place between them but that the adviser will respect the client's confidentiality. The adviser should ask the client, in the light of that, to confirm that they have no objection to the person accompanying them being a party to the discussion which is about to take place, and to hear the advice which the adviser will be offering to their client at the conclusion of that meeting. This will give the client the opportunity to invite the other person to withdraw if the client realises that they would prefer the discussion to remain confidential between themselves and their adviser. If they do not ask the person to withdraw, the adviser should make a note of who was present at the discussion.

As part of their duty of confidentiality the adviser has an obligation to communicate at all times directly with the client. It will sometimes be inconvenient to ring a client and find they are not available. It may be that an urgent message needs to be given to the client and there is a willing family member who offers to take that message. No matter how tempting that offer might be, an adviser will refrain from discussing their client's case with anyone else, even their closest relative. Even where a client tells an adviser that they consent to the adviser giving information about their case to close family members, the adviser will exercise caution in doing so in terms of the likely impact on their client's case. In particular, the adviser can never be totally confident that there is no conflict between the client's needs and those of a close relative, partner or friend, for example in relation to money, housing or property rights.

If a client does indicate to their adviser that they are agreeable to the adviser leaving messages for them, or speaking to others to give or receive information, the following guidelines will assist.

Guidelines for speaking to a client's associates and for leaving messages

- If a client authorises an adviser to communicate with another person, this should be confirmed in writing to the client by the adviser.
- Where clients do continue to attend meetings or interviews with others, the adviser will acknowledge this as being the client's right but will check on each occasion that the client is happy for that other person to be in attendance.

• Care should be taken not to leave a client a message on their landline telephone since the adviser can never be sure who will hear
the message. This also applies to the adviser leaving a message to
call them back as the adviser will be identifying themselves and
possibly also leaving contact details. The client should always specifically authorise their adviser to leave messages for them in their
absence.

Dealing with other family members or friends

Following on from this, the question of how the adviser should handle
regular interceptions or messages or information being relayed to
them by a client's family members or friends can sometimes be problematic. It can be the case that another family member can be of great
assistance in supporting the client and in remembering details which
the client may perhaps be too distressed to recall, perhaps due to the
client's emotional involvement with their legal problem. There may
also be instances where a client is in a personal relationship where
they are clearly being guided by a partner or parent, for example,
and the client is quite used to that arrangement. That person may
have been responsible for bringing the client into contact with a legal
adviser. If an adviser appears to be ignoring or sidelining that person
it may be unsettling for the client, and may even have an adverse
effect on the client's relationship with their adviser or indeed that
other person.

There are of course times in our lives when we feel unable to make
a clear-headed decision and when we welcome and are grateful for the
close guiding hand of a friend or relative. Where this does appear to
be the case for a client, the adviser will nevertheless ensure that they
are receiving instructions from their own client and that the client has
given those instructions both directly and without any excessive influence (as opposed to guidance and support) being imposed on them
by another individual.[2] The adviser will not only do this in interviews

2 Rule 6(c) of the SRA Code of Conduct 2011 refers to 'duress or undue
influence' when taking instructions and is probably worth setting out in full as
it is accessible and helpful in these situations: 'It is important to be satisfied
that clients give their instructions freely. Some clients, such as the elderly,
those with language or learning difficulties and those with disabilities are
particularly vulnerable to pressure from others. If you suspect that a client's
instructions are the result of undue influence you need to exercise your
judgement as to whether you can proceed on the client's behalf. For example,
if you suspect that a friend or relative who accompanies the client is exerting
undue influence, you should arrange to see the client alone or if appropriate

where the client is accompanied by others, but will record the client's instructions to them in writing to give the client a further opportunity to consider for themselves exactly how they want their adviser to proceed on their behalf.

In the rare circumstances where another family member or individual repeatedly intervenes and repeatedly purports to be acting in the client's best interests in offering their opinions or stating what it is the client wants, the adviser will need to consider their position. They may need to decide if they still have a contractual adviser/client relationship built on the foundation of mutual trust and confidence, or whether the client has unwittingly broken that link by allowing another person to intervene in the conduct of their case. While the adviser should have every sympathy with a client who appears unable to prevent such a course of action they may, in such a situation, no longer be able to continue as the client's adviser.

8.5 Deadlines set by courts or opponents

Where the resolution of a client's case involves the use of court or tribunal processes, the time frames provided by these processes will inevitably impact on the conduct of a case and will need to be adhered to by both adviser and client. There are many penalties associated with a failure to comply with the rules of a tribunal or court, and these include not being able to pursue a claim or case, having a defence to a claim or case struck out, or facing an order to pay the legal costs of an opposing party. We will look at these procedures in further detail in chapter 17. In terms of the impact on the planning of how a case might progress, it is not an infrequent occurrence for planned hearings to be postponed or for hearings to take place at short notice which can be unsettling for a client but which the adviser will need to deal with on their behalf. In addition, whether a client's matter is in a court or tribunal system or not, their opponent (such as a landlord or an employer) may impose deadlines on them or their adviser as to when they would like replies to letters or a course of action to be taken or agreed to by the client. The adviser will be prepared for this to

with an independent third party or interpreter. Where there is no actual evidence of undue influence but the client appears to want to act against their best interests, it may be sufficient simply to explain the consequences of the instructions the client has given and confirm that the client wishes to proceed. For evidential purposes, it would be sensible to get this confirmation in writing.'

happen, as they themselves will at times engage in a similar process for the benefit of their clients. As long as requests are reasonable, the adviser will comply with those deadlines, making sure that the client has been advised of the efficacy of taking such a step and is happy for it to be taken. The adviser may also impose deadlines on when they expect replies to letters or certain commitments to be given to their client. Both adviser and the client will maintain awareness of these uncertainties, the impact that they may on their agreed timetable and the necessity to accommodate their actions around that timetable.

8.6   Time recording

In the charitable or not-for-profit sector, advice work will in many instances be driven by external funding, including legal aid funding, which will inevitably impact on the time which can be allocated to each client's case. Furthermore, all legal advisers will have in place systems for recording the work they do. Time-recording systems will vary according to whether a client is fee paying, legally aided or being advised by a service funded by a grant or charity. This process of time recording or reporting will need to be balanced with the adviser's requirement to manage their time and work in the best interests of each of their clients.

Advice skills

Interviewing

9.1   Planning and preparation

The process of effectively interviewing a client is one of the most significant skills deployed in legal advice work. The interview will be seen as the primary vehicle for building on the adviser/client relationship, for ensuring that the adviser is aware of all the relevant aspects of the client's problem, and as a mechanism of agreeing action to be taken to take the matter forward. Legal advice and often some practical advice is also provided as part of the interviewing process.[1] All client interviews conducted by an adviser, no matter how brief, or no matter how experienced the adviser is, will require prior planning and preparation.

Pre-interview checklist

Advisers will vary as to how they carry out their interview preparation. The steps set out in the checklist below may not be necessary on every occasion, but may stand as a useful guide for the adviser to focus on the key issues to be addressed.

Pre-interview checklist
- Put together a summary of facts already known about the client's problem, as a result of initial telephone conversations or letters or emails received from the client.
- Compile a note of gaps in knowledge of facts or events which need to be filled by further questioning.
- Produce an outline of what the legal problem appears to be.
- Outline the advice which might be offered, including a note of any preliminary research the adviser has made relating to the client's legal problem.
- Suggest lines of enquiry or development which might arise out of the first interview.
- Organise any particular arrangements which need to be made for the first meeting (eg, arrange for an interpreter).
- Make a note of how much time the adviser has planned to allocate for the first interview.

---

1   For a general overview of good practice in client interviews see also the Legal Advice National Occupational Standard SFJGA6 'Develop and manage interviews with clients' in appendix D.

The interview environment

As well as preparing for the process of taking instructions and advising in the interview, the adviser will carry out some practical preparation. Even where space is at a premium an interviewing environment should be appropriate and will ideally be confidential, comfortable, child-friendly (if the client is accompanied by children) as well as safe and hazard-free for both adviser and client.

Confidentiality

We have already looked at the obligation on the legal adviser to keep their clients' matters confidential. This will include the contents of discussions and interviews and so an interviewing environment should ideally only contain the client and the adviser. Where there is no choice but to use a room occupied by another caseworker, that person would need to be alerted in advance that a client interview is to take place. They will be aware of the client's requirement for confidentiality and it is customary for that other occupant to be briefly introduced at the outset of a client interview and for that person to also assure the client that they are aware of the client's requirement for confidentiality.

Comfort

The client should be made as comfortable as possible and their needs for drinks and comfort breaks should be borne in mind by an adviser when preparing to interview.

Child-friendliness

A client may have no option but to bring small children to an interview due to childcare arrangements. If at all possible this should be accommodated; some, but not many, office environments are child-friendly. It may be that the agency has volunteers who can spend time with small children in an area where they can still be seen by the adult. If children do accompany parents, guardians or carers to interviews, the adviser may need to be realistic about how long an interview is likely to last and may need to plan for a split interview.

Risk assessment: health and safety

Advisers will also be alert to the more regulatory aspects of health and safety. Owner or occupiers of a building have a legal obligation to ensure that their lawful visitors come to no harm through any fault of the occupier.[2] Public liability insurance taken out by the organisation will provide similar protection. In addition the law requires any business environments with employees to have risk assessment procedures in place to ensure the health and safety of their employees is being monitored.[3] Furthermore, in addition to providing a safe environment for the client, the same approach should be adopted for the adviser. Advisers seeing new clients or clients who they know may behave unpredictably should ensure that the layout of the room allows for them to be safe and, if necessary, to leave without any obstruction from the client. Some organisations have alarms or alert systems in place to protect their staff. This may seem to be cautious but, unfortunately, from time to time clients may place their advisers in possible risk situations by their behaviour, whether involuntary or not.

For the same reason, if an adviser has arranged to see a client off-site, for example in the client's home, there should be safeguards in place for the adviser who is working away from the office. This is likely to include a note being left in the office diary as to where the adviser is, that they have taken a mobile phone with them and how long they expect to be away. If the adviser exceeds their expected time away, the agency should have procedures in place to check on their safety.

9.2   Elements of an adviser/client interview

Once the adviser embarks on the interview process, they will be using a number of skills and approaches to ensure that they are in full possession of the relevant facts, can advise their client effectively, and can use the interview process to progress towards a resolution of the client's problem.

Introduction

As outlined in chapter 7, as a practical preliminary to embarking on the interview process the adviser will begin by outlining what will

---

2 See Occupiers Liability Act 1957.

3 See, for example, Management of Health and Safety at Work Regulations 1999 SI No 3242 reg 3. In practice this means that someone in the organisation will be nominated to identify and reduce any risks or hazards to the employees' health and safety, both physical and environmental, as they go about their business.

happen in the interview. This will include the adviser listening to the client's story, and questioning and probing for any additional details they may require. They will note early on what the client wants to achieve by way of an outcome and will ensure they refer back to that at regular intervals as the interview progresses. They will explain that they will be keeping a running note of everything being said in the interview. They will be pausing at regular intervals to summarise and review progress and decisions made as well as doing so at the conclusion of the interview. They will be offering the client advice towards the end of the interview, then awaiting any further instruction before agreeing with the client on next steps. They will also explain that they will write to the client to confirm and record advice and any agreed plan of action, which will help to allay any fears the client might have that they must remember all that takes place in the interview.

Listening to the client's story and asking questions

At the outset the adviser will need to obtain from their client all the facts which are in the client's possession (a process we have already explained as taking the client's instructions). This will inevitably involve asking a number of questions of the client, as well as listening to what they want to say. Later on in the interview they will also take from them their instructions on how they wish to go forward in the light of the adviser's input. Furthermore, the adviser will need to question the client for any comments they may have on the adverse aspects of their case, and/or on a conflicting set of facts which may have been put forward by others.

When seeking to obtain the facts, the adviser should begin by asking open questions ('what happened?' and 'what happened next?') but should then be 'funnelling' those questions, or making them more focused, in order to get as much detail as possible. For example, if a client says they went to a meeting with a housing officer representing their public sector landlord in which their rent arrears were discussed and then sorted out, the adviser will ask them specifically if they can recall what figures were stated by the housing officer as being the arrears and what exact arrangement was entered into by the client in that meeting to pay off the arrears and how it was to operate.

Any necessary questioning to obtain the full picture should be as detailed as possible. If anything is overlooked it could be to the client's disadvantage. It could be brought out for the first time in a meeting or hearing by the client's opponent and thus affect the ability of the adviser to use it in any way which is helpful to the client because they have not had the opportunity to deal with it in advance.

The adviser should also be asking questions which are designed to test out what the client is saying and to ensure that it can be held up for scrutiny or that it cannot be challenged. If, for example, there is a letter from a landlord stating the amount of rent owed, and the client denies that they owe this much, the client must be asked why they think the landlord has come up with that figure based on any evidence of rent payments made which the adviser is shown.

In questioning a client the adviser should be non-judgmental. If the client discloses that they have behaved in a manner which the adviser themselves believes to be unwise or even reprehensible, it will not be for the adviser to comment on that behaviour. Instead their role will be to advise as to how that behaviour might affect any desired outcome on the part of the client.

Noting and interpreting the client's answers

The adviser needs to record what their client tells them. This will be looked at in more detail in the next chapter but it should be noted that a key element of advice work is to make full notes of what is said and what action is agreed during client interviews. At the same time as recording, the adviser will nevertheless ensure that they remain engaged with their client and avoid giving the impression that their main source of contact is their screen rather than their client, as they record the process of the interview.

As part of recording the adviser will need to decide how the answers they record will flow into the issues they are exploring. For example, in preparing for the interview the adviser may have already seen a copy of a letter sent by a landlord to a client in which a higher level of rent arrears is referred to than the figure put forward by the client. The adviser will note that disparity as they record it. The adviser should not pepper their notes with comments (eg, 'client's/landlord's figures are wrong') but should be interpreting what they hear or read ('client's figures differ from those set out in landlord's letter – check this with client – write if necessary to landlord?').

Summarising

As part of the questioning process, the adviser should be regularly summarising what the client has told them. This gives the client an opportunity to reflect on what they have said and if necessary to correct it or add to it. The adviser should also summarise their advice, including advice on agreed courses of action reached in the interview. A client may, for example, agree to pay off rent or mortgage arrears as a result of advice given during the interview and the adviser will be summarising what impact that will have on the conduct of a court action or court hearing the whole process of which is under discussion as part of the interview.

Reviewing and reflecting

This aspect of the interview involves the adviser taking stock at various points in order to reflect on the stage reached so far. This will be particularly relevant where the adviser has begun to advise the client that their prospects of achieving their desired outcome are more limited than perhaps at first envisaged by both the adviser and the client due to external developments or further information provided by the client as the interview progresses. The adviser will be reflecting with the client on what the implications are for the client if, for example, the adviser has advised that the client has little prospect of paying off their rent or mortgage arrears. For example, if the client's desired outcome is to keep their home, the adviser may need to review how that will stand up to the advice that the level of arrears is likely to mean that a court could make an order for repossession of the client's home.

Advising

The skills and the process of advising both in an interview and in letters, emails or by phone will be looked at in chapter 10. Advice lies at the heart of the adviser/client relationship and there are a number of skills to be acquired and tips to be assimilated in order to advise effectively.

Making decisions

It should be the case that decisions which are made which affect the client, and which affect the way in which their problem gets resolved, should be made jointly. The adviser should not take ownership to the extent of telling the client that they have no option but to pursue a course of action or that the adviser will pursue a particular course of action for the client. Indeed, it is likely to be at this stage of the interview, once the facts are known and advice offered to the client, that the adviser will take the client's further instructions and will ask the client, in the light of any advice or new advice, what course of action the client now wishes to take. This will be a part of the process of making a decision about how the case will go forward. There can often be a process of negotiation between the adviser and client leading to decisions which affect the conduct of the case but, even where the decision is not one which the client came into the process expecting to reach or agree to, it should be arrived at jointly.

Agreeing next steps

Following on from the verbal advice provided and the joint process of making decisions as to the best way forward to resolve a case, the aim at the conclusion of each interview should be to agree what next steps need to be taken. These may involve both the adviser and the client. The adviser will have provided oral advice on the law and how it impacts on the facts of the client case, on the strengths and weaknesses of the client's case and on the most efficacious route to be taken to resolve the case in the client's favour. They will offer to follow that up with a letter of advice. In addition, if there is an opponent or another party involved in the client's matter, the adviser may offer to write a letter or email to them or make certain enquiries on behalf of the client. As we saw earlier, the contents of communications to be sent out to anyone else will need to be approved by the client before they are sent. For the client's part, they may agree to start to outline a statement to bring to the next interview or to locate additional documents to show the adviser. The adviser should be able to give the client a more realistic estimate at this stage as to how long it will take to conclude the matter and reach a resolution to the client's problem.

9.3 Adviser's skills used as part of interviewing

Listening

We have already made mention of the adviser's listening skills in chapter 4. Here we will see how they are used in the context of interviewing. In asking the client to outline their story, the adviser will ensure they listen to everything they are being told no matter how lacking in relevance it may appear to be at first sight. Questioning will have the effect of clarifying what is and is not important or relevant, but it is helpful to hear as much as possible of what the client wants to say rather than to keep cutting off their flow of information on the basis that it appears to be irrelevant. More is better than less, and filtering can be done by the adviser once they have heard and seen what the big picture is.

A skilled listener will hopefully be able to tell when there is another, hidden, agenda which, once brought to the surface, can reveal the true extent of the client's problem, for example that their debts have in reality been incurred by another person. In addition, some clients will have greater difficulty in communicating than others, and patience will be required in order to elicit from them what they need to say. Many vulnerable people in our society spend much of their time being talked to or told what to do and are given less of an opportunity to be heard and listened to than the more articulate and independent members of the community. Alternatively, as suggested earlier, the stress of the legal problem facing a client may make a normally articulate client tongue-tied. If the adviser comes across to the client as a good, non-judgmental listener then they will hopefully have a strong chance of finding out from the client all they need to know in order to provide an effective resolution.

Sensitivity to the client's needs

The adviser should not only be conscious of the client's physical needs, for breaks or rests during a long or stressful interview, but should also be aware of their need to be understood, offered sympathy in a constructive and professional manner, and overall to be believed and their problem recognised and not trivialised. If they are taken seriously at all times by their legal adviser it will make a substantial difference to their self-esteem and their ability to manage any obstacles or set-backs in the conduct of their case.

Understanding the specific nature of the client's case

In terms of providing solutions for the client there may be a temptation for the adviser to say that they have seen these cases many times before and are aware of how best to resolve them. They may be tempted to provide standard advice for this type of legal problem. Although they may find themselves reciting the same law to a number of clients in terms of its meaning and impact, they should nevertheless bear in mind that each client's story will have its own features and that the adviser's task is to resolve the problem with that particular client in mind and for their benefit. So the adviser should be regularly checking with the client that they have understood what the client is saying about their specific problem and how it impacts on them in order for the adviser to advise on a way forward appropriate to that client.

Keeping control of the interview process

Although much of what should happen in an interview should involve joint decisions, the adviser should nevertheless ensure that they maintain overall control of the interview process and not allow the structure of the interview to fall apart. This can happen when the client wishes to intercept, make comments, or offer information in a random order or once that stage in the interview has been passed. Although the adviser will need to be flexible to a certain extent as to the order in which they conduct the interview, they should keep a firm hand on the structure. If, for example, the client seeks legal advice right at the outset, and prior to giving any instructions, the adviser will confirm to the client that they will be in a position to provide advice once they have established the full facts and agreed with the client on the main issues to be decided upon to reach a satisfactory conclusion. They will be able to assure the client that they will as part of the interview process be summarising and reviewing as outlined above.

Time management

Finally, it will be up to the adviser to manage the time spent interviewing, ensuring important or urgent matters are outlined and dealt with in the time allotted and showing that they are keeping track of time and are able to use it effectively. They will ensure that they are not interrupted by calls or messages in order to keep focused and use their and their client's time efficiently.

9.4   Mapping the interview process

Sometimes an adviser will only see a client once for an interview in order to provide helpful advice and to offer a resolution to the client's problem. As we saw in chapter 1 this is the typical process followed by advisers who are part of the LawWorks clinic scheme or who do evening advice sessions in their local communities.

If the adviser is going to be involved in following a number of stages through in order to reach a resolution of the client's problem there are likely to be milestone interviews arranged. The following is a possible pattern of what each interview is likely to be able to achieve.

Interview stage	Purpose
First interview	• Sets the scene; • adviser/client relationship is formed; • client gives initial instructions about the facts or what their problem entails and seeks help in resolving it; • initial advice is offered to the client; • next steps and review process are agreed.
Second interview	• Discussion and advice offered on any replies to initial letters written or any steps taken by the adviser to attempt to resolve the client's problem; • further tactics for resolution discussed.
Third interview	• Preparation for any court or tribunal hearings; • evidence which will need to be gathered, preparation of any witness statements or documents.
Fourth interview	• Discussion of any final stage reached in the client's case (which may or may not involve a resolution); • final advice on the outcome of the case and on any steps to be taken by the client hereafter and/or by the adviser to bring their file to a close.

Where there may be tribunal or court hearings to prepare for, there are likely to be a number of preparatory interviews between the adviser and the client focusing simply on that process, including one which takes place at the hearing venue itself. Otherwise it is likely that there will instead be repetitions of the second stage interview as further steps are made towards a resolution of the client's problem.

9.5   Obstacles encountered as part of the interview

Time

In spite of any careful time management and planning, interview time may begin to run out. The client may have limited time and may, for example, have to contend with tiredness where an interpreter is involved, or with the competing demands of a small accompanying child. If the interview is taking longer than anticipated, it is best to acknowledge this and agree to re-schedule in order to continue with and complete whatever that interview was designed to achieve. Any priority tasks which need to be carried out by the adviser or client can be agreed and acted on prior to the rescheduled interview.

Conflict of interest

As we saw in chapter 4 the legal adviser should have access to a system in their organisation which checks to see whether they already advise someone who is likely to be in opposition to the client in relation to a particular case. Simple examples of this will be where a legal service is instructed by both landlord and tenant or employer and employee in litigation. If this is the case, the organisation will be regarded as having a conflict of interest and the second client will need to be informed that the adviser cannot also act for or advise them. This can hopefully be identified and dealt with even prior to the first interview. It may happen that in spite of checking, the conflict has not emerged and may not do so until the interview is underway. Parties may use different names or fail to disclose a pertinent fact which gives rise to a conflict. If it does emerge during interview, the adviser will outline the nature of the conflict and cease to take the interview any further, offering the client the option of taking independent advice elsewhere.

Problems taking instructions

Apart from any practical difficulties of clear communication which a client may have, an adviser may get a sense that the client is deliberately withholding relevant information or is becoming unreasonably defensive. If it is proving difficult to elicit from the client any clear or consistent information, the adviser may need to reiterate what they need to be told in order to assist the client. If their instructions are incomplete, it is likely to limit their capacity to assist the client. Where the failure to communicate what is required is more fundamental and underpins the whole process of the interview, the adviser may need to consider whether the required element of mutual trust and confidence which is essential to the adviser/client relationship still subsists. Where the adviser considers that it does not, they will have the entitlement to terminate the process having explained to the client their reason for so doing.

Case does not go to plan

Finally, it may be the case that information or documentations is provided for the adviser in the course of the interview which will lead the adviser to revise any advice given at an earlier stage. They may be required to change advice from that of a positive outcome for the client to advice which informs the client that they have a poor or no prospect of success. Where the course of the case is radically altered for the worse, the adviser will need to discuss with the client at the interview how that will affect the way in which they can continue to assist if at all. They will offer to record that situation in writing for the client so that they can consider it and decide if they are able to accept it as the appropriate, if somewhat unforeseen, outcome to their case.

CHAPTER 10

Giving advice and recording advice

10.1   Preparing to advise

Giving advice is at the heart of the advice worker's environment. It can take many forms, from the practical to the complex legal. It needs to be accurate, helpful and relevant to the client's situation and above all it needs to be clearly understood by the client so that they can act on it. It can be offered in a number of situations and it should be offered as part of the interview process outlined in chapter 9.[1] Preparation can be done even prior to an interview as to the type of advice likely to be given and how positive that advice might be, although this will inevitably need to be consolidated or revised as a result of more information being received from the client.

10.2   Advising during the interview: success and outcomes

A client may ask at the outset of the interview how they will fare; will they win the case, recover the money, obtain asylum or get out of debt. Even though such advice may not be able to be provided at that early stage, it will need to be given. It cannot be avoided by simply repeating the facts of the case and agreeing the next steps. The client needs to know why the next steps are to be taken and why they are appropriate in the circumstances. The advice that the client is seeking is whether, on the facts they present to their legal adviser, they will achieve their desired outcome and/or one which provides a legal solution to their problem. It is nevertheless quite common for the adviser to indicate that any advice they do provide in a client interview on such issues as these may be subject to review or consolidation once they have read over any documents supplied to them by the client during the interview or have carried out further enquiries or research.

During the course of the interview, the process of advising is likely to be arrived at by the adviser being satisfied that they have dealt with each of the matters outlined in the following ten questions:

1)   What law is relevant to the client's situation?
2)   How does that law in general operate and has the adviser made sure the client has understood this?

---

1   As with the previous chapter, the Skills for Justice Legal Advice suite of National Occupational Standards provides a standard to complement the process of interviewing and advising – see appendix D, SFJIA1 'Provide legal advice to clients'.

3) What is the impact of the law on their story, the facts they present to the adviser?

4) How does that impact translate into a possible resolution of their legal problem?

5) Is that resolution likely to be favourable – if so, how favourable?

6) Are there any unfavourable aspects of how the law impacts on their legal problem?

7) Can the unfavourable aspects be overcome, and if so by what methods or tactics?

8) What are the financial implications of any advice provided, including any financial risk or outlay for the client?

9) What advice is being offered to them on this particular occasion as to likely success and possible outcomes?

10) Will further advice be necessary dependent on what actions are agreed between the adviser and the client as next steps?

Questions 1–4: The law and its impact on the facts of the client's case – how that might translate into a possible resolution of the client's case

Looking at these first four questions, the worked example below will hopefully illustrate how, as the interview progresses and the client's story unfolds, the adviser will begin to pinpoint the relevant facts and apply the law to those facts and determine its impact on the client's situation.

This example relates to a client seeking advice on their recent dismissal from their job:

'One sneeze and you're out'?

FACTS

1. Client has worked in their job for three years – has a contract and is described as an employee. Works behind deli counter of large supermarket.

2. Client was at work behind the deli counter six weeks earlier and was allegedly observed by staff and customers to sneeze in the vicinity of open food displays.

3. Client was dismissed for gross misconduct. Company rules stipulate that employees who work in fresh food areas must not attend work when unwell with certain illnesses.

LAW
1. The Employment Rights Act 1996 gives employees with more than two years' service the right to pursue claims for unfair dismissal. See section 108.
2. The Employment Rights Act 1996 s98(2) allows an employer to fairly dismiss an employee for the reason of conduct. An example would be failing to follow company rules. Gross misconduct would include a serious example of failing to follow company rules.
3. Dismissal must be a reasonable response to the act of misconduct. See section 98(4). Case-law confirms this requirement.

IMPACT OF LAW ON FACTS
1. As an employee working for over two years this client would have the legal status to bring a claim for unfair dismissal.
2. Client may have a claim for unfair dismissal. Would have to convince an employment tribunal that the employer's decision to dismiss was not a reasonable response to the incident under investigation.
3. On facts presented so far this may be possible given the one-off nature of the incident.

So far so good; the client may have a claim for unfair dismissal if on these facts they can establish that the employer's decision to dismiss was not a reasonable one.

How do they establish that the decision was not reasonable? 'Reasonable' is a word which comes up rather frequently in a legal context. It appears in statutes and other written laws and in cases where guidance has been offered by senior judges as to what is an appropriate yardstick for making future decisions arising out of similar circumstances.

So when advising on how well a client's case may go the adviser will invariably also use the word 'reasonable' in terms of the client's prospects. But they will exercise caution in this respect for a number of reasons:

- More facts may emerge at a later stage which will have a bearing on the success of the case.
- Even where decisions or actions appear to be wholly unreasonable, the courts or tribunals will still need to hear evidence from all relevant parties which will factor in to their view as to what was or was not reasonable.
- Where there are two parties in opposition seeking the decision of a judge to settle their dispute they are inevitably allowing the judge

to be the final arbiter which in itself carries an element of risk for both parties.

So even though some advice and indeed some promising advice has been outlined in relation to the above employment dispute, the adviser will nevertheless be aware that the law will not necessarily come to the client's aid due to some or all of the above factors impacting on the progress of their case.

Questions 5–7: The law and its impact on resolutions, favourable or unfavourable

The adviser's role will be to highlight both the favourable and unfavourable aspects of the client's case in the light of how the relevant law impacts on their case. So, the adviser will next embark on the process of looking at these positive and negative aspects and weighing up how the case might be resolved in the light of these.

Following on from the imagined facts above, the adviser may note the following information also supplied by the client and consider its helpfulness or otherwise in terms of a favourable outcome.

Favourable

- Client had a good work record and no history of any disciplinary problems in the past.
- Client had that day returned to work from being off sick with a heavy cold.
- Client was fully aware of the rule about not coming to work with a bad cold but had been issued with a fit note by the doctor the previous day.
- Client had an internal disciplinary hearing where she had explained all this. She had moved away from the food and turned her back when she realised she was going to sneeze.

Unfavourable

- Client was told at disciplinary hearing that the decision to dismiss had been made not because she might still be recovering from her cold but because her employer had formed the belief that she had sneezed in the vicinity of food.
- Client had also been observed sneezing earlier in the day and had carried on working.

Was it reasonable to dismiss for one sneeze?

At this stage the adviser will remind the client that the law simply expects the employer to behave reasonably in choosing dismissal as an option. The adviser will point out that the employer will have concerns about customer care, health and safety, and the need for employees to follow internal procedures. They will advise that an employment tribunal will carefully consider all the employer's reasons for applying a strict policy. The adviser will add that they would nevertheless aim to persuade the judge that the employer's rigid approach of dismissing in the light of one sneeze was not reasonable, and that the employer should have taken into account not only the employee's good record, but also her fit note and her version of events which would have greatly minimise any health and safety risk or impact. Depending on further information, the adviser will offer advice on possible success, likely to be expressed in percentage terms. At this stage the adviser may be likely to offer a 55 per cent chance of success.

Question 8: Factoring in financial implications

The adviser will need to advise the client also what the financial implications are for the client in pursuing a claim or case. The costs of paying for a case to go into the employment tribunal system will vary according to the type of claim and the size of case. Fees are payable to start off an employment tribunal claim and also at various stages in the preparation for a hearing, including a fee for the hearing itself. Costs, as we have mentioned earlier and will return to later,[2] can also be imposed by a tribunal on a losing party. The adviser's own fees, if there are any to be paid, will also need to be factored in as part of the whole financial picture. All these figures as outlined will form a part of the advice offered to the client on their likely prospects of success in pursuing a tribunal claim as they relate to the advice as to the risks associated with pursuing a claim.

Question 9: Advice on likely success

Advice on prospects of success will then be further summarised and refined after discussing the positive and negative aspects of a client's case. Lawyers will often refer to their advice given on prospects of success in a case as being advice on the 'merits' of the case. Where there

2   See section 16.3.

is the possibility of the client recovering or being awarded money, the advice will be on 'quantum', meaning the likely amount the client may obtain. Put simply, the advice will take two forms:

- Will the client succeed?
- If so (where relevant), how much money are they likely to recover or obtain?

Even where the client's chances of success seem slim the adviser will be thinking of as yet unknown factors which may affect the client's prospects of success as the case develops, some of which we have outlined above. They will also be mindful that the case has yet to develop further and further information may have an impact on their continuing to advise on the merits of a case. This further information will include:

- more information provided by the client;
- more documents disclosed by an organisation (such as an ex-employer) from whom the client is seeking redress;
- other steps which the adviser and/or client could take to move towards a favourable resolution, such as obtaining further documentation or other witness statements to support the client's story.

Question 10: Future developments and further advice

The lack of certainty associated with any as yet unknown future developments will have a bearing on the weighting of the percentage offered in favour of the client succeeding. The adviser will in any event be regularly reviewing their advice, based on how the problem unfolds and develops. Advice given in a first interview or a first advice letter will refer to that possible uncertainty and will be realistically based on the information provided so far.

10.3 Communicating advice effectively

Confidence

An adviser's confidence may sometimes be affected by their awareness that the client will place great significance on any advice they are given and will want to act in reliance on it. This is quite understandable, and as the adviser progresses they will gain confidence in their ability to offer well-honed advice.

There are two aspects to this concept of advising confidently. The first is that an adviser should be able to assure their client that they know their subject area and are experienced in dealing with similar situations. The second is having the confidence to know their limitations in a given situation. In other words, if a client presses an adviser for advice but the adviser needs to consider the matter further or pursue some further research, they should have the confidence to decline to advise in detail until they are in a position to do so, which is infinitely more preferable than feeling pressured into advising prematurely.

Plain language

Given that advice will be so important to the client it will be necessary to ensure that it is communicated in a way in which the client can understand it. In particular, if the advice includes explaining how a court case or a legal claim may develop, any legal jargon should be avoided and, if written, the advice should be broken up into sections. It is perfectly possible to offer advice to a client which involves outlining the law in an understandable way. For example, the use of the phrases 'merits' and 'quantum' referred to above may not resonate with every client and it may be preferable to use phrases such as 'likelihood of success' and 'how much the claim is worth'.

Professional attitude

The client will expect their adviser to adopt a professional attitude when giving advice. They will expect the adviser to put advice, favourable or unfavourable, in neutral terms and not to comment on advice they offer. If, for example, the client feels they have been badly treated by a third party and the adviser agrees with that, and advises that they can take action, the adviser should not adopt a partisan approach in relation to that third party.[3] The adviser will tread a fine line between adopting a sympathetic stance and an empathetic one. The client does not require the adviser to step into their shoes emotionally but will expect them to offer a positive way out of their problem which may well include the client being able to obtain a just result over a difficult or unpleasant opponent.

---

3 In a recent outline of the court-based mediation process (for which see chapter 15), *Advising and representing clients in mediation* by David Smith, it was noted that one of the obstacles to reaching a resolution lay with the participating solicitors over-identifying with their clients and allowing their own personal interest in a case to block avenues to open discussion as part of the mediation process.

Communicating advice in different contexts

As part of an interview, or in a letter or during a telephone advice session, a client should be offered comprehensive advice on the likely outcomes and prospects of success, taking into account the facts and issues relevant to their case. This comprehensive advice can either be provided as the main service to a client or as part of the conduct of an ongoing adviser/client relationship. It forms the cornerstone of the adviser/client relationship.

Advice is not always given to a client in a formal setting. Informal contact between adviser and client may include travelling together to and from courts or tribunals, sitting in waiting rooms or possible chance encounters, for example when a client calls into the adviser's office to leave or collect messages or documents. Where advice is given in these settings it will be of equal importance and value and should be noted by the adviser and as with more detailed advice, recorded for the client as we shall see below.

Supplementary advice

At various stages there will be the opportunity or the requirement to offer a client advice in much smaller segments which relates back to the overall picture the adviser has painted in their comprehensive advice or which develops the advice already given. The client with the job loss outlined in the scenario above may, for example, later produce a copy of a document she has been able to locate which provides guidance to managers about when it would not be appropriate to consider dismissing in relation to apparent health and safety breaches. On seeing that document the adviser may decide that the client's prospects of success on the unfair dismissal claim improve somewhat and they will advise accordingly.

Practical advice

At all stages of the adviser/client relationship the adviser will also be offering practical advice to their clients. Clients will need to know, for example:

- how to prepare for a tribunal or court hearing – what to bring and what to wear;
- how long interviews or court attendances are likely to last;
- whether they can take friends or children to tribunal or court hearings;

- who will help them in an emergency if the adviser is off sick or the office is closed.

All these matters are part and parcel of advice-giving. Where such practical advice is provided in person, it will be recorded as having been done so by the adviser in their own record, a process we will now proceed to examine.

10.4   Recording advice

The recording of advice is an essential part of the adviser's skills. It is important for a number of reasons.

Why record advice?

- The adviser needs to have a clear record of their advice to refer back to.
- The client also needs a clear record of advice as summarised to them by their adviser in writing and taken from the adviser's notes, and will want to refer back to it to see how it fits in with any developing chain of events.
- The adviser may need to record advice for a funder or organisation supervisor.
- The adviser may at times be absent or taken ill and the organisation will need to see the record of their advice in case another adviser has to step in.
- The organisation will have insurance in place in relation to the possibility of negligent (wrong, inappropriate or inaccurate) advice being given to clients, and insurers will need to see the record of advice given where there is a complaint or claim raised against the adviser and/or the organisation for the advice given.

What to record

There are two aspects of recording. The first is the process of the adviser maintaining for themselves a running record of all contact with the client which is legible (if handwritten), faithful to what was said and agreed, and which records events and contact with the client in a logical sequence. The second is to record in writing the advice provided to the client both by way of an initial letter of advice to the client and also as a case progresses any further supplementary and practical advice.

How to record

The way in which the adviser will record their client contact and advice will vary according to the procedures or systems in place in the adviser's workplace. There are likely to be centralised case management systems for recording certain aspects of the adviser's work (for which see chapter 12) as well as paper files or folders kept in respect of each individual client.

Nevertheless the following general guidelines may assist in terms of recording:

Recording advice checklist

Method of recording
- Will advice be recorded by way of handwritten notes, on a pre-set form or on to the computer?
- If using a combination of these methods – what information needs to go onto the computer or the pre-set form and also what handwritten notes need to go onto the client's paper file or folder?
- Does the paper file show what information has been recorded onto the computer?

Timing of recording
- Is recording taking place as the interview progresses?
- If so, can the adviser still fully engage with their client?
- Is the record being made later and/or added to or being completed later?
- If so, are the interview notes sufficiently detailed and is there a diary note to confirm when the record will be completed (this should if at all possible be on the same day that the client was seen or spoken to)?

Style of recording
- Are interview notes written in a clear accessible way – could another adviser read and understand them?
- Are they in jargon-free language?
- Is the style of recording free from commentary or personal opinion?
- Is the same style used for all clients? If not, is there a good reason for this?
- Is there a hierarchy of detail? In other words, providing full details of everything the client has said, then isolating the relevant facts, the advice provided in interview, with less detail of practical advice, for example how to find a tribunal office or what forms to use to make court claims?

- When drafting advice letters are they logical and reader-friendly for the client – are they easy to follow?
- Is it clear in the advice letters at which point the adviser is providing advice – is the advice properly headed as such?

10.5 One-off advice or ongoing case: concluding the client interview

There are some advice-giving situations where the adviser and client will only have contact on one occasion. Typical of these will be where the adviser is taking part in an evening advice session as a volunteer for a host organisation as we saw in chapter 1. Alternatively, where there was an expectation of an ongoing adviser/client relationship developing, the advice may need to be entirely negative which will mean that there is nothing further the legal adviser or service is able to do for that client in that situation.

One-off advice

Where the advice is part of a one-off advice session it will usually involve advice on not only the likely success and outcomes for the client in a particular case, but also what further steps the client may be able to take to resolve their legal problem themselves. In chapter 7 we looked at a fictitious case of a ruined holiday where advice might be offered to take legal action against the holiday company. This type of query is typical of one which a host agency may refer to its volunteer legal advisers on the basis that hopefully much ground can be covered in one advice session with a view to arming the client to take the matter further forward themselves.

If a client comes to a one-off advice session (even where the advice is not followed up in a letter but recorded on a form) the adviser is likely to proceed with such a query in the following manner:

- They will check that they have no conflict with the holiday company – do they perhaps act for them in their own day-time job – if they do, they will not be able to advise the (second) client in front of them that day.[4]

---

4 See chapter 4 where we discussed the protocol where an adviser believes they have a conflict of interest.

- They will take instructions on the full facts, perhaps filling out the client's story from details already provided in the advice session's referral forms drawn up when the client contacted the host organisation.
- They will explain to the client the relevant law – the duty to provide the holiday contract in the manner outlined in the description provided by the company and in a way that the holiday-maker gains enjoyment from the experience.
- They will tell the client that there are legal cases which have established that a claim for distress and disappointment for a booked holiday can lead to compensation being awarded to the holiday-maker.
- They will advise the client based on the facts of their case, on their likely prospect of success should they take the company to court.
- They will also advise the client on other options for resolving the claim such as letter-writing or a reference to the company's trading standards association.
- They will outline how small claim for such claims operates in the local county court[5] and refer the client to websites or other sources of information concerning procedures. They will also tell the client about small claims court mediation services as a way of avoiding court hearings.

Overall (and this is the key to these 'one-off' advice sessions) the legal adviser will be giving the client clear advice and pointers as to how they will be able to carry on pursuing this matter utilising the legal advice now provided to them. This advice will be a tool for the client in providing them with the confidence to continue to pursue what they now know to be their legal right.

Negative advice and an end to the advice process

In either of these advice-giving situations, either one-off or envisaged as ongoing, there is always the possibility that advice given will be wholly negative. It may be that on paper and in advance of seeing a client the case or legal problem looked to be one which would be favourable to the client or at least worth pursuing in spite of any possible unfavourable angles; then, once detailed instructions are received,

---

5   These are claims worth £10,000 or less where fees and procedures are relatively accessible for a litigant in person to pursue their legal rights – see chapter 17 for more on the civil court processes.

the advice reluctantly may have to be that there is no case for the client to pursue or defend.

Even so, the adviser would, as described above, provide for the client the same amount of information as to how the law operates and impacts as well as legal advice on the likely outcome, explaining why they have to advise there is no case for the client. In the example we outlined earlier in this chapter relating to the job loss, on a different set of facts, where an employee might have repeatedly ignored health and safety procedures, or where there was evidence of similar behaviour occurring and warnings ignored, the advice may have to be that the dismissal was fair and that a claim for unfair dismissal would not be successful. Nevertheless, the adviser will keep an open mind during an interview and while being realistic should not be too quick to assume a poor outcome until they have explored every avenue for and with the client.

Where it has been agreed that a client's case is going forward with their adviser, the next step will be to progress their case for them in a number of different respects as referred to earlier in chapter 7. One of these will be the way in which the adviser will advocate for their client, which is the subject of the next chapter.

CHAPTER 11

Advocating for the client

11.1   The meaning of advocacy

Many people who see the word advocacy will associate it with a barrister or solicitor who appears in court and presents a court case for their client. While this word does describe this function it is important to know that advocacy has a wider meaning as well. An integral part of the adviser/client relationship will be built on the adviser's willingness to engage with others as their client's advocate and to utilise the skills of presenting and defending their client's position with external parties. Although there are quite specific and sometimes high-level skills involved with formal advocacy which we will refer to in this chapter, it is also worth noting that an adviser will be employing advocacy skills on a more everyday level and may do so instinctively without putting a label on what they are doing. In that more general sense the activity describes the process of 'pleading' for another and speaking on behalf of that other.[1]

11.2   Informal and formal advocacy settings

Informal

Being a champion for the client: setting out and pleading their case with an outside party[2]

An adviser can in many settings act as the client's champion by offering to speak, make calls or write letters on behalf of the client and in doing so will represent what the client wants to say to others and plead or argue the client's position in order to achieve a result. They will hope to persuade the other party of the correctness of their client's position or of any injustice they have suffered in order to achieve the client's desired outcome. The adviser will be both acting as the client's

---

1   See Oxford Dictionary: 'Advocacy: 1. *public support for or recommendation of a particular cause or policy.* 2. *the profession or work of a legal advocate.*' (The origin is from the Old French word (via Medieval Latin) 'advocare' = summons, call to one's aid. Indeed the modern French word for a lawyer is an 'avocat').

2   See appendix D and the National Occupational Standard SFJDA3 'Act on behalf of clients in informal proceedings', which outline the skills and knowledge involved in representation in informal proceedings. The distinction made in this book is between the process of pleading on behalf of the client by phone or in writing and that of exercising advocacy skills in person, whether the proceedings are informal or formal, and the associated skills of these two processes.

voice, putting the client's case for them, and using their powers of persuasion to effect the desired outcome.

Advocacy in non-court or tribunal settings – adviser pleading by letter

There are a number of decisions which can be made which affect people's lives where the setting is relatively formal but the decisions are more administrative than legal. In many of these venues it would not be usual for an individual to attend a meeting or hearing with a legal adviser, sometimes due to concerns that it might over-formalise or legalise the process.[3] An adviser may, however, be instructed to write a letter on behalf of a client who has to attend a meeting or hearing themselves which is part of an administrative process and where a decision is likely to be made affecting the client.

In order to look at how the adviser might utilise advocacy skills to assist a client in this type of venue we will look at the example of a school pupil being excluded from school for a disciplinary offence. That pupil's parent has certain rights to seek to influence the outcome of the decision.[4] Let us say that her daughter aged 14 has been excluded from school on three separate occasions in a term by the head teacher for what he regards as a repetition of a serious disciplinary offence, that of wearing earrings at school, which is not permitted under the school uniform policy. On each occasion the pupil has allegedly said that she does not care what the uniform policy is and that she intends to carry on wearing the earrings. She has been suspended for a total of six days.

In these circumstances the girl's parent has the right to make representations to the school governors while they deliberate whether they will confirm the head teacher's decision. Both the girl and her mother, who agree that they both want the same outcome,[5] come to see the adviser and ask the adviser to write a letter to the governing

---

3 A good example of this would be an employer's internal disciplinary hearing (which we briefly referred to in the example in the previous chapter) where the law allows for the employee to be accompanied by a work colleague or trade union representative but not by a legal adviser – see Employment Relations Act 1999 s10.

4 The School Discipline (Pupil Exclusions Reviews) (England) Regulations 2012 SI No 1033 provide the legal framework for how school pupil exclusions should operate. In addition, the Department of Education has provided statutory guidance for those involved in this process, including the parent and/or their representative appearing before an independent review panel.

5 See section 6.3 on how to approach a child or young person as a client.

body asking for the suspension to be overturned. The girl's story is that she was given the earrings by her grandmother whom she is very close to. She thought that it would only be a breach of the school rules if she had jewellery on display and has been able to hide the earrings most of the time behind her hair. She says she has tried to explain this to the head teacher.

After some discussion it is agreed that the adviser will advocate to overturn the suspension by setting out the following points in a letter:

- pointing out the disparity between the pupil's and the head teacher's version of events;
- stating that if the pupil's story were to be believed it would place her in a more favourable light;
- requesting that the disciplinary panel accept the pupil's story;
- pointing out that the pupil's actions were not deliberate but mistaken;
- explaining that there was a strong family reason for her wearing the earrings and the reason was not capricious;
- stating that although the wearing of the earrings may have had an unsettling effect on her school mates it did not impact on their welfare or education;
- expressing that she has missed six days of schooling including the preparation of an art project on which she is a team leader;
- expressing on behalf of the girl and her parent their regret and apology for the disciplinary breach;
- asking the governors to overturn the decision to exclude her for all these reasons and to allow the girl to continue to have an unblemished school record.

In setting out these matters in a letter written on behalf of the client, the adviser is not only setting out the client's story on her behalf, but has also moved into 'pleading' with the panel of governors in order to achieve the client's desired outcome to overturn the exclusion decision.

Law or no law?

In writing such a letter a legal adviser may well also include a reference to the law and procedures surrounding school exclusions and refer to the parent's right to take the matter further.[6] The letter may make it clear that the adviser is familiar with the relevant legal

---

6 The regulations referred to above (note 4) would allow a parent to ask an independent review panel to review a governing body's decision to uphold an exclusion.

principles surrounding such decisions as part of seeking to persuade the governors not to uphold the head teacher's decision.

Even where an adviser is not operating in a legal setting or does not employ any law in advocating for their client's desired outcome,[7] this type of advocacy process can be most efficacious for the client. If the parent wishes to attend the planned governors' meeting, the adviser's letter paves the way for and prepares the client for that meeting, where she can refer them and herself to it to keep her thoughts in order and her arguments on track.

Formal

Pleading in a formal setting

In some administrative venues such as boards or panel meetings, an adviser may be permitted to, or instructed to, represent a client in person. More commonly such advocacy will be conducted in the more formal and legalistic tribunal or court setting. Here the skills associated with that more legalistic process of advocacy will be deployed.[8]

In some legal venues the court will expect the advocate to be qualified as a lawyer before they can address the court on behalf of their client. This is what is known in legal parlance as having a 'right of audience'.[9] Legally qualified personnel will have undertaken training in the process of advocacy and will have studied the laws of evidence.

---

7 There are advice services which offer to speak on behalf of a client caught in an administrative process where an adviser will not necessarily advocate by placing their arguments in a formal legal setting. In some cases this can be a positive advantage as some decision-makers may adopt a more rigid approach if they feel they are being 'lectured to by a lawyer'.

8 See National Occupational Standards in appendix D: SFJDA7 'Prepare cases for representation in formal proceedings' and SFJDA4 'Represent clients in formal proceedings' for more background to this section.

9 A barrister will have a right of audience in all courts and tribunals and at all levels of the court system (which we look at in more detail in chapter 18). A solicitor will also be able to appear in all tribunals and at most levels of the civil and criminal court system if they have a higher right of audience (see chapter 2) for the higher courts. A lay person representing themselves can also appear in any court or tribunal. Otherwise there are certain venues where a non-qualified advocate may speak on behalf of and represent their client. In the main these will be all tribunals at each tier or level of that tribunal process and also what is known as the small claims court in the civil court system. Finally, the courts will allow a silent adviser to sit with a lay person representing themselves and give them whispered support. That person is known as a 'Mackenzie friend'.

The idea of appearing in settings of this type to advocate for a client can be quite daunting even for a trained advocate.

In a number of civil legal venues, advisers, whether legally qualified or not, will be able to appear and advocate for their clients. Examples include school exclusions review panels referred to above or tribunals dealing with welfare benefits entitlements, school special educational needs and employment disputes. They may also represent clients at court duty sessions in relation to housing repossession cases or in the small claims court. These venues will also be frequented by trained and qualified lawyers and so where the venue is adversarial[10] there may be a mix of these advocates and those who are trained but not legally qualified appearing before a judge or tribunal. Each forum, panel or tribunal will have its own rules and procedures and will expect all those appearing there to be familiar with these. They will not necessarily expect an advocate who is not a trained lawyer to use any formal advocacy tactics, although if they do so this will be acceptable and in many cases welcomed as a way of streamlining the process.

In formal settings, as we will see below, there are a number of preparatory and tactical steps which an advocate will engage in as part of their approach to advocating. They will also be aware of the appropriate dress code for the relevant venue and will familiarise themselves with what mode of address to use in presenting their case in a court or tribunal. Once they are invited to advocate they will be exercising skills which they will either have formally studied or which they have acquired through experience guidance and observation, some of which we will also examine below.

11.3 Preparing to advocate

In some of the situations referred to above, such as attending a housing duty court advice session, the advocate will have very little time to prepare. As they wait to be called into court they will take details from a client of their rent or mortgage arrears, their efforts to pay these off,

10 An adversarial tribunal, such as an employment tribunal, will involve a judge hearing two opposing views and then making their decision in one or the other party's favour. In an inquisitorial tribunal, for example a special educational needs tribunal or benefit tribunal, the tribunal will listen to representations made by or on behalf of an individual affected by a legal or quasi legal (administrative) decision but will be there to decide on the correctness of that body's decision.

and their financial liquidity, and will gather as much detail as they can concerning the way in which the landlord or mortgage company has dealt with the matter to date. They will then, on instructions, seek to persuade a judge of the efficacy of reaching a decision which is lenient on their client but which takes into account how the law operates in these circumstances, as well as weighing into the balance the legal rights of their opponent ultimately to obtain judgment in their favour.

A number of skills are at play in that process of 'last minute representation' not least of which is the ability to think and act quickly on behalf of the client. We will look at how some of these skills are deployed in practice by the advocate below, starting with the preparation normally carried out where the advocate has been instructed in advance to represent a client in a formal hearing.

The formal venue – rules and procedures

The adviser will first familiarise themselves with the venue they are about to engage in as an advocate as well as how its rules and processes operate.[11] The advocate will also ensure they know how that jurisdiction can reach a decision and what kinds of decisions its rules may allow it to make. In the case of a panel or tribunal there will be set procedures for hearings specifying the order in which people will be allowed to address them, whether questions can be asked, and to whom these questions can be put. Some panels or tribunals will be able to reach a different decision from whoever made the original decision and/or be able to hear evidence as well as listen to representations. Others may not be allowed to hear any evidence, and will only be able to review the evidence before the original decision-maker as part of making their decision. In each of these circumstances the advocate will need to know whether they will be allowed to present evidence to allow for a fresh decision to be reached or may only be allowed to make representations as to the correctness of the original decision. Civil courts also provide for how advocates should present their cases, which in the simplest terms can be expressed as allowing each of the advocates representing a client to have their turn in presenting a case, as well as putting their opponent's case to the test, before allowing a judge to decide in favour of one or the other adversarial party.

---

11 Usually referred to as the jurisdiction – the legal venue in which a hearing is taking place and the rules and procedures associated with that jurisdiction.

The client's case

An adviser needs to know the client's case thoroughly. This involves not only knowing everything their client has told them about their legal problem, but also what aspects of it are relevant to highlight any injustice, or to persuade a court or tribunal to reach a decision favourable to the client. This will inevitably involve consideration of how they intend to use the law and/or or any legal or regulatory guidance to support their client's case and what arguments, both tactical and legal, they have been thinking about in order to put the case at its best and seek an appropriate resolution. We saw an example of that process being developed above in the adviser's letter to the school governors where the adviser moved from setting out the client's story or instructions to making representations designed to overturn a decision to exclude a pupil from school.

As well as the strongest aspects of a client's case ('I thought I was not breaking the school rules when I did what I did') the advocate will have explored all additional angles, including the awkward corners ('I agree that I was warned and suspended on three occasions for the same offence'). They will try to anticipate what a panel, tribunal or opposing party may say to counter the client's assertions and be ready to address these points ('Why did the pupil keep repeating the same breach of rules?'). The advocate will present evidence from their client to ensure that what their client wants to say will be accepted ('The pupil genuinely misunderstood how the school rule operated').

The opposition case

In most adversarial venues the two opposing parties will have had an opportunity to look at each other's documents or witness statements, and sometimes even their legal arguments as part of preparing for the hearing. The advocate will then not only prepare to represent based on what their own client has said but on what their opponent is likely to say, and will be prepared to deal with that in terms of countering or overcoming any opposing views which might damage their client's case.

Even where the process is not adversarial but involves an administrative decision-maker coming under scrutiny by a panel or tribunal, the advocate should be well versed in the details of that decision and the circumstances in which it was reached in order to challenge it at the hearing.

Organisation of documents

In terms of practical preparation, the advocate will prepare their own 'hearing file' so that they can easily find documents as they present their case. They may use highlighter pens, page dividers and post-it notes to organise a well-prepared pack. This will reflect the order the panel or tribunal expect papers to be set out in, as well as containing the adviser's own copies of statements, preparation notes or documents ready for them to refer to during the hearing.

At the start of that file it is helpful for the advocate to have a document setting out key dates and incidents which lead up to the necessity of resolving a dispute. Some jurisdictions ask to see those. Even where they do not, this document, usually called a chronology, can assist both the court and tribunal as well as those appearing before it, to be reminded of these events. Key events or incidents will be set out neutrally and quite briefly and the contents of a chronology can often be agreed on between two opposing parties in advance of a hearing.

In some jurisdictions a panel or court will themselves prepare a set of documents for a hearing and will expect everyone who appears at the hearing to have these documents in the same order. It is usually the case that the more formal proceedings become, the more likely it is that panels or courts will dictate how representatives prepare their documents ready for a hearing. The following checklist contains the types of documents most commonly used in formal hearings, including administrative panels or tribunals, but will be subject to variation according to the nature of the case and the rules of the relevant jurisdiction.

Documents checklist

- An outline or timeline of what happened up to the point necessitating this process of having a hearing (chronology).
- The key documents setting out the case stated for and against as required by the relevant court or tribunal (pleadings).
- A set of documents recording what has happened to or has been seen by anyone wanting to give evidence to this effect (witness statements).
- A further set of witness statements prepared by expert witnesses. These may be doctors, surveyors or other professionals providing an expert opinion to assist the court or tribunal (expert statements).

- A set of additional documents usually drawn up and agreed either by a tribunal or court or by two opposing parties, the contents of which are designed to support what the witnesses and their advocates want to say. These may include decision letters or other correspondence which a witness may have seen or written. They are usually set out in subject headings and date order beginning with the earliest.

All these documents and statements will, once they are finalised and ready for a hearing, be referred to as the 'hearing (or trial) bundle'.

Statements, questions and submissions

Witness statements

In preparation for the client's role in a hearing, the advocate will assist the client in finalising a statement to support their case. The client will be required to read out or confirm the contents of their statement during the hearing and will be asked questions on it. The advocate will ensure it is in the client's own words and includes all that the client needs to say. It will be in the form of a factual account of what the client heard or saw or what happened to them, and will not require them to provide any legal opinion. It will be set out in short paragraphs, flow in time sequence from one event to the next and, where relevant, refer to documents (as part of the trial bundle) which the client has seen or written in order to underline for the court or tribunal the truth or credibility of what they are saying. There is a sample witness statement set out in appendix A in which a client is describing what happened when she took some curtains in for dry cleaning. It will be seen that the statement is set out in plain language and simply outlines what that sequence of event was from her perspective.

If there are other witnesses who the advocate considers will support a client's case, factual or expert, these will also prepare statements in advance. Sometimes a client will ask if they can bring along a witness who will give testimony to their honesty or good character. This type of evidence will, however, rarely add to what the judge or panel can observe by hearing that client's own evidence at first hand.

Questions

As well as the advocate's own witnesses there may be witnesses giving evidence on behalf of a client's opponents. In an adversarial setting an advocate will be allowed to put questions to witnesses called by the opposing side. This process is known as 'cross-examination'. It is part of the wider map covering of the rules of evidence and the skills of advocacy studied by barristers (and also now more commonly solicitors) in preparing for their key role as advocates in court. Whilst it will not be possible to outline this process in full in a book of this nature it should be borne in mind that cross-examination can be crucial to highlighting the key aspects the advocate's own client's case, and persuading a court or tribunal to accept that case. Cross-examination questions should be prepared in advance and if at all possible refined during a hearing once the evidence gets underway. Ideally each question the advocate wants to put to the witness will be written out, relating to the various topics the advocate wants to test out with that witness. The aim is to attempt to elicit answers from a witness which are either favourable to the advocate's client's case or which in some sense throw doubt on the credibility of that witness. Questions should be short and they should where at all possible be designed to elicit a short yes or no answer to elicit the required admission.

In a simple example of a criminal case where the advocate's client is defending a charge of theft in a workplace, the advocate wishes to rely on their client's alibi defence that they were elsewhere at the time the offence was committed. They may prepare a series of six short questions to a witness whom they know will allege that their client was observed at the scene of the crime. These might look like this:

Q You have told the court that you were not at work on that particular Tuesday haven't you?

Q You have also told the court that your CCTV camera was out of order on that same day haven't you?

Q You have been shown a copy of the defendant's sick note for that date haven't you?

Q You have also produced to the court records of the CCTV system being under repair that day?

Q So you could not have witnessed my client allegedly taking money from the till on that date could you?

Q Nor could this have been recorded on your CCTV camera could it?

The advocate will anticipate a short positive response to the first four questions followed by negative responses to the final two, all of which will hopefully assist in supporting their client's alibi defence.

Submissions

In some formal venues an advocate will also prepare what are some-times called 'submissions'. The contents may also be referred to as 'summing up' and in some civil courts advocates will refer to them as their skeleton argument.[12] They may be presented at the end of a hearing where each advocate or representative is permitted to sum up their client's case in a final effort to persuade a court or tribunal of its good qualities. Even where the formality does not call for such a process it will always be useful for the advocate to prepare a short document to have with them in order to remind them of these salient points. It will summarise the law relevant to the matter in hand, high-light its relevance and applicability to their client's case and outline how evidence heard has assisted that case. How it is set out will vary from one individual or jurisdiction to another but it can be a useful way of getting a case back to its basics at the point at which it may have become quite bulky and detailed with all the documents and evidence prepared for the hearing to take place.

11.4   In the hearing: tips and tactics

Once a hearing gets underway there are a few tips and tactics which will allow an advocate to keep their case on track and present it at its best.

Flexibility

A key feature of advocacy is being prepared to deal with the unex-pected. In advance of the hearing, the advocate will be aware that what their client will say and what evidence is put forward by others is likely to conflict and they will prepare to deal with that. However, if matters progress even further during the hearing, any variations from that pre-planned pattern will also need to be accommodated. Questions prepared in advance may need to be modified in order to deal with unexpected developments, perhaps by way of statements made by other witnesses while giving evidence, or questions asked by a panel or the last-minute production of documents. There will be no benefit in doggedly sticking to a prepared set of questions or submissions if evidence which emerges on the day is not favourable to that line of

---

12 This is one of a number of expressions used in the preparation and conduct of a hearing which are referred to and explained in the glossary in appendix F.

argument. The advocate will be required to be quick-witted in adapting to these developments in order to keep control of their client's case.

Making concessions

If it seems that certain aspects of a client's case are not going well then it will often be better to make concessions but still make a case for other aspects. Planning might be made to advocate for more than one outcome, all being advantageous to a client, if things do not go as well as expected. An example of this might be to argue that if a pupil's suspension from school can be overturned, instead of a return to a totally clean record, a lesser disciplinary sanction such as being on report or under review might be an alternative and less unpleasant outcome for her. It should, however, be remembered that whatever concession might be made on the client's behalf during the course of a hearing will require their instructions even if that requires seeking a break during a hearing to discuss options and review what is being asked for.

Looking for opportunities

Where an opportunity arises to strengthen the case, which the advocate has not foreseen, they should be prepared to grasp it. An example might be an admission made by a witness which will assist in highlighting the client's credibility as with the cross-examination questions prepared and outlined above. If such a helpful advantage arises, it is usually best to make a note of it and refer to it in summing up a client's case at the end of a hearing rather than to spend time underlining its helpfulness at the time it emerges.

Accepting outcomes

Flexibility can also mean that both the adviser and the client should be prepared for the possibility that the case may not go according to plan. Even where a case is very well prepared and argued it can be possible for the outcome to be different from what was predicted or hoped for. This is usually referred to in civil cases as the risk of litigation. For example, a client's case may not come across exactly in the way it was planned to. It may not impress the person hearing it in the manner hoped for, or the client's evidence might not come across as well as anticipated, perhaps due to the stress of taking part in the hearing.

Both adviser and client will need to accept that the damage has been done and that it may well limit the client's chances of a successful outcome. The adviser cannot ignore it or brush it aside but will deal with it as part of the advocacy process, usually by trying to place it in context as they sum up the strengths of their client's case.

11.5   The language of advocating in courts and tribunals: an introduction

For someone relatively unfamiliar with the formal court processes we will look in chapter 18 at how to navigate the courts and legal systems in more detail. In the meantime it may be helpful to provide an overview of some of the 'lawyerly' aspects of court and tribunal language associated with advocacy which hopefully will help to prepare a lay person or non-legally qualified advocate for some aspects of formal court and tribunal representation.

Jargon	Everyday meaning
1. Addressing people in court	
My opponent	The person who represents the other party (the employer, the landlord, Home Office etc)
My friend	The same person as above
My learned friend	The same person as above but that person like me is a barrister
Your honour	A circuit judge in the county court
Sir/Madam	A district judge in the county court or the magistrates' court or a judge in a tribunal hearing
Chairman or Madam Chairman	The person in the centre of a tribunal panel of three who is running the tribunal

Jargon	Everyday meaning
2. Expressions used by judge or tribunal chairman	
Appearing before me, or appearing	Stating that you are the person in the proceedings who is representing a particular client
Opening your case	This is asking you to go first and present your case by calling witnesses
Not to lead a witness	Asking you not to give the witness the answer you want as part of your question (eg, 'You didn't take the money did you?')
Inviting you to cross-examine or saying 'this is now your witness'	Inviting you to ask questions of another party's witness which are designed to help your client's case (eg, 'Do you agree that my client could not have been seen by you at work on the date in question?')
Asking you to sum up or present your submissions	At the end of the hearing or meeting asking you to summarise what you believe has happened and the points which you think have been established in your client's favour
3. Hearing documents	
A statement of truth	A sworn statement at the foot of a statement of case or a witness statement that indicates the truth of the contents of that statement
A bundle	A set of documents which everyone has copies of and which the court or tribunal will be asked to read or refer to and which a witness will also be asked to refer to
A paginated and/or indexed bundle	A set of documents with page numbers and an index referring to what each document is called and what date it was produced

Case progression and case management

CHAPTER 12

Case management on individual files

12.1   Introduction

Case management focuses on a requirement for the adviser to demonstrate that certain steps and checks are taking place on each matter
they handle for a client, that there is a file opened for each matter or
case and that they have a system for managing all the files or cases for
which they are responsible. A case management system embedded
in a legal advice service should be consistent across the organisation
and will be the basis for demonstrating good practice and compliance
with any professional conduct or other legal requirements. It should
be able to show, for example, that the organisation is aware of, and
is complying with, its obligations in relation to how information is
processed, so that the requirements of the Data Protection Act (DPA)
1998 are being complied with.[1]

Most advice organisations, no matter how small, will have such a
system, whether it is paper-based or a software package. The paper-
based file will store papers or documents relating to the client's
case as well as complementing the computerised file. Typical of the
documents stored on these systems will be copies of letters sent and
received, memos of discussions (usually called attendance notes),
summaries of interviews, records of telephone calls and copies of
emails. This means that there is a clear paper trail in the office to back
up that on the computerised system.

The three most significant case management procedures are:

- file opening and procedures;
- evidence of ongoing file management;
- file-closing procedures.[2]

12.2   File opening and procedures

There are a number of procedures which should be followed in
embarking on a new case or file for a client. Even where the advice
may only cover one interview or a telephone call, there will still be a

---

1   Under the DPA 1998, where data is kept in relation to an individual they will
    have certain rights in relation to accessing information on them where the
    information is held in a relevant filing system – see, for example, DPA 1998
    s7. The Information Commissioner's website provides further guidance – see:
    www.ico.gov.uk.

2   See National Occupational Standards in appendix D: SFJIA2 'Manage legal
    advice cases' sets out these three activities as the three elements in managing a
    client's ongoing case.

requirement to record that contact and the outcome of it. Each new file opened will be allocated a reference number linked to the organisation's central system for recording files. The system may relate to client groups, case work teams and numbers of files opened, and will also include the reference of the adviser who will have conduct of the case.

Contact details

The contact details of the client should be recorded on the file. Name, address and landline number, with mobile and email address included if possible, for ease of contact. These details should be accessible but not externally visible in order to retain client confidentiality. The name and reference number of the person advising the client should also be easily accessible so that others in the organisation are aware of who is responsible for that case.

Check for conflict of interest

We have already referred in chapter 4 to a situation where it will not be possible to act for or provide legal advice or representation to two clients with opposing interests in the same case.[3] As the adviser opens a new case they will check on the organisation's case management system for any possible conflict. The organisation should have the facility for an individual to carry out conflict checks by a matching process across the list of clients. The adviser will then note on the file that the conflict check has been carried out.

Key dates and milestones

The file should record in a distinct area of the file, (in the case of the paper file most usually on the outside flap), what the important dates are in respect of that particular matter.

The first category of key dates are deadlines. These may relate to the date by which a court or tribunal hearing has to be commenced or when the hearing of a case is to take place.

There may also be milestone dates which carry significance in relation to when steps may need to be taken on a file. Examples might be a date when a road accident took place or someone's date of birth, as both these dates might have an impact on when they might need

---

3 See section 4.3.

to start off a personal injury claim. They may be dates when a child reaches their legal majority (18), which might affect a housing application or a benefit calculation, or the date on which a divorce petition is made absolute by a court, or when an employee's notice period runs out.

The adviser will be taking responsibility for ensuring that deadlines are complied with and will note and review key dates linking these to a central record of those maintained for each client's case which the organisation will have in place. Court or tribunal hearing dates will be recorded there, together with the name of the case worker taking responsibility for those.

Funding and costs

At the start of the case, funding will be discussed with the client and also noted on the file in a separate place. At the same time the adviser will initiate a running record of time spent and costs expended on that file. Computerised case management systems usually provide a built-in time-recording system matched to each file.

The organisation's procedures and client care letters

As outlined in chapter 7,[4] part of what the adviser will do when they first meet their client will be to introduce the client to the organisation and its services. It is usual for this information to be contained in an initial client care letter with two copies provided for the client so that they can keep one and return one signed as having been read. This letter is usually sent out in advance of the first interview. It will contain the information outlined above as well as details of any funding or costs arrangements relevant to the conduct of the client's case; and a statement that both the adviser and the organisation will keep confidential all information they hold on the client. Most legal advice services are also required to carry out money laundering checks which require them to verify the identity of their new clients by reference to original documents such as passports or utility bills. If so, the adviser will explain to the new client the purpose and process of this requirement[5] and it is also likely that this requirement will be referred to in

---

4　See section 7.1.

5　The Money Laundering Regulations 2007 SI No 2157 and the Money Laundering Regulations 2012 SI No 2298 both have implications for legal services in terms of liability for any possible wrongdoings by association with those who approach them to become clients or who are their clients. These will

the client care letter. An example of a standard client care letter is set out in appendix A.

Setting up a system

At the start of a new file the adviser will not only be complying with the computerised case management system in terms of conflict check, central diarising and time and activity recording, but will also set up a system for running their paper file. This system will vary from one organisation to another but will be applied for all that organisation's files to allow for checks and reviews to take place and for others in the organisation, where necessary, to step in and handle an aspect of an ongoing case. In any event it is likely that a paper file will be organised on the following lines:

- a place to record the client's contact details;
- a place to record key milestones and dates;
- a way of recording each activity carried out by the adviser on the client's case as discussed below;
- a way of recording time spent, and costs incurred, on a running basis;
- a place to keep copies of all letters and emails sent.

In the same place will be kept notes of phone calls both made and received and memos or attendance notes (for which see later under 'Progressing the file') which are kept in date order. Most advisers refer to this as the correspondence section or tag, and will tag each of these pages in reverse date order (with the most recent on top) for when the file is next picked up for consideration as to the last action which occurred and what the next step should be. It is also:

- a place to keep documents which might have been brought in by the client (letters, emails or notices they have received for example);
- a place to keep court papers, hearing dates or orders or directions sent out to the parties.

However the system looks, once it is set up, it will be necessary to ensure that it is maintained and does not slide into disarray.

usually involve making document checks to verify identity and/or electronic checks concerning any possible fraudulent identities or activities.

12.3   Ongoing file management

Once a client's file has been opened and begins to progress, evidence of a number of activities will be reflected on it.

Ongoing advice letters

Advice given to the client will continue to be recorded by letter or email. We saw in chapter 11 that even where advice is not given in the formal surroundings of an interview, it must nevertheless be recorded for the client. As the case progresses and further advice letters are sent to the client, copies of these will be kept on the correspondence section of the file.

Keeping attendance notes

Reference was made above to attendance notes. These are part of the running actions on a file. Each time a client is contacted or spoken to, especially as part of a client interview, that activity will be summarised in an attendance note. The note will record and summarise the conversation which took place, and state what action is agreed as the next step. A note will also be taken of any discussions or contact with an external party where actions were agreed.

Examples of how attendance notes might be recorded and used in that context are provided below in relation to a client with an imminent court hearing concerning their mortgage arrears. When speaking to another person, including the client, the note will refer to the adviser 'attending' that person.

Attending client Mr Y who is facing repossession of his flat due to mortgage arrears possession. Client telephoned to say that father-in-law has offered to lend him £2,000 and would this be enough to avoid next week's court hearing? I reminded him that £3,500 was still owing but would write today with this proposal to the building society's solicitor. Advised a short adjournment more likely to be agreed by them than a postponement or withdrawal of their claim for repossession.

EH 2.6.14. 10.30 am. Time spent: 10 mins

Attending Ms A of MoreLaw re the case of Mr Y by phone

Ms A rang to say that she had received my letter sent by email seeking an agreement to a postponement of the repossession proceedings and had spoken to her clients the Big Building Society. They would be prepared to ask the court to adjourn the court hearing next week to the first available date the court has in September, on the basis that the payment of £2,000 offered by my client is received in their account two days before the hearing. He should also be telling the building society how he intends to clear off the rest of his arrears. I indicated that I would take my client's instructions on these proposals and call her back.

EH 5.6.14. 3.45 pm. Time spent: 5 minutes

It is important to make and maintain attendance notes, and to record these in date and time order, especially where events are likely to be moving quickly, as they are in this example. The final note makes it clear that a number of other actions will need to be taken on this aspect of the client's case prior to that imminent hearing if he is to obtain the adjournment or postponement he is seeking.

Organising documents

As we have seen, as part of file opening, documents will be kept in separate sections in the paper file in a logical order. As the case progresses, if the paper file begins to become large and unwieldy, a second file can be set up, or the various types of documents separated out into separate paper folders. Correspondence folders and document folders may be separated out with file reference numbers duplicated on each folder.

Whenever a client brings in documents of whatever nature, they will be scanned or copied and the originals returned to the client. Original documents will not be kept unless required to conduct the client's case. If original documents such as passports, wills or marriage certificates do need to be kept as part of the conduct of the client's case they will be kept in a secure place such as an office safe.

Details of experts used

If an expert, such as a barrister, surveyor or medical consultant, is approached for an opinion in order to assist in the resolution of a client's case, there will be a note of where they are drawn from. Any lists or details of experts and the way in which they are selected must comply on each occasion with the organisation's equality and diversity policy. There should also be a note that the client has been consulted on the selection of an outside expert to assist with their case.

Prioritising activities

It should be clear from the file which activities are to be considered more important, either in terms of what they mean to the client or in terms of how quickly they need to be carried out. The file will contain a note of priority activities, with deadlines in ranking order of importance, which is regularly reviewed by the adviser.

Updates for the client

The file should show that the key dates and milestones which need to be recorded in a separate part of the file are being followed through as agreed. This is likely to be in the form of an attendance note which effectively the adviser is addressing to themselves and which they attach to the correspondence section of the file. Progress and updates will also be reported to the client in writing. In addition, if costs are relevant to the client's case they should be referred to regularly and an update given to the client of the position on costs. If the adviser has drawn up a case plan for themselves they will be regularly referring to it to review progress.

File reviews and supervision activities

Where the organisation's structure includes supervisors of the adviser's activities, a supervisor will monitor and review an adviser's handling of a case. Whichever form this supervision takes, it should be recorded on the file concerned as well as in a central record in the organisation. A chart showing how this process usually operates is provided in chapter 13.

Linking client's matters

If a client has more than one case or query with the organisation, files may need to be linked with common reference numbers or systems particularly if the client's matters may be interrelated, examples being a client with a rent arrears problem being dealt with by the organisation's housing adviser and a housing benefit query being dealt with by the debt and welfare benefits adviser.

Systems for prioritising work and reviewing workload

As well as prioritising activities on an individual client's file the adviser will have a system in place for prioritising work in order to ensure that they are running all their files and cases equally efficiently. How they set up the system will vary, but using a diary or an electronic diary with reminders is probably the most effective. A system which involves piling papers or files on the adviser's desk in some sort of priority can be unreliable and lead to confusion. The adviser will be regularly reviewing their entire case load and monitoring progress on each file, bearing in mind that the client who does not contact the adviser regularly may still need as much attention as the one who does.

12.4 **File-closing procedures**

File-closing procedures are not only operated by individual advisers in a set pattern but will also be incorporated into the organisation's procedures and systems so that it is clear across the organisation which files and matters are still ongoing and active and which are not.

It is important for the adviser to regard the closing of a file as being part of the conduct of that case and to properly reach and record the end of the process for the client. The conclusion of a court case or hearing may not necessarily conclude that client's case. Further paperwork may need to be completed within a specified time, costs paid out to a client or invoicing done. Following a set procedure ensures that no final or ancillary matters have been overlooked in concluding a case and closing a file. This will include confirming to a client that there are no outstanding financial transactions or documents required to be returned to the client before their case is closed, then recorded as being closed and finally archived.

The following matters will be attended to as part of the file-closing procedure:

- **Recording the outcome:** A letter will be written to the client which records the final outcome of the case and which goes on to confirm the agreement reached between the adviser and client that no further steps will be taken by the adviser. This not only gives the client an opportunity to have a written record of the outcome but it is also a way of confirming that both the adviser and the client are of the same mind, that it is indeed the case that there are no more steps to be taken on the client's behalf, no loose ends to be tied up and nothing which the adviser has promised to do which may have been overlooked. A standard letter[6] is then usually written to the client (often accompanied by a client satisfaction questionnaire) stating that the file will be closed, put away in an archiving system, and that all the client's original documents have been returned to them.

- **Dealing with costs and compensation:** Where the client has been paid any compensation by another party, the file-closing procedure and final outcome letter to the client must clarify the exact position. All legal fees or costs owing by the client to the adviser or another party will need to have been paid. There should be no money owing to, or owed by, the client when the file is closed.

- **Dealing with documents:** Where the adviser has possession of any original documents belonging to a client for the purposes of conducting that client's case, these documents will be returned to the client and a note of that made in the closing letter.

- **Archiving the file:** Advice organisations and services will have in place a system of archiving a file at the end of the client's case. Practising solicitors will be required by the terms of their insurance cover to keep files for at least six years after the case is closed: the legal limitation period for any claim against a solicitor for negligent advice.[7] Advice organisations that do not employ legally-qualified staff will also have in place insurance arrangements for the advice they give, and their insurers may also require files to be kept for a minimum period after they are closed. The adviser will be aware of the insurer's requirements and who will take responsibility for archiving files which have been closed. The archiving process involves keeping a store of files in a safe storage system and maintaining a regular review of them, whereby files archived more than six years earlier will be shredded or incinerated.

---

6   Usually known as the 'client closing letter' which tends to be quite short and simply contains the information set out above.

7   Practising solicitors are required to maintain professional indemnity insurance for this purpose and any claim or case will be handled by a solicitor nominated by the insurer. The six-year limitation period is the period in which contract claims must be brought and any claim against a solicitor will be based on the contract they entered into with that client.

CHAPTER 13

Case management as part of an organisation

13.1   Introduction

In the previous chapter we looked at the file and case management procedures followed by an adviser which will at times be complemented or mirrored by the organisation's central case management system. Here we will look at some other aspects of case and other management practices which are organisation-wide and which an adviser will be participating in as part of their work. These include supervision activities, appraisals, making referrals and dealing with complaints, all of which are carried out typically in a legal services organisation.

13.2   Supervising: rationale and good practice

An adviser may either supervise or be supervised as part of managing their case load. Some organisations operate teams of legal case workers, which may be hierarchical, with senior staff having overall responsibility for the management and supervision of the team's workload. Members of such a team may have differing levels of expertise and experience which will be reflected in the work allocated to them. Supervision is of particular importance in a legal advice setting as it provides checks on the quality and accuracy of advice given and ensures that advisers are complying with any professional conduct rules as part of the advice-giving process.

It may also be a process which assists the individual and the organisation in monitoring and meeting targets. These may relate to costs estimates provided for clients or in the not-for-profit sector, to dovetail with any requirements set by external funders for service delivery. Supervision will also serve to ensure standards of service are maintained at the levels set within the organisation and will provide support and encouragement in terms of staff development. Many legal services organisations will have a business plan or equivalent where goals have been set to provide and develop the service, and the activity of supervision can assist in monitoring the progress of that plan. A typical set of targets set internally might include the following:

- The provision of certain types of legal services.
- Identifying client groups for whom the service will be provided.
- Aiming to take on or complete a given number of cases or enquiries within a specified period.
- Providing reports or feedback on work activities to managers or trustees.

- Complying with legal or professional requirements as part of service provision, such as health and safety, equality laws, money laundering principles and professional conduct requirements.
- While many of these activities relate to management processes, supervision will play a role in contributing to them.

The supervision process – monitoring goals and developing capacity

The supervisor will be supporting the adviser to provide a quality service and to develop their own capacity to the full. They will identify the adviser's strengths and weaknesses, challenge deficiencies where necessary, and support and encourage compliance with the organisation's goals of delivering a quality legal advice service. The process will allow for advisers' strengths and different ways of working to be accommodated. Some advisers may have strengths in the way they communicate in writing, others in face-to-face client contact. Some will be more confident at negotiating resolutions or in conducting advocacy. Any particular strengths and skills demonstrated by the adviser will be built on by the supervisor as part of the supervision process.

People skills

A supervisor should have the necessary interpersonal skills to develop a rapport with those they supervise. This includes the ability to be accessible and flexible at all times and not just during formal supervision sessions. Informal discussion may take place, for example as to what advice should be offered to clients or the best way to word a letter or prepare for a hearing. In formal supervision sessions they will be non-judgmental in recording observations. Neutral and non-critical language will be used in discussions and records, even where offering criticism or voicing concerns.

Recording and reviewing objectives

The supervisor will also look for aspects of the adviser's work which still need development and set objectives for them to meet. The obstacles encountered might relate to time management or certain aspects of client care. In addition, long-term objectives may be set for the adviser such as developing knowledge in a new area of law or embarking on advocacy activities for clients. This process of setting

objectives will include regular reviews highlighting both good practice and any deficiencies in advice work.

13.3   Being supervised

Within the organisation there should be some guidance for employees as to how the process of supervision operates, ideally by way of
an office manual or equivalent. This should answer the following
questions:

- Is it supervision of file conduct alone?
- Does it include appraisals, meeting and setting objectives?
- Will it include goals for personal development?
- Is it linked to any performance pay or review systems?
- How often will it take place?
- Where will it take place?
- How much preparation will the adviser be required to do for
  supervision?
- What sort of record will be made of supervision meetings and
  where will that be kept?
- Will there be follow-up or review processes built into supervision?

Knowing the process will hopefully assist the person being supervised to prepare for formal sessions and to engage in them in a constructive fashion.

Knowing when to seek help and support

It will be important for the adviser to understand that the purpose and
process of supervision is not to be a prop or safety net but to support
and develop good practice in advice work. The role of the supervisor
is not to compensate for the adviser's lack of ability or to take on the
work they have not done but to assist in building the adviser's capacity
to function within the organisation's framework.

An adviser will also need to feel confident that they can seek help
and support when they are dealing with new or unfamiliar territory,
such as unforeseen developments in a case or a difficult situation arising with a client. The supervisor can use their experience to attempt
to resolve such issues. Thus an important part of being supervised is
to know what situations would be aided by intervention and which
situations the adviser should be learning to manage themselves. An
adviser who is unsure when to seek help and support from their

supervisor should be asking that question of their supervisor to help them understand the boundaries of responsibility in the supervisor/ adviser relationship.

Chart of supervision activities

The activities referred to in the chart overleaf will hopefully now be familiar as they show the supervisor ensuring that case management is being properly adhered to as part of how the adviser is delivering an effective advice service. They are offered as a fairly typical example of how specific supervision on an adviser's file might take place. The file reviews in the first column will involve the supervisor reading over and discussing with the legal adviser the activities they are undertaking on their clients' files. The supervision process involves the supervisor monitoring the processes set out in the remaining columns.

13.4   Appraisals

Appraisals of individual staff in an organisation may take place as part of supervision or may, more usually, be carried out as a separate process, which will involve more input from the adviser being appraised than the process of supervision usually involves. They are now being used more consistently across the legal services spectrum in order to foster individual staff development in terms of their primary function of delivering an effective legal advice service. The process will usually focus on the appraisee's development from their own perspective including what goals they might be aiming for either professionally or within the organisation. In this sense the process of carrying out appraisals is not strictly part of case management in an organisation but will hopefully contribute to effective and high standards of work as well as a sense of job satisfaction for the staff being appraised.

13.5   Referrals

An organisation will allow for referrals to be made and received both internally and externally for a number of different reasons. We will look at the circumstances in which each of these referrals is likely to take place and what steps will be involved. Referring a client or case either to another caseworker in an organisation or to an external

Chart of supervision activities

File reviews	Legal or good practice compliance	Organisation compliance	Client care	Adviser development
1. Evidence of file-opening and closing procedures being followed	Evidence that the adviser is aware of and complying with the relevant discrimination laws, health and safety regulations and data protection law and guidance	Evidence that the adviser is aware of and complying with organisation requirements, especially concerning equal opportunities policies and procedures, health and safety of staff and users, complaints procedures	Evidence that clients have been introduced to the service and are aware of their role in the adviser/client relationship	A system of reviewing the adviser's work for each client and recording on the client's file the process and outcome of those reviews
2. Evidence that interviews, telephone calls and other contact is being recorded	Evidence of privacy checks being adhered to and confidentiality rules are being observed	Evidence that the organisation's recording systems, including time recording, are being complied with	Evidence that all advice, including oral advice, is set out in writing to the client	A system for appraising the adviser's progress in terms of the processes of their advice work and any goals or objectives which the supervisor and the adviser may have agreed
3. Evidence of the adviser acting impartially, maintaining client confidentiality and a constructive client-care relationship	Evidence that the adviser is aware of good practice and/or professional rules in relation to conflicts of interest and interpersonal skills of advice-giving	Evidence that the adviser is complying with the organisation's guidance on checking for conflicts of interest	Evidence of an organisation-wide commitment to client-related skills	A system in the organisation for updating or training advisers in procedures in these areas and in client care skills

File reviews	Legal or good practice compliance	Organisation compliance	Client care	Adviser development
4. A system of keeping files which shows a clear order of advising and taking steps for a client	Evidence that the adviser is aware of the importance of file management in relation to being transparent and accountable about the process of giving good advice	Evidence that the system complies with the organisation's set procedures	Evidence that the client is aware of any timetables or time limits and/or their part in meeting these	A system which encourages high standards of advice and record keeping and accountability for the processes of giving advice
5. A system of diarising dates and key deadlines, and informing clients of these	Evidence that the adviser is complying with legal or other requirements to keep to deadlines and is aware of the consequences of not doing so	Evidence that this system is linked to or part of a central system for recording key dates and deadlines	Evidence that clients are aware of key dates and deadlines and of any active steps to be taken by the adviser and/or themselves to comply with deadlines	A system for supporting advisers in relation to any pressing targets and any related time-management issues the adviser may have
6. Evidence of appropriate advice being given to the client	Evidence that the adviser is familiar with the area of law or advice being offered, by reference to research methods being referred to on the file	Evidence that the organisation is arranging for training and updates for advisers in their areas of advice	Evidence that advice is appropriate to the client's needs	A system for ensuring advisers are receiving training and development in their subject areas

source will have an impact on the organisation, both internally in terms of tracking their work flow and externally in terms of demonstrating how they operate, what work they are able to manage, and who they refer to and why as part of their business ethos.

Internal referrals

Where an adviser refers a client to a colleague in their organisation to deal with a separate matter, the referring adviser will provide a file note or memo to their colleague in which they provide as much information as possible about the matter being referred. The client will have given their consent to confidential information about them being passed on to a different adviser. The referral will ideally contain the following information:

- A brief overview of the referring adviser's role in assisting the client in order to provide a background.
- Any financial circumstances which might be relevant to a new case being taken on (fees payable or legal aid forms to be completed).
- A brief overview of the matter which the client has sought the referral on, with any gaps in the referring adviser's knowledge to be made clear so that they can be filled in.
- The client's contact details and the best way to contact them and the most convenient times to arrange appointments for that client.
- A statement that the client has asked for the referral and is agreeable to it being to this named adviser.

Finally, a note should be made on the referring adviser's file that they have discussed another matter with the client and have referred that client to a colleague in the organisation in relation to that matter. A copy of the referral memo should remain on the file.

Note that, as we have outlined earlier, some clients' cases will be handled by two separate advisers who will provide advice and assistance to achieve a common goal for the client from two different perspectives. One example, as we saw earlier, was the housing benefit claim linked to rent arrears. Another might be a serious injury or assault caused to an employee which proceeds first as a criminal claim and, after this process is completed, either a personal injury and/or an employment discrimination law claim. Two different advisers may deal with each of these aspects but will keep in close contact to ensure that an appropriate outcome is finally achieved for the client.

External referrals

Referrals to a different specialism

This model of referral is most like the internal referral outlined above. Here the adviser has been told of a problem by their client that the adviser does not have the specialist skills to resolve. The problem may be linked to the one which the adviser is handling or it may be a separate one. The adviser may be able to refer that specific problem to another organisation. Where the two matters may be interlinked, the adviser will aim to provide the same information outlined above where they refer internally to a different specialist and may well maintain contact with the referred adviser in terms of possible overlap.

Referrals to a different level of service

Some advice agencies may only provide initial or one-off advice due to how they operate or what resources they have in terms of staffing. This limited, but highly useful, service will involve advising clients, by telephone, letter or in person. Once a limit has been reached in relation to the services that organisation can provide, it may be able to refer the client elsewhere for further assistance, and in doing so will often helpfully inform the receiving organisation of 'the story so far' and may provide copies of the client's relevant documentation as well as the client's contact details.

Lack of resources

This type of referral may take place where the advice service would normally have the capacity and resources to assist the client with that type of problem but at that particular time is not able to assist due to a shortage of resources.[1] An arranged referral to another organisation carrying out that type of work may be possible in order to meet in part a client's expectations of the service being offered as being available to all. Furthermore, if good referral links are established with other local organisations, the organisations can work together for the good of the local community in providing referrals when resources are temporarily limited in one of those organisations.

---

1 The Solicitors Regulation Authority (SRA) Code of Conduct 2011 at rule 2.01 states that solicitors are 'generally free to decide whether to take on a particular client'. The rules will allow a solicitor to decline to take on a client or case where they do not have sufficient resources (or the necessary competence) to do so.

The information provided for this type of referrals will be more limited as it is unlikely that the first organisation will have done any or any work of substance for the client. It may extend no further than contact and availability details for the client with a description of the nature of the problem being referred and a note of any deadlines for action to be taken. The receiving organisation then takes the client on from the beginning and the client is not required to explain their problem to more than one adviser.

Client changes adviser

Sometimes a client will inform their adviser that they wish their case to be transferred to another advice organisation. The reason for this may not be given to the original adviser who is not entitled to know it unless it is obvious or is offered to them. This is different to the situation where the adviser or the client has initiated the termination of the adviser/client relationship due to a breakdown in that relationship. When a client changes to a new adviser for a different, neutral reason, and when the adviser's papers are requested by another adviser, they need to ensure that the client has given written consent to the new adviser to request the papers. This is a safeguard for the client and both of the advisers. The referring adviser should copy their entire file and send it to the receiving adviser by recorded or guaranteed delivery to ensure its safe arrival. They will then follow the file-closing procedures set out in chapter 12.

Receiving a referral

An adviser who receives a referral in any one of the situations outlined above will ask the new client to sign a written authorisation requesting the referring organisation to send their papers on to them which will signal the process of a complete transfer of an ongoing case. The receiving adviser will expect to be informed of any imminent deadlines or work already carried out for the client on that matter. They will inevitably require the client to go over similar ground with them as the previous adviser at the start of their instructions in order to ensure that they have the full picture. They will then proceed to case manage the client's file as with any of their other files.

Keeping a record of referrals

Some organisations will keep centralised records of both internal and external referrals made by their advisers. This will not only make it easier for a receiving organisation to get back to the referring organisation with any queries, but will allow the referring organisation to monitor referrals it makes in order to identify patterns and trends as to whom referrals are made and why. Monitoring referrals made will also ensure that clients are being offered a range of options and that the referral system complies with the organisation's equal opportunities policies.

13.6 Dealing with complaints

It is never pleasant to be on the receiving end of a client's complaint. An advice organisation's procedures will nevertheless allow for complaints to be made and properly dealt with and for each adviser or person who comes into contact with the public to be aware of that procedure and to communicate it to their clients in the appropriate manner.

If a client expresses unhappiness or concern which falls short of a complaint, the adviser should have a strategy of openness and willingness to listen. If, for example, a client says that they have rung their adviser more than once before they speak to them or does not think their adviser's letters to them are clear, the adviser should be able and willing to remedy these shortfalls by explaining fully what the reason for any apparent delay or unavailability was, and reiterating advice given, ensuring that the client understands it.

If the client does wish to enter a formal complaint in line with the organisation's procedures, the adviser will hand that aspect over to the organisation's nominated complaints officer who will process the complaint in line with those procedures, including time frames set within these. Assuming the client is still instructing that organisation a decision may need to be made as to whether the same adviser continues to deal with that client's case. If the organisation's insurers have been informed of a complaint they will provide guidance as to whether the case should be proceeded with. Organisations will keep records of formal complaints which will form a part of their overview of quality checks and allow them to monitor them for any patterns they may wish to address as part of their overall service delivery.

PART 5

Case resolution

CHAPTER 14

Building up the client's case

14.1   What is meant by a 'case'

So far we have referred to the client approaching an adviser with a legal problem and we have noted that the adviser will need to clarify for themselves and with the client the exact nature of the problem so that they can start to resolve it. We have made various references to the client's 'case', including that outlined in chapter 11 in discussing the process of advocacy. Although the word 'case' is often associated with a court or tribunal hearing, it does have more than one meaning in the context of legal advice work. It can mean:

i)   A file which an adviser has on a client. Advisers will often refer to the 'cases' they are conducting or will refer to their workload as their 'caseload'.

ii) A matter which has been entered into a court or tribunal system. Courts and tribunals will allocate numbers and other references to cases when they come in to their system and they are referred to as cases, whether or not a hearing takes place.

iii) A summary of a client's position in relation to a legal issue. For example, in a criminal trial a defendant's case may be that he was elsewhere when the alleged crime was committed and so has an alibi.

iv) The facts, evidence and legal arguments which make up the totality of what a client assembles in order to reach their desired outcome. In the example given in iii) above, the facts might be that the client wishes to establish that he was elsewhere at the time the offence was committed, the evidence is that he has kept a train ticket used to travel elsewhere, and that he also has statement made by himself and other witnesses to attest to his being there on the day and time in question. The legal arguments will concern the defence of alibi and how statute and decided legal cases[1] might assist him in mounting a successful defence. All these go to make up his 'case' in defending the allegation of a crime committed.

It is this last meaning of a case that will be addressed in more detail in this chapter. We will examine the process by which the adviser arrives at the point where they have assembled all the necessary building blocks which make up the client's case. They will start by looking at the facts and sorting them into relevance. They will match these to the relevant law and arrive at a point where they have identified what

---

1   See chapter 19 'Legal research', which provides more information about the sources of law used by advisers to assist them in arguing a client's case.

steps need to be taken to resolve the case and what obstacles might lie in their path along the way.

14.2 Identifying and agreeing the facts of the case

Facts of the case

As we saw in chapter 7 the starting point for the adviser is to take from their client full details of their story, what has happened to them and how that has affected them. As this process is taking place, the adviser will be filtering information provided in order to identify the relevant facts. These may not all emerge at the outset as a third party may have information in their possession which the adviser is as yet unable to obtain. Nevertheless the adviser will find out as much as they can from the client, noting all they say, and will start to highlight those facts which are likely to be more relevant as part of building up the client's case.

Sorting into relevance: a holiday pay claim scenario

As an example, a client may state that they left their job recently and believe that their employer owes them some holiday pay. The adviser will make a note of everything the client tells them about this situation but will also elicit and note facts more relevant to what they are likely to advise will be a claim for unpaid holiday pay against the ex-employer. The less relevant facts will still remain a part of the adviser's notes but identified as such. This is how their notes relating to what is relevant might look once the client has told their story:

Type of fact	Relevant	Less relevant
How long client worked there	X	
How much client was paid	X	
No written terms or contract	X	
How much holiday she took last year		X
Where she went on holiday		X

Type of fact	Relevant	Less relevant
The reason given for not paying her holiday pay when she left the job		X
How much paid holiday she took this year	X	
When she left the job	X	
Why she left the job		X

In terms of the relevant boxes above, an adviser considering a worker's legal rights to holiday pay will be aiming to establish:

- How much the client was paid by way of wages or salary under her contract. This will be the basis of the calculation of the figure for any holiday pay owed.
- Whether the holiday year and annual entitlement was written down in a contract. This will supply the correct basis for calculating entitlement.
- If not, the date upon which the client started her job. This will provide an alternative basis for calculating entitlement.
- How much paid holiday the client had taken in that or any previous holiday year up to the date she left the job. This is relevant to what might still be owing at that date.
- The date the client left the job. This is relevant to what is owing and to the correct jurisdiction to make a claim.

So, crucially, the adviser wants to establish what was owing to the client by way of holiday pay at the date she left her job and when that was. In thinking about this, the adviser is already bearing in mind the legal basis for such claims. They will summarise this information for the client to ensure that the client is satisfied that it is correct. At this stage the adviser will be less concerned with the circumstance relating to the termination of the job, although they will note these in case they have an evidential value to support her claim.

14.3 Legal or legal-based research to identify the relevant law

In identifying these relevant facts the adviser is starting to apply the relevant law to the client's claim. They are aware of how to calculate a holiday year both as set out in a worker's contract and where it is not set out in the contract, and how much annual leave a worker is entitled to by law and how to calculate that. They are also aware of what the law says about the requirement to pay any holiday pay owing on the termination of employment. They are also thinking of what legal jurisdiction such a claim can be heard in as that relates to how long ago the client left the job. Even if they do not know the exact answer to how each of these legal principles and procedures operate they know that these are relevant to legal entitlements in this area of employment relations. To confirm their thinking and supplement their knowledge they are likely to research the following sources:

- **Statute law** in relation to who is legally entitled to have paid holidays, how their holiday year is calculated, how much paid holiday they are entitled to each year as well as how much they can be paid when they leave.[2]
- **Case-law** where available to support such a claim; one aspect the client may raise, for example, is that they are owed holiday pay from previous years and the adviser will research if recent case-law might assist this aspect of their claim.[3]
- **Court or tribunal procedures** which allow for such claims to be heard and any time limits within which claims might need to be started off, how such claims will proceed, and any fees involved in bringing the claim.

14.4 Identifying and agreeing the issues

Once the adviser has established the relevant facts and researched how they are matched to the law, they will proceed to identify the issues in the case. These will be both the matters which the adviser

---

2 The relevant statutory instrument here is the Working Time Regulations 1998 SI No 1833, which give workers all these rights whether or not these rights are set out in a statement of terms or a contract.

3 There are a number of cases decided in the European courts which have an impact on how employers may need to approach the carrying forward of unused holiday entitlement.

is seeking to resolve for the client, as well as the matters which are in dispute between two parties. In the first approach, the adviser may draw up a list of questions which need to be answered in order to resolve the client's case and will check with the client to ensure that they agree that these are the matters which have to be resolved.

In the above example these may be:

1) What was the client's take-home pay?
2) How much holiday did the client take in the current holiday year?
3) When did that holiday year commence?
4) How much was left to take when she left the job?
5) When did the client leave the job?
6) How does that number of days or weeks translate into a figure owing for holiday pay?
7) Was there any holiday pay owing from any previous holiday years and if so how much?
8) What jurisdiction will she need to make a claim in?
9) How much will that cost her?

After some discussion clarifying all these points, the client and adviser may be able to agree that these questions will be answered as follows:

1) Weekly take-home pay was £200.
2) Client had taken three weeks' holiday in the current holiday year.
3) Holiday year ran from April to April.
4) She was owed two weeks' holiday pay when she left.
5) She left her job six months earlier in December.
6) The amount she is owing is therefore £400.
7) She had no holidays owed from the previous holiday year.
8) Claim will need to be made in the small claims court as the time limit for claiming in an employment tribunal has expired.
9) She will not be required to pay any fees as she is in receipt of certain state benefits.

The adviser has now established the basis for setting out how the entitlement arose, what it is in figures, and where the claim needs to be made. They have reached the point where these issues can be addressed by applying the relevant law in an appropriate way.

Issues between the parties

Once two parties are engaged in a legal dispute they may decide to identify jointly the aspects of the dispute which require resolution with the intervention of a court or tribunal. They will describe these aspects as the 'issues between' them or the 'issues in dispute'. If the dispute enters into the court or tribunal system, these issues are often ordered by a judge to be agreed between the two parties as part of preparation for a hearing. The adviser is therefore likely to start with the questions they agree with their client which need to be resolved, and later develop these into the issues of dispute between the client and their opponent.

Let us say this client shows her adviser a letter in which the ex-employer is disputing the amount of two weeks' holiday claimed, based on their assertion that she was owed three days' holiday and not two weeks'. The letter goes on to state further that three days' pay was sent out to her last month in the post by cheque and so for that reason they owe her nothing. The key issue of dispute, therefore, is that she claims two weeks amounting to £400 and they state it was only three days amounting to £120, which she has now been paid.

Having read the letter the adviser may check again with their client the information she has already supplied. If she confirms it as being correct and states that no cheque or payment has been received by her, the adviser will then start to address the issues in dispute to be resolved between the parties. These are likely to be translated into a series of questions or issues which, if answered in her favour, will give her the benefit of the amount she is claiming, and if in the ex-employer's favour will mean she has no claim. The issues might be expressed as being as follows.

Issues in the case of Ms Z v Mr D her ex-employer

- When did Ms Z's annual holiday year commence?
- Did she take holidays in that period?
- How much holiday did she take?
- Was she paid for those holidays?
- How much was left untaken at the date Ms Z left her job?
- Was she paid for that?
- If so has she received that pay?

If the issues are drawn up between the parties or for a court or tribunal, they will be described in a neutral fashion with no opinions added as to the correctness or otherwise of a party's position and no reference to any evidence a party might be able to produce to resolve any issue in their favour. This will allow an independent arbiter, such as a judge, to decide on each of them based on the evidence they see or hear in order to reach a decision in favour of one party or another.

14.5   Explaining the case to the client

This process of the parties setting out the issues in dispute will also have been discussed with their respective clients. Moreover, the client, as well as having received advice on the strengths, weaknesses and any financial aspects of their case, will be asked if they have understood how the adviser has translated the client's story into the client's case.

The client in the above example will be asked if she understands how, for example, a claim for unpaid holiday pay is translated into a claim which takes into account how the law requires the claim to be set out and how it will uphold the claim. She will be asked if she understands how that claim will be put to an opponent or a court or tribunal so that it is presented in its best light. She may also be asked to assent to conceding certain aspects of the case where there are weaknesses or areas of dispute if there is evidence which supports her opponent's case. In the example above, this might involve a possible acknowledgement that she was owed less holiday pay or had been sent some or all of the money she was entitled to. The legal adviser is therefore not only drawing the case along but involving the client throughout that process.

14.6   Building up the client's case

Setting out the adviser's role in progressing the case

We have already begun to see how a set of relatively simple instructions require a fair amount of factual detail to be elicited in order to test those facts against the relevant law, as well as in the light of any opposing views put forward to resist claims or legal rights. Further instructions and further information or documentation received will add to this ongoing development until a point is reached where a case is ready for resolution. The various means of resolving a case will be looked at in the next three chapters. As the case progresses towards a resolution, the adviser will be explaining to the client the process that both adviser and client are now involved in and what each of their roles are in engaging in that process.

The adviser's role: focal contact point and primary conduct of the case

The adviser will explain to the client what steps they will take in order to progress their case in order to resolve it. The adviser will be the client's point of contact with all those involved in their case. They will make representations to others on behalf of the client and will, where necessary, argue points in relation to that case with any opponent. Where an adviser takes on responsibility for progressing a client's case and is authorised by the client do so, they are referred to as 'having conduct of the case'. They will inform other parties, including courts or tribunals, that they have the client's permission to conduct the case on behalf of the client. Some outside agencies will require the client themselves to confirm in writing that this is the case.

Using outside expertise

In addition, when outside expert help is sought or required, the adviser will offer to arrange that for the client. The adviser will be able to call on experts such as doctors, surveyors or barristers to assist in resolving a client's case by perhaps advising on or giving evidence on one or more aspects of the case. A medical consultant may be able to confirm the nature or effect of a client's disability, a chartered surveyor may be asked to provide an opinion on the cause of disrepair in a tenant's rented flat or a barrister to represent a client as their advocate in court. In selecting such an individual, the adviser will ensure they choose an appropriate expert drawn from as comprehensive a list as possible, not least in order to comply with the organisation's equal opportunities policy. They will also ensure that the client is happy with their recommendation.

Explaining how cases are put

The client should, by now, not only understand the way in which the adviser is framing their story in order to translate it into a legal case or claim, but also understand how their case will be put by their adviser to the opponent or other organisation involved. Where the adviser needs to argue legal points they should explain to their client how the arguments will be set out. They will also explain to the client the resources they have used to build up the case, any legal principles, statutes or legal guidance which they have relied on or interpreted. The client should have any law relevant to their case explained to them in an accessible way using plain language, as well as how the adviser will use it to assist in the progress of their case. Many clients find this valuable and say that they have undergone a learning curve in pursuing a legal matter in terms of finding out about, and discussing with their advisers, how the law operates and impacts on the outcome of their case.

Maintaining the momentum of the case

The adviser will also confirm to their client that they will keep the client's file under review and will continue to take any necessary practical steps to progress the case. These will include:

- Continuing to correspond with any outside agency or opponent ensuring that all relevant information is exchanged with them.
- Where agreed, commencing a claim in a court or tribunal on behalf of the client.
- Agreeing with any tribunal or opponent what the issues are in the case and what are the differences and points of agreement.
- Continuing to research any relevant background to the case, such as policy documents, statutes or regulations.
- Regularly reviewing the case with the client and ensuring that they are happy with and understand how it is progressing.
- Testing out with the client how their case is standing up to further developments which emerge along the way.
- Making decisions with the client about the strengths and weaknesses of their case and about strengths of the case which should be better highlighted or weaknesses which should be discontinued.
- Being fully prepared for any meetings or hearings with the client or others involved in the client's case.

The adviser will be thinking the case through and regularly returning to it in order to ensure it progresses including, where appropriate, being prepared to change direction or take on board new developments or facts as they emerge either from the client's perspective or from any opponent.

The client's role

The process of resolving a client's case involves the client as well as the adviser. In addition to supplying information and documents, the client is likely to have other functions to perform.

Supplying instructions

Throughout the conduct of their case the client will not only give the adviser information but tell them what they would like the adviser to do, especially in the light of any unforeseen or new developments in their case. They will be continuing to instruct the adviser.

Preparing statements

It will often be useful for the client at an early stage to set out their story in the form of a statement they write out themselves describing what happened to them. Later, the statement may be formalised into a witness statement if there is to be a court or tribunal hearing. In the above example, the client will set out in her witness statement what her holiday pay entitlement is, what is owing to her and what, if anything, she has received or been told she will receive. The adviser will ensure that all the relevant information is in the client's statement and will hone and polish it together with the client. Nevertheless it should be the client's own statement and not that of their legal adviser and will be set out in plain language.

Understanding how evidence is used

What a client says in a statement, or what appears in documentation, will count as evidence or proof of what the client's case is and may be used to persuade an opponent or court or tribunal to accept the client's case and to agree to the client's desired outcome. The client will need to understand, therefore, what counts as evidence and how that evidence can be used to persuade other people of the truth of what the client is saying.

There are rules of evidence which trained court advocates will be familiar with.[4] Generally, evidence can be said to amount to what a person says or has written, and is factual unless it is the opinion of an expert such as a medical practitioner. From the client's perspective it does not involve an outline of the law or a person's opinion as to the correctness of their own case. If it relates to what a person said or did

---

4 These will vary according to the type of case. The main distinction in the court system relates to what amounts to criminal evidence and how it must be presented and that for civil cases. Tribunals have a less rigid approach to how evidence must be presented, but on the whole tend to mirror the system in the civil courts. There are a number of guides on the rules and law relating to evidence which might be useful for those less familiar with this topic, some of which are aimed at the student audience learning the rules of evidence and the techniques of advocacy.

it should if possible be verified by other evidence to confirm it. At the beginning of this chapter we looked at the example of alibi evidence in a criminal case with other witnesses being prepared to say that they saw the defendant elsewhere at the time the offence took place. The defendant had also kept his train ticket to show he was elsewhere on the day in question.

14.7 Putting the case for the client

Part of the adviser's role is to relay confidently and accurately to another party or organisation what their client's case is. It may be expressed somewhat more formally than when it is set out for the client, but essentially the facts will be the same.

A professional approach to putting the case

An adviser should put the case to the other party simply, accurately and concisely. It will comply with their client's instructions as agreed. The adviser will be courteous to their opponent or the organisation they are putting the case to. They will not hide information or use tactics designed to annoy or alienate an opponent. They will avoid delaying and will maintain a firm stance as to their belief in the correctness of their client's case without allowing themselves to argue with or hector their opponents. There are still individuals who adopt an aggressive or combative stance when faced with a claim or complaint, but their style is best not copied. In addition, a calm and professional approach will impress the client and make them realise that their adviser is free from any personal motives in the way in which they put their case.

Knowing procedures in putting the case

We saw in chapter 11 that the adviser who is advocating for a client will need to know the rules and procedures of any organisation or court or tribunal system in which they are operating in order to resolve the client's case. They will demonstrate to an opponent or decision-making body that they know what those procedures are and how they will be required to follow them including, where necessary, a willingness to utilise them to best progress their client's case.[5]

---

5 See chapter 17 for more on this.

Knowing the other person's case in putting the client's case

As well as knowing what their own client's case is, the adviser will make sure they have understood an opponent's case and are aware of the facts and documents surrounding it. This will enable them to engage knowledgably with their opponent, to see any gaps or flaws in their case and to take advantage of those where appropriate for the benefit of their client. It will also allow the adviser to advise their client better on the strengths and weaknesses of their own case as details of an opponent's case emerge. This is likely to be part of an approach the adviser might use to reach a resolution without the necessity of a final hearing, as we shall see in the next chapter.

CHAPTER 15

Resolving the case: no court or tribunal

15.1   A letter of claim

Once the adviser is clear about their client's story, case and instructions, and once a jointly agreed plan of action emerges, it is likely that the first step the adviser will take in terms of communicating with an outside party or opponent is to write a letter of claim. Having advised the client privately concerning what their claim is and how well it will proceed to a satisfactory conclusion, a draft letter of claim is then prepared, approved by the client and sent to the opponent. This letter is written to inform the opponent of the adviser's role in acting on behalf of their client in relaying instructions, and also to summarise the positive aspects of advice given to their client on their case. It sets out the nature and basis for their client's claim, usually in terms of putting it at its best. It also offers an opportunity to avoid formal or legal proceedings on the basis that the opponent admits to the client's case and is prepared to meet their claim. This step will only be taken where the new client is putting forward a claim or asserting a right and there will, of course, be a number of advice situations where the client is having to defend their position or resist a claim. In those instances the client may well be bringing a letter of claim they have already received to the adviser and seeking their advice on how to respond to it. Either way, that first letter to an opponent is the usual preliminary step on the route to resolution.

In some situations a letter of claim must be sent before any court claim is commenced. The most significant of these will be virtually any claim in the civil court system.[1] It should in any event be at the forefront of both the adviser's and the client's mind to try to avoid the stress, time and expense of taking matters through the court system.[2] The letter of claim, sent prior to any legal proceedings being commenced, not only has the function outlined above of setting out a client's case but is also offering the opponent the opportunity to avoid

---

1   As we shall see in the next chapter, the civil courts place a heavy emphasis on requiring a would-be claimant to write to their opponent prior to starting off a court claim. In the case of *Burrows v Vauxhall Motors Ltd* 1998 PIQR P48 CA, the Court of Appeal said that if a party did not do this they would more than likely be ordered to pay their own and their opponent's costs whatever the outcome of the case. The civil court rules (Civil Procedure Rules or 'CPR') refer to these as 'pre-action protocols' which are mandatory, for example, in relation to claims for personal injury, housing disrepair or housing claims for rent arrears. See CPR r44.2.

2   As elsewhere in the book we are concerned with the civil court system rather than the criminal court system, where inevitably a client will have very little choice about whether they go to court or not.

litigation by reaching agreement and meeting the claim as framed in that letter. A typical letter of claim is set out in appendix A.

The letter of claim can herald the start of resolving a client's legal problem. We shall see below how, following on from that letter, it can be possible to reach a resolution to a legal dispute without the necessity of using the formal court or tribunal procedures, and in some instances, in a way that can be legally binding. In this chapter we will look at some of these processes and then, in the following two chapters, at other ways in which cases can reach a resolution.

15.2   Communications with opposing parties

It is quite common for an adviser to resolve a client's legal problem using the traditional tools of communication: letters or emails, telephone calls or attending meetings with or on behalf of their clients. Sometimes the adviser will be dealing with an opponent who has no advice or legal representation and, as we shall see in chapters 20 and 21, the adviser should afford that person courtesy in how they deal with them but will not be able to cede any ground simply because their opponent is unrepresented. In resolving a claim which avoids litigation, the adviser is using their skills to achieve the same or a similar result to that which a judge or other decision-maker might have provided. They will present to that party a number of (sometimes apparently conflicting) positions in order to achieve a result. These are likely to be:

- Presenting a strong view of their client's likely success if they were to engage in a conflict-based process.
- Pointing out the risks of losing the case for the opposing party: these may relate to financial loss and loss of reputation.
- Indicating that within a specified time period the client will move on to the next stage of starting a claim or applying to a tribunal.
- Indicating that their client is also mindful of risks and so would be prepared to forgo the threatened claim and reach resolution by an alternative route.
- Suggesting a resolution which would satisfy their client and hopefully be satisfactory to their opponent.

The final point is likely to be put in a manner most favourable to the client and will reflect the terms of a successful outcome in a court or tribunal. There are, however, circumstances in which this stance might be accommodated to produce an outcome which is still favourable, but which may involve making some concession, as we shall see later. First, we shall look at how advisers communicate in order to arrive at a resolution for a client.

Effective correspondence

In setting out the points listed in the previous paragraph to an opponent, the adviser will use everyday language interspersed with any necessary references to the law. All their communications with an opponent will be framed in this way, adopting a stance which not only protects their client's position but one in which they are seen as willing to assist their client and opponent in the interests of a speedy resolution.

Any first letter sent out on behalf of a client, whether it is a letter of claim or not, is setting a precedent for the adviser's approach and how they portray both their client and themselves to the outside world. Furthermore, once dispatched, the letter or email is in the public domain. If a case fails to be resolved, early letters can sometimes form the backbone of any subsequent case. In any event, they could well be produced in a court hearing and be read by a judge. For this reason, many advisers follow the rule of writing every letter to an outside party on the basis that at some point in the future it may indeed be read by a judge. This helps to keep their correspondence relevant to the matter in hand and also firm but courteous.

A lengthy letter is less likely to be read in detail than a letter which gets across its points succinctly. Paragraphs and sentences should be short and concise. A letter which covers one side of A4 paper or an email which does not require the reader to scroll down is ideal as it can be easily and quickly read. The letter must be seen to flow from one point to another. As we have seen above, an initial letter written on behalf of a client will follow the format of introduction, outline of claim or case and seeking a remedy or resolution. It may even be worth using short headings in a letter to reflect these different points. Furthermore the tone used in correspondence will not seek to judge, criticise or condemn the recipient unnecessarily. Any comment as to how the client feels about their loss or treatment will be made in a factual and not an emotive setting.

Emails

Emails are used as a matter of course and have the effect of being able to speed up communication. Where quick resolutions are hoped for they can be of significant advantage, especially where it is hoped to resolve a dispute prior to reaching a deadline. Even where time is against the adviser, they will need to relay emails received to the client for their instructions. Thereafter, in responding to an opponent's emails, use of the 'reply' or 'reply all' button should be avoided because long strings of messages may end up being sent or copied to those for whom the reply is not intended. Furthermore, should these 'strings' of emails ultimately be read by a judge as part of the documents in a case they are hearing, it will be unnecessarily burdensome for them as they attempt to follow the thread of the correspondence.

Telephone calls

Where advisers are communicating with an opponent by phone, the process is even speedier. It will be important not to be drawn into any change of approach which is not in the adviser's remit and is beyond instructions. An opponent may resort to various tactics in the course of a phone call in order to persuade an adviser to shift their client's position. Examples might include:

- Indicating that the adviser is not aware of certain matters relating to their client which place their client in a bad light.
- Indicating that they do not have the means or the ability to meet the client's stated remedy and offering an alternative instead.
- Indicating that they or their client have already spoken to the adviser's client and reached a different resolution.
- Indicating that, between themselves, as professional advisers, they know better than their respective clients and that they can therefore reach a resolution in a more helpful way. This often translates as a resolution which is more favourable to the opponent.

Whatever is said to the adviser, they should be aware that they cannot shift any ground without their client's consent. If a resolution is proposed, the adviser will state that they will take their client's instructions, as well as recording it in writing and communicating it to whomever they have been speaking to.

15.3 Attending meetings or external interviews

Sometimes an informal meeting can be set up as a mean of resolving the client's problem. The meeting may be with a housing department or a benefit agency or a school. It may even be with another legal adviser who represents an opponent. The adviser may accompany their client or may go on their behalf.

The adviser will prepare, both with the client and on their own, what they need to say and aim to achieve in that meeting. They will allow themselves time to get to the venue. They will take with them any papers or files which they will need to refer to and ensure that these are kept safely throughout the time they are away from their office. They will check in advance who will be at the meeting, their names and their role in the organisation. Finally, they should find out how long has been planned for the meeting.

If proposals or resolutions are offered during the meeting, it will be quite reasonable for the adviser to ask for time so that they can discuss these with their client before proceeding. If the client is not present, the adviser will only be able to make progress to the limits of whatever instructions they have received in advance of the discussions.

At the same time as participating in a meeting or discussion, the adviser will need to take full notes and, if necessary, write those up as soon as possible afterwards as their record of the proceedings. This will be done even where there is a record-keeper present.

At the conclusion of the meeting and before the participants depart, the adviser should check:

- if all present are agreed on the outcome of the meeting;
- any agreed action or next steps to take to resolve matters under discussion;
- who will take that action or follow up those steps;
- who will record the agreed outcome – the organisation or the adviser; and
- whether that record will be sent out to all interested parties and by what date.

15.4 Keeping the client informed

Whatever process of resolution is being used, the client will be kept informed as to how matters are faring, advice will be provided on any twists and turns in the process of resolution and further instructions taken. Advisers will avoid allowing themselves to agree without instructions to any proposal to resolve or settle a dispute by an opponent, even under pressure of that opponent's tactics, or knowing their own concerns about the merits of a client's case, or being under pressure of deadlines.

Where the adviser has indicated privately to their client that there are weaknesses in the case they will not disclose these to any external source. If an opponent does nevertheless seize on a weak aspect and rely on it in order to force the adviser to agree an outcome less favourable to the client, the adviser may, in confidence with their client, suggest it as a possible way forward. As we shall now see, there are ways in which this can be achieved without too much loss of face or without giving too much away at the price of not being able to argue the client's best points before a judge.

15.5   Reaching and recording a resolution

Simple and speedy

It is somewhat rare, unfortunately, for the letter of claim we referred to above to produce the exact outcome sought, although this may occur from time to time.

A simple example might be a letter written to a dry cleaning shop seeking a refund of money paid for the cleaning of a set of curtains which came back shorter. This set of facts is set out in the letter of claim in appendix A. The client had already been into the shop on more than one occasion. She had paid £50 to have the curtains cleaned but stated she was no longer able to hang them as they no longer fitted. She was therefore claiming the cost of the curtains as well, valued at £450, bringing her total claim up to £500, as a result of the alleged negligence of the dry cleaner in ruining her curtains when providing this service.

The adviser sets this out in their letter to the dry cleaner as well as referring to the likely cost, disruption and outcome in favour of their client of a civil court case. In response, the dry cleaner sends the adviser a letter enclosing a cheque for £500. The letter does not state that the dry cleaner admits they were in the wrong but offers the money as a gesture of 'good will' on the basis that the client is a good customer.

In these circumstances the client will be informed of the positive outcome and will be sent her cheque. The adviser will then write a short polite letter to the dry cleaner accepting the sum on behalf of the client as a settlement of her claim.

It will rarely be necessary for any other formality to be entered into since, in these circumstances, all the adviser is doing is confirming that the dry cleaner has complied with their legal duty towards a consumer by making reparation for the breach of their obligations to provide an acceptable standard of service. The outcome will also be recorded by the adviser to the client. Occasionally, when such a speedy resolution is offered a client may think it is worth going back and asking for more. In these circumstances the adviser will remind the client what their original advice was, what the client's instructions were, and what it was agreed that the adviser would seek on their behalf prior to the opponent being contacted, and that this is what they had achieved.

Less simple and speedy

In many circumstances where a letter of claim has been written, an opponent will not come back with an offer or, alternatively, may come back with another proposal. Where no resolution is offered, the matter may end up in a court or tribunal (for which see chapter 17). Where a lesser resolution is proposed or offered, even where the client has been advised that their case is a strong one, the client may agree to this lesser offer on the basis that 'a bird in the hand is worth two in the bush'. Accepting a lesser sum (but not necessarily the arguments in favour of so doing) will mean that the client does not have to await the uncertain outcome of a court hearing which may take many months to happen and will involve the client paying court fees which may or may not be recoverable.

In the above example, the dry cleaner may alternatively make an offer of £300 and a free voucher for future cleaning, again, as a gesture of good will but not accepting liability. To avoid prolonged correspondence and rising costs, and especially where the client is paying their adviser, the client may well agree to accept the lesser sum. In these circumstances, where resolutions are offered which are near to the client's best case, the adviser will write to accept the sum, not as being what the client believes they are entitled to, but only in the interests of a speedy resolution. Again, the response need only be short stating simply that this is the basis of acceptance.

Sometimes the process of reaching a resolution between the two parties may be more prolonged. Staying with the above example, let us say the dry cleaner responds by saying that when the client brought the curtains in to the shop for dry cleaning she stated that she needed them cleaned as soon as possible as she was holding an important business meeting in her house later that week and wanted her curtains to look clean. The dry cleaner told her that curtains of that fabric would need to be sent away to be cleaned which would take up to two weeks. They would be able to do the job themselves in a matter of days but could not guarantee the outcome as the process did carry risk for that colour and fabric. As a result, but only again as a gesture of good will they were only prepared to refund to her the £50 cost of the cleaning process.

When this letter is relayed to the client she agrees that she did require the job to be done quickly but states that there was no warning of risk issued to her. The adviser is now, however, alerted to a possible risk in terms of the matter going before a judge. Either their client will be believed or the dry cleaner will be believed which might make a substantial difference to what, if anything, their client might be able to recover. The adviser advises the client to consider a settlement at a lower figure. She states that she would settle for the £50 but asks the adviser to ask for a higher sum, but lower than the sum originally requested given the advice she has now received on risk.

Without prejudice

A series of letters, emails or telephone calls may then ensue whereby figures and points of dispute are exchanged between the adviser and the dry cleaner or their adviser if they have one. Once it is clear that some negotiating is going to be necessary to try to reach a resolution, letters and emails sent or telephone calls embarked on following this pattern of debate will always be preceded or headed by the words 'Without Prejudice'.[3]

This phrase allow parties to try to reach a resolution of a claim or dispute without any prejudice to their right to air their case in front of a court or tribunal. The court or tribunal where such a case may end up will not be allowed to know about or see any correspondence headed in this way. This allows for the corresponding parties to make concessions which, if aired in open court, could be damaging to their respective client's cases but which could be made in the interests of achieving a settlement. In the example above, in the light of the risk pointed out to the client concerning what was said when she took the curtains in for dry cleaning, the client may be prepared to admit that she was warned of some risk, but will want the adviser to push for a better sum to be offered on the basis that the dry cleaner should not have accepted the job if they were not able to offer an acceptable service. If there is a discussion 'without prejudice' which does not result in a resolution, none of this correspondence will be shown to

---

3 See chapter 16 for more on negotiating skills.

a presiding judge or decision-maker, which will then allow parties in that venue to put their best points freely in seeking a decision or judgment.[4]

If an agreement between the parties is reached through this route then it must be recorded in an open letter or email, in other words, one that does not have the words 'without prejudice' preceding its contents. This is because, at that point, an open agreement will bind the parties as to its terms and, depending on the type of claim or possible future legal forum that it might have been decided in, it may even be capable of forming a contract between the parties which they can refer back to in the event that one or the other does not comply with its terms fully. For this reason it has to be a resolution openly recorded between the parties.

Stages at which cases are resolved

In all the examples above the client's case appears to have reached a resolution at a relatively early stage. However, it is worth stating that a claim, case or dispute can be resolved at any stage. As we will see in the next chapter this can happen either prior to any legal proceedings being taken out (instead of issuing legal proceedings, particularly where a client indicates that this is not something they want to do), or at the same time as legal proceedings are in train and moving towards a final hearing. The phrase 'doorstep settlement' refers to where a case can be resolved even on the doorstep of a court (or indeed partway through a claim or case being heard) on the day of a hearing. In these circumstances, there will be face-to-face meetings and discussions taking place between the parties, with each adviser's client being consulted or involved in the discussions where appropriate and with a written record (sometimes also reflected as a court order of the terms of settlement) drawn up to reflect the outcome. Many claims and cases are settled in this way, which some may question as being the best use of time and resources. However, even when best endeavours are used by all concerned this may be the only manner in which a resolution can finally be achieved.

---

4 The process of 'without prejudice' correspondence is not as simple as perhaps referred to here. There are court decisions which provide guidance as to the circumstances and contents of such communications which would need to be borne in mind when drafting of this nature takes place because not all such correspondence is immune from later disclosure to a court or tribunal, in spite of the intention of its authors.

15.6 Client resolves their case

In some advice-giving situations, the adviser will be able to give the client the necessary information and support in order for the client to resolve the matter themselves. As we have already seen, a typical example of this process is the pro bono adviser offering a one-off advice session.

The volunteer advice service helping the client to resolve their problem

The advantage of the volunteer advice service is that more clients can be helped as less time and fewer resources are utilised in relation to each client. Furthermore, the aim is to assist the client in resolving the matter themselves once they have had some preliminary advice and assistance. The disadvantage, however, is that some clients will still find it hard to resolve their own problems and will realistically find the limited help they are offered insufficient, a situation which a volunteer adviser will be all too often aware of and unable to remedy in the limited time which they have to offer. Nevertheless, this service may be suitable for clients who are, for example, using the small claims court in the county court to resolve disputes over money claims or consumer matters. It may also be used for clients using a tribunal service such as the First-tier Property Chamber, or a welfare benefits tribunal.

An advice service's process of self-help resolution

If an agency does run a service which is geared towards assisting clients to resolve their own problems, the following approaches will usually be employed in that process:

- **An initial advice session takes place.** This is likely to be the key interview and may last up to an hour or even longer. At the interview the client will be given information about the law, advice on the merits of their case, advice on how to resolve the case, and advice on likely outcomes of following a given approach to resolving the case. The interview will, in effect, serve as the main advice route for the client to resolve their problem.
- **A letter of advice will be sent to the client by their adviser.** Sometimes, but not always, the service will also provide a letter of advice for the client, very much in the style of the advice letter we have

already referred to as being the first step the adviser takes following the first client interview. The advice letter will confirm that
from that point on any further steps will be taken by the client and
this will include taking responsibility for complying with any deadlines. Furthermore, the client will be reminded that they should
not name the advice organisation as being their legal representative to any third parties. This is important since, if a client errone-
ously holds an organisation out as being their legal representative,
there could be serious implications in terms of the steps that a
third party might then expect that adviser to take on the client's
behalf. Furthermore, the organisation is unlikely to be insured in
the self-help context to do any more than advise.

- **A letter may be drafted by the adviser for the client to send to the
  organisation or individual with whom they have a dispute.** This
  will often be drafted by the adviser for the client. It will be written setting out the client's case and at the same time seeking a
  resolution.

- **The client will aim to be able to resolve the matter directly with
  their opponent.** The letter drafted by the adviser may produce the
  desired outcome or the client may be able to steer their way into
  the county court or a tribunal system using leaflet and online guidance to help them understand the process. Many individuals find
  that the process of resolving their own case or problem is empow-
  ering and gives them back a sense of control over an area of their
  lives which was causing them stress or unhappiness. Others do
  not fare well in the legal or another similarly formal system, and
  the statistics show that these are more likely to outnumber those
  who have legal representation. In general, clients will need to be
  advised that courts and tribunals should only be used as a last
  resort. We will return to this issue in chapter 20 with some tips
  and tactics for the 'litigant in person'.

CHAPTER 16

Resolving the case: alternative dispute resolution

16.1 Alternative dispute resolution: meaning and processes

What is ADR?

We saw in the previous chapter that legal advisers can use their skills of drafting and negotiating to avoid the process of a formal court or tribunal case and to reach a resolution acceptable to both sides in a dispute. The negotiating skills they use will also be looked into in more detail below.

Over the years this approach to resolving a dispute has come to be referred to as 'alternative dispute resolution' or ADR. This process of utilising a method to resolve a dispute by agreement between the parties rather than decided on by a judge or decision-maker, is now firmly embedded in the legal system as a recognised route to resolution.

ADR can take a number of different forms and follow a variety of procedures, often related to the type of legal dispute involved. It can in some cases result in a resolution which places each party to the agreement under certain obligations, carrying a penalty for those who do not comply with the agreed outcome. It requires an open mind and one in which essentially the parties attempt to put aside their differences in order to try to find a way of reaching a resolution. This chapter will provide an overview of the various activities which provide an opportunity to bring a dispute to an end, all of which go under the general umbrella description of ADR.

What should be emphasised at the outset is that it must be seen both by an adviser and a client as a necessary route to resolving cases. Lawyers are sometimes criticised for 'racking up costs' in a case, pursuing a dispute right up to and including a full trial simply in order to enhance their fees, in circumstances where they could have achieved a resolution much earlier and more speedily. This may still be true for some practitioners but for most, fortunately, ADR is not only seen as a necessary step towards achieving the right outcome, but one in which their lawyerly skills will be put to the test.[1] The concept of ADR does not involve accepting defeat or a lower standard of result.

---

1 Any such non-conciliatory tactics are in any event now very much frowned upon by the courts. The key case warning of costs penalties for failing to consider ADR is *Halsey v Milton Keynes General NHS Trust* [2004] EWCA 3006. In the more recent case of *PGF1 1SA v OMFS Company Ltd* [2013] EWCA Civ 1288, the Court of Appeal stated that, where an invitation to enter into ADR was met with 'complete silence', that alone would be enough to merit a costs penalty even though there was in the end a last-minute settlement. The judge issued a costs penalty 'pour encourager les autres' (to set an example to others).

It does involve achieving a helpful result without the cost, stress, time and risk involved in taking the matter through to the end of a legal process.

The processes

As we saw in the previous chapter there are some types of claim in the civil courts where a letter of claim must be sent prior to claims being issued. This is known as the 'pre-action protocol'. The civil court rules also offer a link to a Practice Direction[2] which specifically refers to ADR and to the options open to parties to use a form of ADR in order to resolve the dispute prior to or instead of a full trial before a judge. This Practice Direction is entitled Pre-Action Conduct and suggests four possible ways in which a dispute can be resolved. These are:

1) mediation;
2) arbitration;
3) negotiation;
4) early neutral evaluation.

The first three of these are the best known and most traditional processes of ADR and we shall look at each of them below. In looking at arbitration we shall also look at conciliation. The last approach is a process which has been used in some parts of the tribunal system[3] so we shall make some mention of that as well.

We will also look at the role of the ombudsman, although it is important to note that someone who refers a complaint to an ombudsman is seeking their decision and is not entering into a process whereby two opposing parties seek to resolve their differences.

---

2 A Practice Direction is a form of guidance issued by the court which those who use the court system need to be familiar with in order to comply fully with a relevant rule. Practice Directions enhance and amplify the court's statutory rules.

3 In addition in the employment tribunal system, for example, there are also specific references to ADR in their rules of procedure – see the Employment Tribunals (Constitution and Rules of Procedure) Regulations 2013 SI No 1237 Sch 1 (Employment Tribunals Rules of Procedure) para 3: 'A Tribunal shall wherever practicable and appropriate encourage the use by the parties of the services of ACAS, judicial or other mediation or other means of resolving their disputes by agreement.' We shall make mention of the various routes to resolution now well established in that process.

16.2   Using ADR

Considering options

The traditional methods of ADR outlined above are not all necessarily cheap or swift when matched with each other or against the process of following through a claim in a court or tribunal. Negotiation is the least formal as it will usually take place between the advisers representing the two parties in dispute. Otherwise a number of considerations will need to be borne in mind when embarking on an ADR route. These can be summarised as follows:

- **Court processes:** Does the venue in which a likely claim or case may end up require the client to have attempted to begin an ADR process? Can they show their genuine willingness to have done this?
- **Choices:** Do they have a genuine choice about the route of ADR to follow? In the small claims court, for example, all parties are offered court-based mediation and no other route. It is, however, a free service provided by the court system.
- **Costs:** What are the costs of the process the client is offered or advised to engage in if any? Can they shop around for a cost-effective ADR service?
- **Speed:** Is the client under any pressure, say, to attend a final court or tribunal hearing or to start a claim off within any legal time frame, and if so have they got time to engage in an ADR process? How long will that process take as opposed to the process of a full court or tribunal process?
- **Frame of mind:** Is the client willing to adopt a more open and conciliatory frame of mind (through their adviser) in order to settle differences and reach a helpful outcome?
- **Outcome:** Has the client been informed of the likely outcome of the ADR process they are entering into? Does it satisfactorily match or indeed exceed what they hoped to achieve in an adversarial legal or quasi legal process?
- **Implications:** Is the client happy with any possible implications for them in accepting the decision of the third person they ask to resolve their dispute? Will they be able to or be prepared to comply with any requirements placed on them at the likely conclusion of the ADR process?

Once these points have been discussed and agreed with the client then hopefully they will be better prepared to enter into the required or chosen process of ADR in order hopefully to save themselves the time, costs and stress of engaging in litigation.

16.3 Mediation

Mediation is perhaps the best known form of ADR. It is also available in a wider variety of legal systems and is a form of ADR which can vary from costing nothing to costing a great deal of money.

Where is mediation available

Court-based service

It is, as we saw above, available for all those who enter into the small claims court system in their local county court where a judge will provide mediation as a free service. As of April 2013 all parties involved in resolving a small claim will be given the opportunity to see if the case might be suitable for mediation by a county court judge instead.

It is also available in the employment tribunal system and there also conducted by a judge. However, it is not offered for every claim but only where a senior judge in the region decides it to be suitable. Furthermore, the respondent (who is always the employer) resisting a claim made by an employee or ex-employee now has to pay a fee for this service[4] and so even where it might be offered they will be carefully weighing up the costs of meeting this fee as opposed to opting instead for a full hearing (where the claim may fail and they may walk away with no financial penalty other than their own legal costs).

The third best known court mediation service is a part of the way in which family courts operate.[5] There is currently no obligation for couples with family disputes to enter into mediation prior to going into the family court but it is highly recommended. As of early 2014 it is also likely to be a mandatory requirement as a prequel to any family law litigation.[6] In addition, the family courts operate a service designed to take the stress out of the process of family separations and divorce. The government set up a service under its education department in 2001 called the Children and Family Court Advisory and Support Service. Not surprisingly this rather long title of the service is more usually referred to under its acronym, CAFCASS. This service is child and family centred and aims to provide resolution

---

4 See the Employment Tribunals and the Employment Appeal Tribunal Fees Order 2013 SI No 1893 art 4(3) – fee of £600.

5 The family courts as they are commonly described are in fact a branch of the High Court. Family law cases are also heard in local county courts. For more on the court structure see section 18.2.

6 See the Children and Families Bill 2014.

in relation to matters such as arrangements for the care of the child where the parents are divorcing. The CAFCASS mediator then refers their file with recommendations to the judge who decides on the legal aspects of the family dispute.

Other courts and tribunals also have mediation services but these three are probably the best known and longest established court-based services.[7]

Community mediation

It is also possible, usually in smaller disputes, to obtain the services of a community mediator. These services are not universal but where they are available they are enormously valuable. They will not all be free to use but will charge a reasonable fee for their services. They will be able to mediate on issues such as neighbour, family or consumer disputes. Many cities or regions will offer these services, either funded by a charity or a local authority. Given that they will all have varying ways in which the service can be accessed or utilised, and in some circumstances paid for, the best approach would be to use a local directory or website to find out more about them.

Commercial mediation

In all the above situations and in a variety of other areas where the law may be used to resolve a dispute, such as property, commercial or business disputes, it will alternatively be possible to utilise the services of a commercial mediator. There are a number of these in the market place and, due to the rising cost of litigation and the focus of some parts of the court system on ADR, this is a growing industry. It would therefore not be fair to isolate one commercial provider as being any more helpful than another, although some, of course, have longer track records than others. These services can at times be quite expensive with the cost usually being split between the two parties. This can create some difficulties where one of the parties has considerably more financial resources than the other. There is no national regulatory framework for mediators, although an adviser recommending a commercial mediator to a client will look for a mediation service where the mediators are trained and where the organisation can offer

---

7 The process has for example been used in special educational needs and
   disability tribunals where parents are challenging the provision of education
   for a child with special educational needs.

a quality mark or kite mark to show that they have achieved certain standards in the field.

The mediation process

Mediation will take place in the form of a meeting or series of meetings in which the mediator will seek to enable the parties to find some common ground and to reach a helpful outcome. The mediator will remain impartial and their approach will not so much lie in helping the parties to argue their differences better or to understand their respective weaknesses, but to assist them in seeing an end to the dispute by opening up the channels of communication and being a lever to allow for changes in a person's position to be made in a positive way.

The process can take some time, possibly a number of days spread out over a period of time. It will usually take place in a neutral setting or, if at court, in an informal room in a court building set aside for mediation purposes. It is quite common for a mediator to place the two parties in separate rooms for the early part of the discussions or indeed throughout the whole process. This allows for the mediator to move from room to room, outlining to each party what the other party is saying or what their various proposals are for moving the matter forward and ironing out the areas of dispute. It also allows the parties to discuss freely among themselves or with their adviser what they want to say to the mediator (and through the mediator to their opponent) and how the process seems to them to be developing. We saw in chapter 14 that an adviser will identify the issues in a client's case – they will agree and outline the areas of dispute, sometimes also with their client's opponent. This type of approach can also be taken in mediation, where the mediator asks the parties if they can agree what their points of difference are and then move through each one to see who can make a proposal or shift a view in order to reach some common ground and hopefully agree a resolution.

Mediation does not produce a legally binding result for the parties but it does have many advantages. A trained or experienced mediator (which will include a judge in the court system) will enable the parties to speak freely but constructively about their differences and will help them to explore any common ground they might have. The mediator will not take sides but may perhaps probe each side to see if they are clearly setting out how they might be prepared to resolve each area of dispute. At the end of the process the mediator will record the decision.

16.4 **Arbitration and conciliation**

Arbitration

For many years arbitration was the only alternative way of resolving a dispute outside court. It is also the process which is the nearest to a court decision, as the arbitrator will make a decision at the end of the process which will be legally binding on both parties. The arbitrator is given the role of deciding on the dispute and makes a decision in favour of one party or another.

Arbitration began as a process in the commercial world and is still commonly used in relation to commercial contract disputes. Many of these contracts will have in them an 'arbitration clause' whereby, if there are disputes as to how any part of the contract should have operated, the parties will be required to go to an arbitrator to resolve the matter. Arbitration can also involve an examination of a dispute concerning the services provided by a professional such as an architect or building surveyor working to the terms of a commercial contract. Unlike other ADR methods, arbitration involves the use of arbitrators whose actions are governed by law.[8] Arbitration also exists as a process in some employment disputes. There are some types of unfair dismissal claims which can be referred by the parties to an ACAS[9] arbitrator. This is also governed by law.[10]

The process of arbitration will involve a hearing, or meeting, or series of meetings with both the parties in dispute being present, and the arbitrator (or sometimes a panel) inviting each party to state their case and then decide on the outcome for them. The rules of evidence which apply in court hearings will not apply in these hearings but it will be possible for witnesses to be called and for documents to be put before the arbitrator as part of the party's evidence. These can, however, be quite formal processes and it is not uncommon in commercial disputes where large sums of money may be at stake for barristers to represent their clients in arbitration.

Although often associated with commercial matters, knowing of the possibility of arbitration in some areas will be of benefit in the

---

8 Arbitration Act 1996.

9 Advisory, Conciliation and Arbitration Service – see www.acas.org.uk. This is a statutory service specifically designed to deal with employment disputes, both in employment tribunals and in the workplace (such as industrial disputes, strikes).

10 ACAS Arbitration Scheme (Great Britain) Order 2004 SI No 753 (also extends to Scotland). However, this service has rarely been used since its inception in 2004.

advice sector. For example, if there is a holiday dispute involving a company governed by ABTA[11] it will be useful to know that this organisation offers a free email arbitration service.

Conciliation

Conciliation is a less formal approach than arbitration in that the latter will result in a decision being made by the arbitrator which both parties will be required to abide by. In conciliation, the conciliator will be used by the parties as a medium for them to try to reach a compromise or a decision which one or both of them agrees to put into action. The decision will be reached by the parties and not by the conciliator. Furthermore, the decision will not be legally binding on either party and so it involves more of a leap of faith on the part of the parties.

Conciliators do not have to possess any particular legal or other professional qualifications, which is usual for arbitrators. However, they will often have received training or have a relevant background which will enable them to talk knowledgeably to each party about the issue and to use powers of persuasion to see if the parties can reach an acceptable compromise. Conciliation has a particular role in the process of compromising employment claims.[12] There are also legal requirements which must be followed in compromising employment claims which have been settled with the help of the ACAS conciliation service and ACAS will advise as to how these will operate.[13]

Conciliation can also take place in the public sector. Some health authorities and local authority services will encourage aggrieved individuals to use their conciliation services and the outcomes may result in changes of policy as well as admissions of below-standard services or unnecessary delays. These are matters which a court cannot always address and so this process may be useful for a client with concerns about public services.

---

11 Association of British Travel Agents. See http://abta.com/go-travel/travel-clinic/arbitration-and-mediation.
12 See ACAS Conciliation.
13 See note 9 above for the ACAS website and how ACAS conciliates in relation to employment or workplace disputes and its role in achieving a settlement of those disputes.

16.5   Early neutral evaluation

We saw above that the civil courts Practice Direction Pre-Action Conduct refers to early neutral evaluation (ENE) as one of the ADR processes. This process involves an independent third party, who can be either an expert in the area in dispute or possibly a judge or barrister providing an opinion or evaluation. The individual is asked to look at both cases at the same time at an early stage and provide an opinion on the strengths and weaknesses of a case and/or a legal opinion on its merits. They will then provide that opinion to each party in identical terms. It may be as a result of ENE that the parties are able to see more objectively how each aspect of the case or matters in dispute are likely to appear to an outside expert such as a judge and this in turn may have the effect of encouraging them to settle their dispute, possibly following one of the routes outlined above. This process has been used with some success in the context of disability living allowance and attendance allowance appeals in the benefit appeal tribunal system.[14]

16.6   Using the ombudsman

The ombudsman service is a process whereby someone who has no way of being able to resolve their case using the law can seek a finding of maladministration (improperly using their powers) in relation to a business or public body. There is a government ombudsman (known as the Parliamentary Ombudsman)[15] charged with dealing with complaints about the administrative decisions made by central government, as well as a local authority ombudsman[16] and others serving various commercial sectors such as finance and banking.[17]

The relevant ombudsman investigates what the decision was which caused the individual to raise a complaint, how that decision was reached and how the public body or organisation handled that person's complaint. The ombudsman can recommend compensation as well as deciding if there has been poor practice or maladministration.

---

14 See *Early neutral evaluation in tribunal appeals*, 2010, a report setting out the results of this process – on the website of the Advice Services Alliance: www.asauk.org.uk.

15 See: opca.enquiries@ombudsman.gsi.gov.uk www.ombudsman.org.uk.

16 See: www.lgo.org.uk.

17 See, for example, the Financial Ombudsman Service: www.financial-ombudsman.org.uk.

These services cannot mirror or supplement a legal process but can provide a decision where no such process can be followed by a complainant.

The ombudsman service takes us more into the realms of a complaints process. Most organisations that deal with the public will have their own complaints process and if this has not produced a satisfactory result for a client they may be able to go to the relevant ombudsman assisted by their adviser. There are time limits for using the ombudsman service and the process involves leaving it entirely up to the ombudsman officer to ask whatever questions or seek whatever documents they decide they need in order to reach a decision. Someone who goes to an ombudsman for redress will be required to show that they have first of all exhausted the complaints procedure of the organisation their complaint is about. It is rare but not unknown for this person to make a complaint using the services of a lawyer or legal adviser. However, an adviser will be able to identify for a client whether complaining to the ombudsman is the right route to take, particularly if they have advised them that they have no legal redress for that type of complaint. Most ombudsman services are user-friendly and can often assist complainants in organising and presenting their case and any relevant documents.

Although, as we saw earlier, the ombudsman service does not involve mediation, it can sometimes be the case that in giving his or her final decision the ombudsman will recommend mediation to see if that process can further resolve areas of dispute still in existence between two opposing parties, such as a bank and its customer or a local authority care provider and the relatives of the service user.

16.7 Negotiation: skills and tactics

As mentioned in the previous chapter it is perfectly possible and indeed common for parties in dispute to reach some form of resolution as a result of negotiating via traditional forms of communication. When engaging in this process on behalf of clients, their advisers use a number of skills. Many law students will study the skills and tactics of negotiating as part of their education or training. There are some common approaches that will be used in order to ensure that the process goes smoothly.

Persuading the other party to agree to your client's outcome

In some circumstances the process of negotiating can mean that the adviser reaches an outcome by persuading someone else to agree to do what the client wants. This might, for example, be to accept a series of offers to pay off mortgage arrears in return for asking a court to adjourn possession proceedings. The adviser representing the client in arrears may use a number of arguments to persuade the mortgage company to do this. For example:

- If they accept the offer now then the arrears will start to be paid much sooner than if they wait for the outcome of a court case.
- If they accept the offer it may be that if the client's financial circumstances improve they will be able to increase it.
- If they insist on going to court they are risking an uncertain outcome or one which would not be what they wanted.
- If the court makes an order for the client to pay off the arrears in instalments it will be for a fixed amount with no obligation on the part of the client to increase it.

Negotiating a settlement of differences

Here skills are used by both parties to put aside their differences in order to try to reach a resolution which they can both accept. The resolution will not necessarily be the outcome which either party wanted at the start, but it will be an outcome which both parties can accept without losing face. The aim of a good negotiator is to learn how to achieve a result which their client will accept. They will reach that point by putting forward persuasive arguments in favour of their client's case while also accepting the case made for the client's opponent. In doing so, it is likely they will have to concede points which were in their favour in order to reach a compromise. This is often referred to as settling a case. Where the case is due to go to court or tribunal, it will be referred to as 'settling out of court' if an agreement is reached either before or during a hearing.

An adviser may be tempted to expend energy in the negotiating process in repeating their client's case to an opponent and seeking to convince the other party of it in order to persuade them to give the client what they want. This is unlikely to persuade an unwilling opponent to see things from the client's viewpoint. A more constructive approach to negotiating a settlement will involve the parties knowing what their opponent's case or arguments are but seeing if, in spite of that, any common ground can be found to resolve the matter in a different way.

The process of negotiating

The negotiation process will normally involve utilising the following tactics:

- **Client's case:** Stating the client's case and inviting the opponent to agree on what it is.

- **Opponent's case:** Taking note of the opponent's case and agreeing on what it is.

- **Common ground:** Seeing if the parties can find any common ground – such as the fact that the client is owed a sum of money (but the amount owed is in dispute).

- **Reason to settle:** Agreeing any common reason or reasons which each party might have for wishing to dispose of the case by settling it. The most common reasons are usually to save cost and time.

- **Conceding ground to achieve a settlement:** Whether or not there is any common ground but both parties wish to achieve a settlement, agreeing on what aspects each party might be willing to move ground on. This can be done without the parties conceding their case.

- **Knowing the limits of what can be achieved:** Sometimes negotiations will involve starting the process by putting forward a higher figure for a money settlement than the figure which the client is actually prepared to accept in order to settle a claim. This will allow the negotiations to continue so that it appears that the client is conceding to their opponent if a lower offer is then made (which in reality will be the figure the client is seeking).

- **Discussing proposals with the client:** Even if the adviser thinks the offer is a good one or the pace appears to be moving fast in order to avoid imminent deadlines or hearings, the client will remain at the centre of the resolution process.

- **Recording:** Often negotiations can begin without warning, say, as part of a telephone conversation ostensibly made for some other purpose. In addition, once a settlement appears likely, there may be frequent calls or conversations to 'fine-tune' the settlement. It is important that all these transactions are recorded, not only on the adviser's file, but also in writing to the client, so that the client is fully up to date with the progress of the negotiations and is in a position to be able to give instructions as to how they want their adviser to proceed.

The negotiator's skills

As well as using these common tactics, the adviser will be engaging in a number of skills as part of the negotiating process.

Preparing a client

Even if there is no indication from a client that they want to settle a case, the adviser should always discuss this as a possible option at an early stage and seek the client's instructions as to what they would agree to accept by way of a compromise should the opportunity arise. This will involve having advised the client of the risks involved in setting out to achieve their desired outcome in full.

Being on top of the case

Negotiations can be initiated by either party, often by an unexpected telephone call being received. The adviser needs to ensure they are at all times on top of their client's case and understand the way their opponent's case is being put so that they can be ready to deal with negotiations at any time. This preparedness will show them to be in control of the situation should they receive an unexpected offer to negotiate a settlement.

Displaying confidence in the client's outcome

There will inevitably be weaknesses in a client's case. Even where the client presents a set of facts which they wish to rely on (such as the fact that they are owed money by someone) there may not be the evidence to support this. They may not have kept invoices or receipts, letters or bank statements. There may have been evidence produced which contradicts what they say. In spite of this, the adviser will present a confident approach to their opponent. If the adviser gives the impression to an opponent that they believe their client's case to be weak there will be no incentive for the other party to offer any concessions to settle the case.

Adopting a conciliatory approach

On the other hand, if the adviser takes a robust and unyielding approach to their opponent they will not necessarily be able to reach any form of compromise. It is quite possible to display faith in the strength of a client's case at the same time as indicating that in spite of that the client will be willing to reach a compromise position. Some aspects of negotiation can be described as 'posturing', where both parties are engaged in using the best aspects of their client's case and playing down the worst aspects to try to reach a point where they each will accept a middle way.

Being professional and courteous

In all conflict situations it should be possible to maintain a position in opposition to someone else's at the same time as showing that person courtesy and adopting a professional approach. This is nowhere more true than when negotiating a compromise of a client's case or position. No positive result will be achieved by adopting a combative approach or indeed by responding to like with like. Sometimes it can help to set ground rules with an opponent as part of the process. These may include not interrupting or not frequently contradicting the other person.

There are of course some situations in which neither negotiating nor the use of traditional ADR routes will achieve a resolution in spite of the adviser's best endeavours and these may result in using a court or tribunal to make the decision for the parties. This is the process we will look at in the next chapter.

CHAPTER 17

Resolving the case: courts and tribunals

17.1 Knowing the appropriate jurisdiction

Introduction

Once it becomes necessary for an adviser to steer their client into a formal legal system in order to reach a resolution of their case, they will have done some groundwork on that process, whether or not they are the person who will ultimately represent their client. They will have familiarised themselves with the particular procedures operating in whatever venue they are about to use. As we shall see in the next chapter, the main court system operates on legal and formal lines which practitioners are constantly having to keep up to date with. The wide range of jurisdictions in our legal system and the different ways in which each operates means that it is not possible to outline each of them here. However, there are some general aspects of becoming familiar with the relevant process which might be useful starting points.

What legal claims is the court or tribunal empowered to determine?

A simple but important point. A client may have been advised that they should be challenging their rent or service charges levels; seeking to appeal a refusal of a benefit or special education provision; or seeking to overturn a decision that they are not to be classed as an asylum-seeker. In each case there will be a specific venue where such matters will be decided on by a judge and in each of these situations the venue will be different. So, the first task is to identify where claims can be made or in what tribunal or court will they seek to assert their rights. Occasionally, but not very often, there may be a choice. For example, it is possible to claim for unpaid wages owed under an employment contract in either a civil court or an employment tribunal in some circumstances. A tenant with a rented property in disrepair may be able to pursue a claim in either a civil court or a criminal court, depending on the type of disrepair. Some family disputes can be dealt with in civil courts or in some cases criminal courts. A careful consideration of the exact nature of the legal claim or wrong needs to take place to identify the correct or appropriate venue for the client's claim to be decided in.

What are the processes relating to that court or tribunal?

The adviser needs to know the procedures to start off claims or make applications, how and when any defence or response to claims needs to be made and how the matter will progress from there. In all legal processes, some form of action is taken by a party to initiate the process. Put simply, in a criminal court the Crown Prosecution Service (CPS) takes a decision to prosecute, in a civil court a claim is lodged by a claimant, and in a tribunal an application will be made by a party who may be called a claimant, applicant or appellant. The process will then be managed by the relevant venue. The court or tribunal will issue orders, instructions or directions aimed at bringing the matter to a conclusion.

Where the process is adversarial, the two opposing parties will each be required to take steps to comply with these orders or directions. So it will be important to be aware of what these steps are, what the time limits are for taking them and what penalties there might be for not complying with them. In most venues it is also possible for a party to apply to that venue for something to happen, for example, for their opponent to provide some relevant documentation or to ask that a hearing may be adjourned for whatever reason.

At the conclusion of that process of preparation there will be a hearing to make a final decision on a date and time fixed by the relevant venue, or possibly agreed in advance by all the parties, including the judge in that venue. These rules and procedures of whatever venue the case is in, can be read at source or read around, as we shall see in the next two chapters. Some are highly complex, such as some types of cases in the higher levels of the civil and criminal court system. But, whatever the venue, it would not be wise to engage with it without knowing how it operates.

17.2   Time limits

A further preliminary step is to keep a clear eye on any time limits imposed by the relevant jurisdiction. Given that it is the venue and not the parties that control the process, once anyone enters into the relevant legal process they will have time limits imposed on them by that venue. These can vary from limits for when defences or responses to claims must be sent in, to the time within which preliminary steps need to be complied with, right up to the time a judge will allow for a hearing or even for a witness to be examined in the witness box. Even prior to legal claims being made there will be limits set by rules or law for how long after an incident or act a claim, application or appeal must be received by a court or tribunal. This makes the diarising process particularly important, since if an important deadline is missed, any fault is going to be laid at the door of the adviser and not their client. Advisers will not only assure the client that they have an eye on these, but also inform the client of any steps they need to take which will assist the adviser in complying with that requirement on time, such as supplying documents to comply with a court order.

17.3   Fees and court costs

Fees

Litigation in the court system is not cheap. Although there are still a number of tribunals where it is free to enter into the process, it is more common for a fee to be paid in order to start off a claim or application. In the civil court system fees do not stop there. Apart from the small claims court, where the only fee payable is that for starting off a claim, fees need to be paid at various junctures. These include paying for preliminary processes as well as paying to take part in the final hearing. In some tribunals this process is mirrored. Clients need to be made aware of this, particularly where they are the initiator of the claim, as their fee bill is likely to be higher than that of a defendant. They need to know the amounts payable from start to finish of a claim. Some venues will allow for a remission (or 'waiver') of fees to enter into the system where a client is on a low income. Their eligibility for this waiver will be assessed by the court or tribunal staff on submission of a form setting out the required financial details.

Fees and fee waivers vary from one venue to another. Information about them can usually be obtained by looking at the website of the relevant court or tribunal or by telephoning that venue. Administrative staff in the court and tribunal systems are usually very helpful in providing practical information about how their systems operate but it should be borne in mind that the court and tribunal system is heavily used but not necessarily heavily resourced.

Costs

Clients will also need to be alerted to the possibility that not only might they be paying their own adviser's fees and costs, as well as any court or tribunal fees, but may also face a situation where they may have to pay an opponent's costs. Costs arrangements also vary from one part of the civil legal system to another and will require more detailed research than it is possible to supply here. Three basic likely outcomes are:

- The legal adviser's fees and additional costs (such as paying for experts) will only be recoverable if the client is successful in their claim or case and this recovery process does not operate throughout the legal system. Where it does, the rate of recovery can be less than the amount they have actually paid their adviser in circumstances where the court assesses the exact sum they are allowed to recover.
- If the case is lost, there may be a possibility that the client will also have to pay the fees and costs already expended by their opponent in taking part in this process.
- There are separate financial procedures and costs arrangements for clients who are legal aided. We will not be outlining these here, but suffice it to say that even a client supported by legal aid funding in respect of their adviser's fees and costs may find that money they might recover (which they feel is their due entitlement) can be reduced in order to repay the public purse out of which the initial costs of running the case were borne. In (admittedly very) rare circumstances they too may be required to pay their opponent's legal costs.

All these rather expensive matters will be aired with a client who is embarking on a legal process. It may well be that much of this expense can be saved by winning a case, negotiating a settlement or engaging with one of the processes of ADR referred to in the previous chapter, but nothing is certain and the best approach is to assume that all these financial risks will need to be faced once the claim or case gets underway.

17.4 Using the formal procedures

As they engage with these formal procedures the adviser is likely to be asking themselves the following questions:

- **Time:** If it is up to me to start the procedure off, am I in time to do so? (See section 17.2 above.) Am I complying with time limits for other stages of preparation?

- **Forms or precedents:** If I am starting the procedure off how do I do so? In any event, what form or form of drafting is required by the relevant jurisdiction? Do I have the necessary information from my client to prepare that form as well as the ability to draft that form in the manner expected? Do I have a precedent on my case management system to assist me in drafting?[1]

- **Mode of delivery:** In sending in claims, appeals, defences or even letters or emails to the relevant venue, what method am I allowed to use? Can I send claims forms or formal applications electronically, or by fax or by post? Will letters or emails be read and accepted if sent electronically? Are there specific rules about how time is calculated for receipt of communications in that venue, for example, to take into account both weekdays and weekends?

- **Preliminary stages:** If the venue expects me as my client's adviser to go there for any preliminary discussions[2] have I diarised that and prepared for it (see below) and am I ready to attend with my papers in order, knowing where the venue is and what is likely to happen at that discussion? Have I alerted my opponent to any specific points I think should be discussed in advance of that discussion?

- **Administrative processes:** Am I familiar with that venue's administrative processes: when and how I can contact administrative staff and what information they may be allowed to give me as to the progress of my client's case? When I do contact, or am contacted by, the venue can I demonstrate readiness for any queries or any last minute change of arrangements?[3]

- **Hearing:** Am I ready for the final hearing in every respect? Even where I am not representing the client myself, has all the necessary preparation been done?

---

1 This will be an example or series of examples of how such forms would need to be completed, based on previous similar applications or cases conducted. Where the court or tribunal requires the use of standard forms these might be downloaded and saved onto the adviser's system for future use.

2 The most common of which, in the civil legal system, is a form of case management discussion or hearing where parties preparing for a hearing will be required to attend a meeting with a judge to discuss further steps they will need to take to prepare themselves for the main hearing of the claim or case.

3 The most problematic of which can be the venue's decision that a hearing cannot after all go ahead on a date planned, due usually to overload in the system beyond the control of either the judge or the staff. When this does happen, advisers need to be accepting and courteous with staff tasked with passing on this often unwelcome news.

17.5 **Preparing the client**

Where an adviser will themselves be representing the client at a hearing they will be preparing their client for their role in taking part in that process. This will involve providing information as well as asking them to take part in certain activities. They will highlight the following aspects of going to a hearing from a client's perspective.

Procedures

Information will be provided for the client concerning the process they are about to enter into, what its modus operandi is, what is likely to happen at each step of the way on the road to a final hearing or conclusion. Most important of all, the client will need an account of what is likely to happen at the hearing in terms of the procedure to be followed throughout that hearing.

Knowing their own case

Some clients may underestimate the stress involved in a judicial process. They may only have seen courts represented in a somewhat glamorous fashion in television dramas.[4] They may themselves have never attended anything as formal as a court or tribunal hearing. In most types of cases, once the final hearing gets underway the client is likely to play a focal role. They may be required to read out or talk to a prepared witness statement and answer questions put to them by an opponent's legal representative as well as by the panel or judge hearing the case and making the decision. This means that the client needs to know the case as well as their adviser. In advance of the hearing the adviser will stress the importance of the client knowing their own case in terms of what they want to say and what documents have been prepared. They will check that the client has a set of papers ready for the hearing in the required format and is fully familiar with their own statement and each document in the bundle so that they can quickly refer to them if required when giving evidence or during a hearing.

---

4 Although cameras are now allowed in both the Supreme Court and the civil Court of Appeal in London.

Formality of a hearing

The adviser will explain to their client that all these venues are relatively formal and require certain standards of behaviour to be observed. Overall the client needs to be made aware that they are likely to be nervous and to find the process tiring, and therefore need to be as prepared for that as possible. Furthermore, the adviser will not only be preparing the client for the cost and uncertainty of leaving a final decision up to a formal decision-maker, but also how the client may feel once they are told the outcome of their case.

Likely outcome

The adviser will have advised the client on the likely outcome of the case but added in the risk factor to that advice. As we noted earlier, courts and tribunals will sometimes produce a different outcome from that predicted by advisers. This can be due either to unforeseen developments occurring during the progress of the case, or simply due to the court deciding to see things in a different light or taking a different tack in approaching the issues. This is why all advice on outcomes needs to be relatively cautious and why there are always risks inherent in embarking on, or being involved in, court or other legal procedures.

Clients who succeed in court or tribunal claims will feel a sense of justice done and achievement at having come through the process. Those who do not succeed in court claims or who have been unable to successfully defend claims made against them may have one of a number of reactions. Some are philosophical and often say at the end of the process that they had a sense they may not succeed. Others may feel bitter and upset by what they perceive to be unjust treatment. This can also arise where they have been successful but have witnessed their opponent behaving in what they regard as a reprehensible manner, or where they are unable to recover money ordered by a court or tribunal to be paid to them.[5]

---

5   Unfortunately, a significant number of successful parties in a court action never recover the money awarded to them under the final decision. A 2013 study by the Department for Business, Innovation and Skills in relation to employment tribunal awards notes that 'overall, half of respondents (49 per cent) had been paid their award in full at the time of the interview, and a further 16 per cent had been partially paid. Claimants in Scotland were less likely to report that they had been paid in full (41 per cent compared with 49 per cent in England/Wales).

Furthermore, a victory in a court or tribunal will not always mean that an opponent will accept that decision or abide by it. Some court and tribunal decisions will be taken further by way of an appeal by a losing party and this will mean a long delay. The process of an appeal will usually be quite legalistic which can have the effect of locking the client out of the process unless they are able to grasp the legal issues. All these matters will therefore have to be discussed with a client who is engaged in such a formalistic legal process to help them prepare for its processes and likely outcomes.

17.6   Referring the client for representation

There are two National Occupational Standards in appendix D which may be of assistance in supplementing the commentary on this chapter as a whole.[6] There are two possible situations where a case or claim requiring a hearing may be referred for representation.

In the first, an advice agency will have the staff and resources to provide advice and assistance to a client facing formal proceedings but not to represent the client at the relevant venue. If they have been unable to settle or otherwise resolve the matter they may be able to contact another local agency, free or otherwise, where representation is offered as a part of the service.

In the second situation, the adviser, by agreement with the client, refers the client's case to a barrister to represent a client in a court or tribunal. As we saw earlier,[7] barristers can now, in some circumstances, take instructions directly from a client to represent them at a hearing, but it is still more likely that solicitors or other legal advisers make such referrals. Where this happens, the legal adviser will remain the client's adviser and will continue to prepare any necessary paperwork. They will attend the hearing or arrange for a colleague to attend and will take a note of the proceedings.[8]

An adviser who prepares a case for representation is, in essence, replicating for the representative what they themselves have done by way of preparation. In setting up the letter or other document of

---

6   See SFJDA7 'Prepare cases for representation in formal proceedings' and SFJDA4 'Represent clients in formal proceedings'.

7   See section 3.2.

8   In some legal venues it is necessary for a barrister representing their client to be accompanied by whoever has instructed them or a representative from that organisation. See, eg www.barcouncil.org.uk/media/58802/court-dress for recent guidance from the Bar Council on court dress for barristers in the various courts.

referral they will also go back to the beginning of the process they entered into with their client and start by briefly outlining for the representative what the client's story is. They will indicate what they believe the be the appropriate legal issues raised by the facts which need to be decided and may even summarise how they themselves see these playing out, referring to advice they have already provided to their client on these issues and on the relative strengths and weaknesses of the client's case. They will tell the representative the date, venue and time of the hearing and will summarise any preliminary steps taken so far as part of the preparation for the hearing. Finally they will summarise what the client's objectives are: what it is the client wants the legal venue to decide for them.

This process is known as 'briefing counsel' (the barrister) and the papers sent to the barrister will be referred to as the 'brief'. The barrister is referred to as being 'instructed' to attend the hearing on behalf of the client (who then also becomes their client once they have received and accepted their instructions). Traditionally instructions to barristers for representation at a hearing will contain papers in a set pattern as set out below, and while not all representation referrals are likely to be as formal as this, sending these enclosures will always be a helpful approach as part of the referral process:

- Letter from court or tribunal setting out date, time and venue for a hearing.
- Copies of court or tribunal pleadings or applications, as well as any orders or directions made requiring the parties to take preparatory steps prior to a hearing.
- Copies, in date order from the earliest on top, of any relevant letters or other correspondence which has passed between the venue and the adviser. Where there are two opposing parties, relevant correspondence between the parties themselves. The relevant correspondence is likely to relate to letter of claim and other open discussions about the merits of each other's case, 'without prejudice' correspondence where efforts have been made to reach a negotiated settlement, and/or correspondence which reflects the steps the parties have made towards a final hearing.
- Where already prepared, a copy of the documents the venue has prescribed to be brought to the hearing, or alternatively, copies of any such documents as prepared by the adviser or agreed between two opposing parties.
- Where relevant, copies of witness statements prepared on behalf of the client and their adversary.

Finally, and as a matter of good sense and courtesy, the adviser should invite the representative to contact them with any additional queries to assist them in representing the client. Contact details including mobile phone and availability should also be provided. If a hearing is imminent, the adviser should be prepared to be contacted on a flexible basis with any last-minute queries to allow the representative to be as prepared as possible for the good of the client.

17.7 Representing a client

We have already discussed in chapter 11 the way in which an advocate should prepare for the practicalities of attending a formal hearing and representing their client there. Once an adviser takes the decision not only to advise but also to represent their client at a hearing they are engaging in the twin activities of maintaining the flow of advice to their client, and continuing with any necessary correspondence or contact with other parties or the relevant court and tribunal in preparation for the hearing, together with all the necessary preparation for that hearing. As we also saw earlier, some claims or cases can be resolved without the necessity of attending a hearing, and that process may also be taking place at the same time as preparation for a hearing. It is never wise to abandon preparation for a hearing on the basis that a claim or case looks as though it might settle, as these negotiations may fail and the adviser may then find themselves on the back foot in terms of being ready to represent the client. So again, being prepared for a hearing is paramount. This will inevitably also involve putting other less urgent cases into a lower category of preparation until this particular matter or hearing is concluded.

As they step into the relevant venue for a hearing, the representative will not only be exercising their skills in advocating or arguing for an appropriate outcome for their client, but will also be handing over control of the process to that venue. They may be able to offer suggestions or approaches to a judge or tribunal as to how they may see their client's case or how their own procedures might be utilised in a smooth running of a hearing. Thereafter they, like their client and any adversary will, once they have played their part in representing their client's interests, have to leave the final decision up to someone else, whose role and training has prepared them to hear evidence and make decisions which are hopefully fair and just.

Using the law

CHAPTER 18

Legal systems, courts and tribunals in England and Wales

18.1 Introduction: navigating the legal system

Part of the provision of legal advice is about being able to explain to a client what will happen if a court or tribunal takes over the resolution of their legal problem. Even if the adviser only practices in one area of law where they might only be using the same court or tribunal for all their cases, it will be useful to understand the whole map of the legal system in order to see where the court or tribunal they use fits in, or what happens if decisions made in that court or tribunal are challenged or appealed. Each part of the legal system in England and Wales deals with different types of legal claims or cases, which we will look at below once we have noted some of its core features.

Constitution

The judiciary forms an integral part of the UK constitution, being one of the three cornerstone elements which make up our constitution.[1] As such, it has powers and discretion to examine a wide range of issues including, on some occasions, how government is exercising its legal duties. These powers give the judiciary independence to interpret our laws and how they operate.

The criminal and civil legal systems have rules which judges follow when hearing cases and which advisers and advocates are expected to know. The rules in the civil court system, known as the Civil Procedure Rules (CPR), were completely overhauled in the late 1990s and now contain many key themes in relation to how claims should be prepared and presented. They provide a comprehensive framework of procedures in the civil court system. They are constantly under review and there are regular updates published each year.[2] At the same time, these rules underpin the fairly wide discretion granted to a judge

---

1 The legislature, executive and the judiciary make up the three elements of the constitution of the UK. These are, in turn, parliament which makes the laws, the government which ensures that the law is functional and operational, and the judiciary, the judges in court who uphold and interpret the law. There has been much ink expended on whether the first and second arms of the constitution are, constitutionally speaking, more powerful than the third, or whether they all maintain an equal balance of powers. Perhaps the best known recent example of this tension arising concerns the question as to whether parliament has the power to replace or remove the Human Rights Act 1998, based as it is on European laws with which the UK is bound by treaty to comply.

2 See the Ministry of Justice website at: www.justice.gov.uk/courts/procedure-rules/civil. The CPR 66th edition was issued in October 2013.

under their constitutional powers in terms of making decisions and interpreting the law. Tribunals, on the other hand, are created by statute or regulations which give them the ability to function. They are therefore sometimes referred to as 'creatures of statute'. Each tribunal has its own rules and procedures which dictate its powers and processes. Judges or chairmen making decisions in this forum have less discretion or facility to consider how they may exercise their decision–making powers than in the civil or criminal court system.

Formality

Those using the legal system for the first time will find it to be highly formal, not only in terms of rules and operation but also in terms of dress and language adopted. It can appear to be outdated and at odds with how other public bodies function. Many expressions are those not used in everyday language, clothes are worn by judges and advocates in a fashion which dates back many hundreds of years, and there is a perception that many judges come from the white male middle class group in society.

The court system is conscious of these trends and while it remains formal for many obvious reasons, it is addressing its image and is more accessible than in previous years. Websites have been set up to help people to understand what goes on in court and how things work.[3] As we saw earlier, some courts now allow cameras in to film their proceedings. There have also been some experiments allowing reporters or other professional observers to use Twitter in court to record proceedings, but these have been the exception rather than the rule, and the judiciary is still somewhat cautious about how the judicial process is recorded, used and represented to the outside world. Efforts are also being made to provide a more diverse legal profession in terms of recruiting new judges. There has also been a relaxation in terms of how barristers are required to dress in some of the courts instead of having to wear a wig and gown each time they appear.[4]

---

3 See, for example, the judiciary's website www.judiciary.gov.uk/about-the-judiciary/introduction-to-justice-system, which provides an overview of the court system in England and Wales and the roles and functions of judges in all parts of it, both civil and criminal.
4 See section 18.5 below.

18.2   The court structure in England and Wales

Courts and tribunals in England and Wales all fall under the control and operation of Her Majesty's Courts and Tribunals Service, created in 2011. This service provides support for the administration of the court and tribunal system and is an agency of the Ministry of Justice.[5] The Ministry of Justice itself provides an overview of the legal system and its services and functions, for example, in the administration and provision of the legal aid scheme.[6]

A flowchart showing the structure of the criminal and civil legal system is shown opposite. This structure has been in place for a number of years, but the most significant recent change to its structure occurred in 2009 when the Supreme Court was created. This not only replaced the House of Lords as the most senior court in the land but also created a separate set of Law Lords who no longer also sit in the upper parliament (the House of Lords) to debate and ratify legislation. They are an independent part of the judiciary whose sole function is to act as judges. Furthermore, since 2005 the most senior judge in the land is the Lord Chief Justice with entirely separate powers and responsibilities from that of government. Prior to that date and for many hundreds of years, the most senior judge was the Lord Chancellor who also held a number of senior posts in government and was the Speaker of the House of Lords.

The criminal legal system

Most of the examples in this book relate to civil law and processes but for the sake of completeness we will also look at both the criminal and civil legal systems and how they function. In the criminal system, rules and procedures are contained in a number of statutes. The Courts Act 2003 deals with many, but not all, procedural aspects of the criminal justice system.

In that system the 'lower' courts are at the foot of the flowchart and the 'higher' ones at the top. The 'lowest' court on the rung in the criminal system is the magistrates' court. The decision to bring a prosecution is made by the Crown Prosecution Service (CPS), who refer to their guidelines and consider whether on the evidence they have seen a conviction is likely and/or in the public interest. They make this decision once the police have referred the case to them

---

5 See: www.hmcts.gov.uk.

6 See section 2.5 note 9.

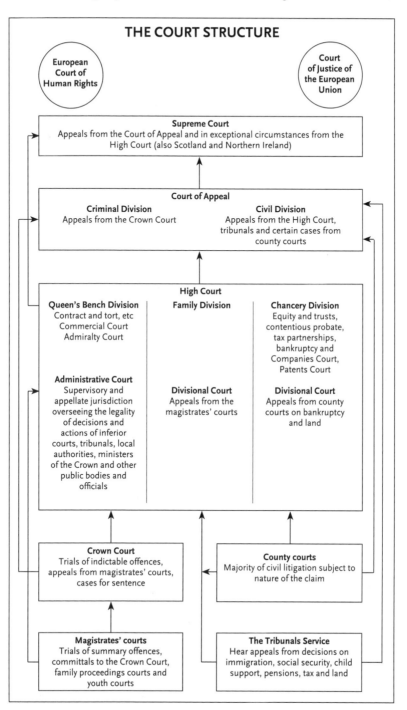

THE COURT STRUCTURE

European Court of Human Rights

Court of Justice of the European Union

Supreme Court
Appeals from the Court of Appeal and in exceptional circumstances from the High Court (also Scotland and Northern Ireland)

Court of Appeal

Criminal Division
Appeals from the Crown Court

Civil Division
Appeals from the High Court, tribunals and certain cases from county courts

High Court

Queen's Bench Division
Contract and tort, etc
Commercial Court
Admiralty Court

Administrative Court
Supervisory and appellate jurisdiction overseeing the legality of decisions and actions of inferior courts, tribunals, local authorities, ministers of the Crown and other public bodies and officials

Family Division

Divisional Court
Appeals from the magistrates' courts

Chancery Division
Equity and trusts, contentious probate, tax partnerships, bankruptcy and Companies Court, Patents Court

Divisional Court
Appeals from county courts on bankruptcy and land

Crown Court
Trials of indictable offences, appeals from magistrates' courts, cases for sentence

County courts
Majority of civil litigation subject to nature of the claim

Magistrates' courts
Trials of summary offences, committals to the Crown Court, family proceedings courts and youth courts

The Tribunals Service
Hear appeals from decisions on immigration, social security, child support, pensions, tax and land

with details of their enquiries and preliminary investigations. Once the CPS decides that an alleged offence should be prosecuted the case will proceed into the criminal legal system.

The starting point for all criminal cases is the magistrates' court, where the magistrates will decide whether they will hear the case or whether it will be referred to the Crown Court. Cases are classified for hearings at one or the other court. Usually, cases of a more serious nature will be heard by a judge and jury sitting in the Crown Court. Alternatively, the magistrates' court will send a case to the Crown Court to be heard from the outset, where the defendant has asked for a jury trial (which they can do for certain types of offences). Cases involving young people (under the age of 18) are heard in the youth courts which are a part of the magistrates' court but the hearings take place in smaller, less formal rooms.

Appeals from the magistrates' courts take a different route depending on whether they come from the family or civil cases heard, or from the criminal cases tried. The Crown Court is where a person appeals against their criminal offence sentence passed on them in the magistrates' court or against their conviction there. Decisions taken in the Crown Court can be appealed further to the Court of Appeal (Criminal Division) and ultimately to the Supreme Court, but permission has to be given by the court making the decision to continue the case with a further appeal. Appeals from the magistrates' court on civil or family cases will go to the relevant division of the High Court civil system, for which see below. It will be seen from the flowchart that the magistrates' court will also hear civil cases either relating to family matters (care orders, residence orders, etc) and some civil matters where fines are imposed, for example in relation to non-payment of council tax or TV licences.

Above the magistrates' court is the Crown Court where more serious criminal offences will be heard and tried in front of a judge and jury. The Old Bailey court in London is a Crown Court, but cases heard there will be serious ones where the judge sitting with the jury to try the case is a High Court judge rather than a circuit judge who hears less serious cases in the Crown Court.

It is hopefully sufficiently well known that cases heard in the Crown Court are decided on by a jury who are all members of the public required as part of their civic duty to carry out jury service. At the end of a criminal trial the members of the jury will receive guidance from the judge on the legal issues and how the law requires them to consider evidence they have heard, but the decision rests with them. Their role is to decide, on the evidence they have heard, whether the defendant is guilty or not guilty. That is, to give their verdict. They will not decide on the sentence to be passed should they hand up a guilty verdict; that is for the judge to decide.

The civil legal system

Whereas a criminal case is brought by the state ('the Crown') against an individual in relation to an offence against the state, civil claims involve private claims between two individuals. Although it may happen that a crime, such as robbery, assault or blackmail will affect another individual's life, the state decides which actions amount to a crime which it has the right to punish perpetrators for committing. As we have seen, the government, in the form of the legislature in parliament, lays down the laws of the land and all individuals in society are bound by this 'rule of law', overseen by the executive and exercised by the judiciary.

The civil system deals with a range of matters which individuals can seek a remedy or decision on in relation to everyday life and their dealings with each other. Claims range from disputes in business dealings, consumers' claims about quality of goods or workmanship, disputes between neighbours, accidents in public places causing injuries, and family or matrimonial disputes or problems. As in the criminal system there is a hierarchy of courts dealing with cases in the civil court system.

Lower court: the county court

The court at the lowest end of the civil system is the county court, which, like the magistrates' court, is a local court. There are county courts in most towns and each district of England and Wales where people will go with their individual disputes. Simple and lower value claims are heard in the small claims court. This is part and parcel of the county court but running on a different speedier 'track' than other claims heard in the county court. Here claims are heard relatively soon after they are commenced with fewer formalities and, where there is a money issue involved, the court will hear any claims worth up to £10,000 (or £1,000 in the case of personal injury claims). Claims at the next level in the hearing system, called 'fast track' claims, will be worth between £10,000 and £25,000, and claims worth in excess of this amount are allocated to the multi-track system. Small claims will be heard by a district judge in his or her chambers (a private informal room in the court). The district judge hears claims in open court as well, where claims worth over £25,000 are heard by a circuit judge who is more senior.

County courts also deal with some family cases, bankruptcy and insolvency claims and claims for repossession of residential property by mortgagees or landlords.

It should be noted that any claim which goes before a judge to decide on a civil dispute will be called a 'trial' (to be 'tried' by the judge) just as it will be in a criminal case where the case is tried by a judge and jury. The difference in the civil system is that the two opposing parties in a case are usually private individuals whereas the two parties in the criminal case will be the state (or Crown) against a private individual.

The High Court

As shown in the flowchart, the High Court divides its business into three main areas, or divisions, with differing cases heard in each of those areas. These are the Queen's Bench Division, the Family Division and the Chancery Division. Judges who sit in each division are specialists in the areas of law they hear cases on.

Queen's Bench Division

Most civil cases (contract disputes, injury claims and other legal wrongs such as nuisance or negligence) are heard in the Queen's Bench Division. Civil claims of a higher value will be heard there, for example a personal injury claim worth over £50,000 will be commenced there as can any civil claim worth over £25,000.

The Queen's Bench Division also operates an administrative court which deals with cases where an individual will be challenging decisions made by public bodies, such as local authorities, as being wrongly exercised or beyond their powers. This process of making an application asking the court to decide on the correctness of an administrative decision or more usually the process used to arrive at it, is called judicial review and is also referred to as public law. It involves the court considering the lawfulness of a decision which has affected one person but which could also have an impact on a sector of society. Examples are decisions about planning, school admissions policies, or care provision. It can be an expensive process but nevertheless one which has been used very effectively to provide checks and balances over public servants in the exercise of their functions. At the time of writing the government is looking at ways of limiting judicial review applications by reducing legal aid availability and the situations in which individuals may utilise this legal process.

Family Division

The Family Division deals with a range of family issues including divorce and claims concerning the welfare of children such as wardship applications. This court also hears appeals from family decisions made in the county courts and the magistrates' courts.

Chancery Division

The third division, the Chancery Division, hears cases relating to some commercial matters, wills and probate (proof of who will inherit a person's property) and a number of other business-related legal claims. There are also a number of other courts dealing with specialised claims relating for example to mercantile law or technology law.

Parties who wish to appeal decisions made in the High Court will do so by way of appeal to the Court of Appeal (Civil Division) and from there to the Supreme Court.

Tribunals

Tribunals also come under the purview of HM Courts and Tribunals Service. Tribunals are classified to deal with separate areas of administrative law, for example, mental health law, education law, land and property issues, criminal injuries compensation, state benefits and pensions. Their usual process is to hear an appeal or challenge from a decision made by a government agency or a statutory organisation with powers to make decisions affecting individuals' legal rights and entitlements.

As the name tribunal indicates, heaings will usually take place before a panel of three people, one of whom – the chair or judge – is a qualified lawywer. They will hear appeals or arguments in favour of, or against, the decision under scrutiny and decide on its correctness or otherwise.[7]

The application or appeal to the tribunal goes to what is known as a First-tier Tribunal. If there is an appeal it is then heard by the Upper Tribunal, and can progress thereafter with further appeals to the Court of Appeal and the Supreme Court. The employment tribunals have their own appeal court, the Employment Appeal Tribunal, where appeals are heard by a panel of three chaired by a High Court judge. Thereafter these appeals may also progress to the Court of Appeal or the Supreme Court.

---

7 As we saw earlier, in the employment tribunals the judge will conduct an adversarial process of presiding over a dispute between employers and employees.

The European Court of Human Rights

On the flowchart, it will be seen that the European Court of Human Rights sits over to the left, as it is a court to which any person may be able to apply if they believe that their human rights have been infringed by any public body (including the government), court or tribunal. The court sits in Strasbourg and the judges are drawn from all the countries which are signatories to the European Convention on the Protection of Human Rights and Fundamental Freedoms.[8] Since the passing of the Human Rights Act 1998 in the year 2000 these rights can be more freely exercised within the UK legal system, and all courts and tribunals must take human rights issues into account when hearing cases and deliberating and deciding on outcomes.

The Court of Justice of the European Union

It will also be seen on the flowchart that the Court of Justice of the European Union (CJEU) sits over to the right. The CJEU (which sits in Luxembourg) encompasses all the other courts in the civil system as a sort of 'umbrella' court. This is because the CJEU may be required by any court to assist in reaching the correct decision by interpreting a law or ruling in line with European law (European law being equally applicable and as much a part of UK law as the laws passed by the UK government). Either a court or an individual can, in principle, ask the CJEU for a ruling on a relevant issue. Usually the referral will be made by the court. Furthermore, tribunals can also refer questions to the CJEU for a ruling. For example, referrals have been made to the CJEU on pension and benefits rights and on employment law rights from the relevant tribunal hearing these types of cases. There are quite complex rules as to how such referrals can be made but, in terms of the structure of the court system, the CJEU is nevertheless a court to which an individual in the UK can have recourse.

Statutes, common law and precedent

Individuals engaging in the court system will need to appreciate how laws are made and the function of the courts in interpreting and upholding them.

---

8 Adopted by the Council of Europe in 1950 and came into force in 1953, now ratified in 47 countries. It largely came into being as a result of the Second World War.

Statutes

Within the UK constitution, parliament drafts and ratifies laws used in the court system. These are either in the form of statutes (or Acts of Parliament), or statutory instruments (SIs). The latter are often referred to as regulations and have as much legal effect in terms of applying and interpreting the law as an Act of Parliament. The content of any of these is subject based, for example a key statute dealing with what family law says is the Matrimonial Causes Act 1973.

Common law

There are also unwritten laws, known as common law. Examples relate to the law concerning acts of negligence committed by others in the context of road traffic injuries or neighbour disputes of some kinds. Even though the law itself may not be written, its operation may be. The civil wrong relating to the injury of another person[9] is not described in statute but there are statutes or regulations which describe how such claims will operate, for example, who should be sued and how blame or damage may be apportioned between various defendants.

Case-law and precedent

The hierarchy of the court system allows for law to not only be enforced but interpreted so that it can be applied by others in the future. This is called judge-made or precedent law. The decisions of a higher court will be binding on a lower court. In other words, a decision made in the Court of Appeal will need to be applied and followed by a judge in the High Court and the courts below when the case to be heard is on the same or similar facts and relying on the same statutory or common law provision. The judge-made decisions in the UK courts which are the most binding are those made in the Supreme Court. We will see an example of how a precedent is made in chapter 19.

Judges in the CJEU will also interpret our legislation by answering specific questions as to what the European laws (Directives) mean and how each member state should apply them in their own legislation. A decision of the CJEU will bind the government of the member state (such as the UK) from where the reference to the CJEU came. Although in some circumstances it is possible to ask the CJEU for a remedy (compensation) in relation to what an individual regards

---

9 Part of the branch of common law known as tort.

as the failure of a UK court to implement their rights properly,[10] the usual approach of the CJEU is to hand down its opinion on the law it has been asked to interpret to the state concerned.

18.3   Judges and staff in the court system

Court staff

Most people who approach a court or tribunal will initially be put in touch with the administrative staff who support the running of the court. They are usually called clerks. Any processing of the necessary paperwork which gets a case into that court's system will be done by them. They will process fees and other monies paid to the court, ensure forms are correctly completed and arrange the timetable of hearings in consultation with the judges who sit at the court.

Cases in all parts of the legal system are allocated case numbers and references and these need to be referred to each time the court or tribunal is contacted. A clerk will not be able to give any advice on how someone should proceed with a case nor can they give any legal advice.

When parties arrive at a court or tribunal to attend a case or hearing they will be guided into the room by an usher who ensures that the formalities for running the hearing are adhered to. That person, for example, will ask those in the court room to stand when a judge or the magistrates come into the room or leave it. In the magistrates' courts and the higher courts, the courts will also have a clerk who sits near the magistrates or judges. They have different functions depending on which court they sit in and are different also from the court office clerks in that their primary function is to assist the persons hearing or trying the case, whereas the court clerks are there to ensure the smooth running of the court or tribunal as a whole.

Magistrates and judges

Magistrates

Most magistrates are not legally qualified. Anyone who is over 18 can apply to sit as a magistrate, who are also known as Justices of the Peace (JPs). They sit as a panel of three (usually called a 'bench'). They

---

10 Often referred to as *Frankovich* claims following the case of *Frankovich v Italy*
[1992] IRLR 84.

are guided on the law by a clerk who sits with them at all times (the magistrates' clerk). This person is legally qualified and well versed in the law the magistrates are asked to deal with. The clerk will confer with the bench during a hearing and will offer advice on the law relevant to each case being heard. The clerk does not, however, take any part in the decision-making process. There are also legally-qualified magistrates called 'district judges (magistrates' court)' and these will try the same sort of cases as the bench and will also hear more complex cases in the magistrates' court. They will sit alone to hear a case and the clerk will be there to provide administrative rather than legal support.

Judges and tribunal chairs

Judges and tribunal chairs (who are a part of the judiciary) are appointed by the government department, the Ministry of Justice (MoJ). The most senior judge is the Lord Chief Justice. All judges are experienced lawyers, either solicitors or barristers, of a minimum required number of years' practice in law. They receive comprehensive training in their functions, as well as in the law they are required to deal with. The training continues on a regular basis throughout the time they sit as judges.

Advisers who appear in front of tribunals or judges in court may be uncertain as to how to address them. The same is true of the individual litigant. Some guidance is offered overleaf.

Although not all the judges in the court system are set out in the table, it lists those whom an adviser is most likely to come into contact with. Knowing the correct mode of address to a judge will show courtesy and will give the adviser confidence to engage with the judge if asked questions by him or her. As might be guessed, if we were to carry on higher through the court system, we would see that judges continue to have more extended (and exalted) titles. Any more senior judges not referred to here may be addressed in court as My Lord or My Lady. Most advisers, likely only to attend a tribunal, county court or magistrates' court should therefore be safe in knowing that the person they address will be addressed as either Sir or Madam, unless they are appearing before a circuit judge in the county court, who will wear a purple robe and who will be addressed as Your Honour.

Court or tribunal	Title of judge	Form of address
Tribunal Chairman/Judge	Chairman (whether male or female) or Judge	Sir or Madam
Magistrates	Justice of the Peace (JP)	Your Worship (but usually Sir or Madam)
District judges (county court)	District Judge (Jones etc)	Sir or Madam
Circuit judges (bigger cases in the county court)	His or Her Honour Judge Jones	Your Honour
High court judges	The Honourable Mrs Justice Jones	My Lady, My Lord
Court of Appeal judges	The Right Honourable Lady Justice Jones	My Lady, My Lord

18.4 Using the court system: protocols, tips and tactics

In this section the emphasis is on some aspects of protocol when using courts or attending a hearing.

Communicating with court staff

- Be ready with the case number and any additional reference initials of a case you are involved in each time you contact the court or tribunal. Put it at the top of all correspondence with the court or tribunal and have it to hand when making telephone calls to the court office.
- Be prepared to put even the simplest request in writing. Court files are still largely in paper version and the clerks will be required to show each step that has been taken on the file.
- Be firm but polite with court clerks when trying to make progress. If you have waited a long time for a reply to a letter or a date for

a hearing you should receive an explanation. However, you may be dealing with someone who has no knowledge of your case or, more importantly, less knowledge than you have in relation to the law or the legal procedures. It will need to be borne in mind that the function of court clerks is to manage court business and not to resolve a party's case for them.

- Be aware of how to deal with cases on the telephone. Some civil court hearings now take place on the telephone. Even if you are acting for a defendant you may have to take responsibility for organising the hearing in advance if your opponent is unrepresented. Make sure you know the exact process of preparing for the hearing by checking the relevant rules of that jurisdiction.

Attending a court or tribunal

Checking in, case listing and waiting

On arrival at a venue for a hearing the parties will be met by a receptionist who may combine a security check with a check of which case they are attending. Most court and tribunal buildings have a daily case list (sometimes called 'cause' list) pinned to a notice board near the entrance, indicating the names of the parties, the times of the hearings and where in the building hearings will take place. There will usually be waiting areas or rooms. All those attending will need to be prepared to wait. Often, courts and tribunals will list a number of cases to be heard at the same time. Those hearing the cases will work their way down the list. Hearings are usually listed in the mornings, at 10.00 or 10.30 am. It is less common for hearings to be listed to take place in the afternoon, although they may not actually be heard until the afternoon.

Clients will need to be warned that courts and tribunals are, on the whole, not particularly child-friendly. Unless the child is part of the case, a court will not usually allow children under the age of 14 to sit in the court. There are waiting facilities but, owing to the length of time often involved in waiting for a hearing, this will usually amount to inadequate provision for a small child. It is rare that drinks machines or refreshments are situated in courts or near the waiting areas of a court or tribunal. If at all possible, therefore, clients should try to make other arrangements for young children.

18.5   Court etiquette and language

Dress and behaviour at court

Dress

The usher in court, the person responsible for getting people in place for their hearings, will often wear formal dress, usually a floor-length black robe over their day wear. They will address parties by their family names and will be polite and helpful. All those who attend for hearings should also dress soberly and conservatively. Lawyers or other legally-qualified practitioners who have studied for and obtained a right of audience necessary in some parts of the legal system will be required to observe a dress code. Barristers, for example, will wear a wig and gown in some courts.[11] Advisers representing in tribunals or the lower courts will also dress according to the seriousness and formality of the environment in which they are functioning.

Behaviour

Courts will also expect people to behave in a quiet and orderly manner both in the waiting areas and even more so once they are in a court or tribunal room, whether they are taking part in or observing the progress of a hearing. In the waiting areas they will expect people to converse quietly so as not to disturb the conduct of the cases being heard. They will not allow the use of mobile phones in the court but will usually allow them to be used in a court building.

Once in court, behaviour should be as follows:

- Stand up each time a judge or magistrate enters or leaves the room – usually an usher will ask all in court to 'rise'.
- Wait until the magistrate or judge has sat down before sitting down.[12]
- Switch off mobile phones. Do not simply put them into silent mode as you are bound to be distracted by them which means that the court will too.
- Do not speak to or address the judge or magistrate from the seating area of the court.

---

11 As from 2008, gowns have been worn in the civil courts. Wigs and gowns continue to be worn in the criminal courts.

12 In many tribunals you will go in to find the chairman, judge and panel already sitting. They will invite you to sit in your allocated place.

- Do not talk to others in court unless absolutely essential, and then only by whispering. Clients should whisper if they need to talk to their representative in court.
- Do not react (facial expressions or vocal reactions) to what is said during a hearing.
- Do not eat, drink or chew gum in court.

We have already looked at some legal jargon in chapter 11 on advocacy. In appendix F will be found a glossary of some terms and expressions used in the court system in connection with hearings. It still remains the case that judges and lawyers use language which is often quite different from everyday speech. In some cases Latin may be used, although the court system is making an effort to minimise its use. The glossary explains some basic but possibly unfamiliar expressions which arise in the course of a hearing. A few Latin phrases have crept into this list where they are still in use.

Legal research

19.1   Subject areas

It will always be necessary to do background research as part of advising. It is rare, in fact, for advice work not to involve some measure of law even if it is about getting some form of support in the community for an older person, or helping benefits claimants to complete forms. Both these activities will include consideration of that individual's rights to care or support, or the possible legal consequences of not completing forms or completing them incorrectly.

Individuals providing advice will be aware that those they advise will set great store by what they are told and will expect it to be accurate and informed. They will be regularly updating their knowledge of their subject area and have a system in place for doing so.

An adviser will usually specialise in one subject area. If, for example, it is welfare benefits law, they will familiarise themselves with the rules and regulations which govern how these rights can be exercised, as well as with the process of applying for benefits or appealing a refusal to award a benefit. They will research any relevant case or law reports to support the legal issues they believe are relevant and will assist in a resolution of their clients' cases. They will build up this awareness by access to the core resource in their chosen practice area, whether a handbook or practitioner's guide.[1]

They may also research how to advise on practical issues arising out of their subject area. Claimants of benefits may need advice on meeting their needs as a disabled member of the community. A delay in receiving benefits may mean that they have fallen behind with payments for consumer goods or rent, which will require some form of practical approach in how they can manage these issues as well. Advisers will be looking to maintain as broad a scope as possible of the advice they can offer by maintaining awareness of the wider picture and by engaging in research and training.

19.2   Sources of reference

In this section some of the usual sources of reference for researching the law or procedures on an adviser's specialist topic will be introduced, with suggestions as to whom they will most benefit and how.

---

1 See, for example, Child Poverty Action Group, *Handbook on welfare benefits 2013–2014.*

Books

There is no shortage of books published on law and practice on any given topic. It may be helpful to categorise law books as follows, each of which are used in different ways:

Core texts and practitioners' handbooks

On the bookshelf of many solicitors' offices or barristers' chambers is likely to be found a series of textbooks on the core topics of English law. Examples will include a book on the law of property (or land law), the law of contract, the law of tort (the civil, mainly common, law relating to legal wrongs)[2] and the law of equity. These books outline the relevant law in some considerable detail from a largely academic perspective. Most of these titles will also be familiar to a law student who will have been introduced to them as part of their studies. This type of detailed textbook is more likely to be used by the legally qualified adviser who will have been first introduced to it as a law student. In addition, large practice tomes such as *Archbold: Criminal Pleadings* for the criminal advocate or *Family Court Practice* for the family lawyer will be kept on the desk of those practitioners for regular reference. They will also be consulted online or taken to court for reference there.

Outlines of or guides to law and legal practice

In addition, there is a wide selection of textbooks or reference books available on each branch of law and practice in varying detail and complexity published each year, written by practitioners or academics. Those outlining how the law operates will deal with one area of law (such as personal injury law) or one aspect of that area (eg guidance as to how the courts assess compensation where such claims are made). Practice guidance books can cover matters as diverse as how to conduct appeals at a particular First-tier Tribunal to the conduct and rules of a coroner's inquest. As with the previous type of law book, some of these books will also be available online as part of a subscription or have website links offering continued updates on their content. This is probably the best type of book to use as a source of reference for most advisers in terms of cost and ease of reference. They usually come in paperback form and are relatively affordable and may have web-based updates to accompany them. They will explain how the

---

2   For example, Megarry and Wade *The Law of Real Property* 8th edn, 2012; *Chitty on Contracts* 31st edn, 2012; *Clark and Lindsell on Tort* 20th edn, 2012, all published by Sweet & Maxwell.

law operates and discuss how courts or tribunals have interpreted it in the recent past and will often provide practical suggestions on how to advise on or represent clients in that area of law.

Any law or legal research book will inevitably go out of date quite quickly, as the law is constantly changing and being updated. Many legal practitioners will therefore tend to buy their standard practice texts online as part of a subscription which includes updates. Caution should always be exercised when buying any book which includes an outline of or explanation of the current law and legal practice, to make sure it has been updated or published to coincide with the latest law and legal developments.

Law studies and crammers

There are also law books aimed at the student market, both degree law students and those studying for professional examinations to qualify as solicitors or barristers. These are usually concise, accessible and accurate and are updated each year for a new intake of students. They often form a useful introduction to a particular legal subject or practice area. To supplement legal studies shortened versions or 'crammers' are available. These tend to be highly condensed and may not outline fully the body of knowledge that underpins the legal topic. Their main function is to summarise an area of law which has already been studied in depth, to aid in revising for examinations or assessments. For this reason they are likely to be less helpful as a practitioner's source of reference.

Journals or magazines

It is quite common for legal advisers and practitioners to subscribe to a journal or magazine in a given area of law as an easy-read method of keeping up to date with their topic. Most practice areas will host regular journals, many of which are also available online, which will provide updates of how the law is being interpreted and developed in that subject area, including developments in judge-made or case-law. They will also contain articles which provide commentary and opinion on the law both in terms of that subject area and in relation to its place in the wider context of law and legal processes. Subscriptions are usually annual and whilst not necessarily cheap will be more affordable than subscribing to the practitioners' volumes referred to above. The contributors are usually experienced practitioners in their field.[3]

---

3 See *Legal Action*, a monthly magazine dealing with topics relating to social welfare law: www.lag.org.uk.

Websites and other online resources

The use of websites and online resources is an invaluable way of accessing information and guidance as to how the law currently operates. Using these in isolation can be limiting as they do not necessarily outline the law in depth, especially where the content is free. Exceptionally, however, some national organisations, such as Citizens Advice, have website reference systems which cover a wide range of law and legal topics in some depth. Here can be found an accurate and up-to-date outline of the relevant law and of steps which can be taken to resolve claims or disputes in an accessible and 'non-lawyerly' fashion.[4] A similar service is provided by some specialist legal organisations, such as Public Concern at Work,[5] an organisation dedicated to advice and support on whistle-blowing claims, and the Equality and Human Rights Commission (EHRC), a body with statutory functions in relation to equality laws which also provides advice and information on equality laws on its website.[6] These resources are useful both to advisers and members of the public looking for information.

Other websites provide access to free case reports across the spectrum of law and can be researched by reference to their topic, date and courts in which they were decided (which will be looked at in more detail below).[7] The higher courts as part of HM Courts and Tribunals Service also provide links to their recent legal decisions.

Some barristers' chambers and solicitors' practices provide email alerts which update the law, tell readers about recent cases, as well as providing a link to their own services. The content of these is invariably reliable and usually free. Email alerters are very helpful as updates or brief commentaries on an area of law but should be used to supplement other more original sources of legal research.

---

4 See: www.adviceguide.org.uk.
5 See: www.pcaw.org.uk.
6 See: www.equalityhumanrights.com.
7 There are a number of these. Examples include a fully codified system such as British and Irish Legal Information Institute: www.bailii.org; or a case check website such as www.casecheck.co.uk.

19.3   ## Researching statutes and statutory instruments

Statutes in books

The meaning, operation and effect of statutes will form an element of the law guidance or reference books referred to above. Some law books also come in the form of statutes and/or regulations, all of which relate to one particular topic. Some have commentary on these statutes usually referred to as being 'annotated', while others may not contain the whole of the statute. It would be highly unusual for an adviser to know in detail each section of a statute or statutory instrument as part of their acquired body of legal knowledge due to the sheer volume of these in existence. They will, however, familiarise themselves with the key statute relevant to their subject area and know how it is mapped out so that they can easily refer to it to refresh their memory or consolidate their understanding. They will also be aware of any secondary legislation which adds to or further clarifies what the main piece of legislation provides for.[8]

It should not be forgotten that European laws are as much a part of UK legislation as home-grown statutes and regulations. These are more relevant for practitioners in some subject areas than others and will form a part of the statutory framework in these areas.

In researching relevant UK legislation it will be noted that a statute is categorised by its title and the year in which it was introduced, for example the Freedom of Information Act 2000. The same is true for a statutory instrument which is given a number as well as a year, for example the Working Time Regulations 1998 SI No 1833. A numbered paragraph of a statute is always referred to as a section and usually abbreviated to 's' (eg, Housing Act 1988 s21). A numbered paragraph of a statutory instrument will be referred to as a reg or regulation (eg, regulation or reg 21 of the Working Time Regulations 1998). The wording of legislation is concise and the proper meaning occasionally difficult to fathom. In their original format on the government's legislation website,[9] Acts and statutory instruments will have an explanatory note, or summary, to assist the reader in grasping the key principles before they apply themselves to the detail.

---

8   See, for example, the Health and Safety at Work Act 1974. This Act has given rise to a range of statutory instruments dealing with specific workplaces and types of health and safety hazards. An example is the Provision and Use of Work Equipment Regulations 1998 SI No 2306, whose subject matter is self-explanatory.

9   See: www.legislation.gov.uk.

19.4 Case-law and research

Case-law

Law, as we saw earlier, is also made by judges in the form of case-law decisions. Case-law underpins and complements legal research in terms of understanding how the courts interpret both statute and common law. In researching this topic it will be necessary to know what is meant by 'case-law' and how it is arrived at. When giving a decision in a case, the judge or judges in the higher or appeal courts will come to the 'nub' of their decision by stating how the law should be interpreted as well as going on to explain why, in the light of their interpretation of the law, they have come down in favour of one of the parties appearing before them. The nub of their decision is referred to as being the 'ratio' of the case or to give it its full expression, the 'ratio decidendi' ('ray-see-oh dessi-den-die'). The nearest translation of that Latin phrase is the 'decided reasoning' of the law upon which the judge is basing his or her decision.

Application

Perhaps the best known example for law students of a ratio in a legal case is in the case of *Donoghue v Stevenson* finally decided in 1932 in the House of Lords.

The facts of the case concerned a woman who went into a café in Glasgow with a friend. The friend bought her a bottle of ginger beer. As she drank it, Mrs Donoghue declared that she had found the remains of a snail in the bottle. She suffered from shock and gastroenteritis and wanted to be compensated by the manufacturer for her injuries. Mrs Donoghue had not formed a contract with the shop as she had not herself bought the bottle of ginger beer. Could she sue the manufacturer, Mr Stevenson, even though she had no contract with him?

The case progressed through the court system in Scotland, arriving finally at the House of Lords in Westminster where the judges examined the common law of negligence in deciding in her favour. The decision confirmed that anyone who takes action which might be 'reasonably foreseeable' so as to ultimately affect another individual should be liable for their actions and the damage they may cause. The decision focused on what became known as the 'neighbourhood principle' in the law of 'tort' or civil wrongs between private individuals, which was the ratio of that decision. The leading judge, Lord Atkin, in giving that decision said:

There must be, and is, some general conception of relations giving rise to a duty of care, of which the particular cases found in the books are but instances ... The rule that you are to love your neighbour becomes in law you must not injure your neighbour; and the lawyer's question: Who is my neighbour? receives a restricted reply. You must take reasonable care to avoid acts or omissions which you can reasonably foresee would be likely to injure your neighbour. Who, then, in law, is my neighbour? The answer seems to be – persons who are so closely and directly affected by my act that I ought reasonably to have them in contemplation as being so affected when I am directing my mind to the acts or omissions that are called in question.

The manufacturer of the ginger beer was ultimately found therefore to have a duty of care to any consumer who might use his product and to ensure that they would not suffer shock or physical symptoms due to his negligence in preparing the bottling the drinks for retail sale. This 'neighbourhood principle' still endures and reverberates in claims concerning injuries, faulty goods and the unintended but foreseeable effects on others of an individual's actions which have caused loss or damage.

In researching case-law, therefore, it will be necessary to not only read the facts of any given decision made, the way in which the law was argued before and considered by the judges deciding the case, but to look for the ratio or nub of the decision made. This can be arrived at by a combination of reading case reports until the ratio and how it is expressed in each case begins to take on some familiarity, or by reading reference books or journals which will outline key principles of law as expressed in decided cases.

Codifying and reporting case-law

Case titles

In order to research case-law it will be helpful to know how it is codified or described. Civil cases will be described by reference to the names of the two parties involved in the case, for example *Donoghue v Stevenson*. The 'v' standing for 'versus' meaning 'against'.

There are some exceptions to this, however. For example, a case in which an individual is challenging a public body's decision-making powers as being wrongly exercised in the Administrative Court will be brought in the name of the Queen. As we saw in the last chapter these claims are known as judicial review proceedings. The title of this type of case is usually in the format of:

The Queen on the application of Jane Jones v The Public Body or:

> *R (Jones) v The Public Body.*

The Queen is the first party, followed by the name of the individual, Jane Jones, who has been affected by the decision and the opposing party is the public body (eg, the Secretary of State for the Home Department), whose decision Jane Jones is asking the Administrative Court to scrutinise.

Law reports

If the title of a case is referred to in a book, article or journal it will usually be made to stand out in bold or italics. It will be given its title, the year it was decided and/or reported, which of the acknowledged law reports it can be found in, and in which volume, the page number of the case in that law report and an abbreviation of the higher court which made the decision will also be supplied. For example:

> *Donoghue v Stevenson* [1932] 1 All ER 123, HL

This needs further explanation. As we know, this was a decision made by the House of Lords as it was then known. Hence the abbreviation 'HL'. A decision by the Supreme Court will have the letters SC instead. The phrase 'All ER' refers to the All England Law Reports and the volume of those reports in the year in which the case was reported as well as the page number the case can be found at. It will also be noted that the original claimant was a Mrs Donoghue. Note that as a case progresses up through the court system, the names of the original parties are reversed with the appellant's name coming first. Here it will be seen that by the time the case was finally decided in the House of Lords Mrs Donoghue's name appears first as she won her final appeal.

In most years there are three volumes of All England case reports. In the civil system, the two most common law reports reporting cases in the higher courts are called the Weekly Law Reports (WLR) and the All England Law Reports (All ER). Some decisions will be reported in each of these reports. Others may only appear in one of these reports and still others will not be reported but can still stand equally as judge-made law.

Some years ago the High Court set out some guidelines as to how cases should be described and referred to in later hearings. There is now a consistent series of numbers and descriptions of each case heard in the higher courts which will, if reported, have added to it the reference to where it will be found in the law report.

The system has been set out by the court[10] for codifying or 'citing' (referring to) cases as follows:

> Judgments will be numbered in the following way:
> Court of Appeal (Civil Division) [2000] EWCA Civ 1, 2, 3 etc.
> Court of Appeal (Criminal Division) [2000] EWCA Crim 1, 2, 3 etc.
> High Court (Administrative Court) [2000] EWHC Admin 1, 2 etc.

Under these arrangements, paragraph 59 in *Smith v Jones*, the tenth numbered judgment of the year 2001 in the Civil Division of the Court of Appeal, would be cited as:

> *Smith v Jones* [2001] EWCA Civ 10 at 59.

The 'neutral citation' will be the official number attributed to the judgment by the court and must always be used on at least one occasion when the judgment is cited in a later judgment. Once the judgment is reported, the neutral citation will appear in front of the familiar citation from the law report series. Thus: *Smith v Jones* [2001] EWCA Civ 10 at [30], [2001] QB 124, [2001] 2 All ER 364, etc. The paragraph number must be the number allotted by the court in all future versions of the judgment. Decisions will still be transferred into one or other of the law reports.

Writing up law reports

Law reports are written up by trained solicitors and barristers who will write out the summary of a case and set out the judgment by reference to exactly what each judge said. Where there is a panel, for example in the Court of Appeal or the Supreme Court, there will be a judgment with full reasons set out by a named judge at the start, followed by commentary from the other judges who tried the case. The decision will have been arrived at by an uneven number of judges to allow for any dissenting opinions to sit alongside the majority decision. Where a judge agrees with or dissents from the majority decision, their commentary or gloss will also be recorded in the law report.

Due to the law of precedent, it will not be usual for decisions of the lower courts, such as the county court, to be reported or referred to (or 'cited') in later cases when arguing a particular point. Some courts and tribunals do keep transcripts of decisions or judgments and in some cases there will also be instances when a decision of a lower court is the only decision or the nearest most helpful decision available on a particular point of law. It will not, however, have the

---

10 This is taken from a High Court Practice Direction: Practice Direction (Judgments: Form and Neutral Citation), 2001.

force of a decision made in the higher courts in attempting to sway a judge.

Citation of judgments or law reports in court

It should be emphasised that both the High Court and the Court of Appeal require that where a case has been reported in the official Law Reports published by the Incorporated Council of Law Reporting for England and Wales, it must be cited from that source. Other series of reports may only be used when a case is not reported in the Law Reports. 'Citation' means the process of an advocate referring to a case they wish to rely on in arguing their client's case before a judge or tribunal.

19.5 Building up a reference system

A new adviser, or one who is starting out on a new advice topic, should at the least have an up-to-date 'overview' or guidance book which they use as a reference for their advice subject, and a subscription to a journal which keeps them in touch with developments in their area of law and related areas. They may, in addition, use search engines to check for any updates on the free sites we referred to above. If they need to read case-law they will hopefully be working in an organisation which subscribes to the case-law reports relevant to that area of advice work or will be regularly checking websites which reproduce case reports, as referred to above. Even where the organisation has a comprehensive reference system, the adviser may supplement this by their own individual one to assist them in keeping up to date. This will vary from one person to another and will depend on what area of legal advice they engage in. Some examples are set out here.

A file of recent cases

The adviser may keep a folder on their computer of recent cases, articles about cases, or case reports which are of particular relevance to the work being done by that adviser. They may have a case running for a number of months on one topic, such as disability discrimination, and will keep a record of all they read on that topic during that period as background reference.

A precedent file

Where the adviser is writing letters or preparing claims for court hearings which are in outline the same, on a regular basis, they may build up a 'bank' of precedents which will be the letter or claim in outline. Some organisations have common banks of such precedents for use by all their case workers.

Peer reviews or mentoring

This can be done informally in the context of team meetings or in contact with other similar organisations and their staff. Views and information can be exchanged about how law or policies are developing in the adviser's practice areas as a means of networking, gaining casework support and keeping up to date with recent developments.

Practitioner meetings

In some areas of legal practice and law there are organisations which function as information exchanges and which hold regular meetings for advisers to discuss or hear a speaker give a talk on a specific topic. Examples are the Housing Law Practitioners' Association (HLPA) or the Immigration Law Practitioners' Association (ILPA). These organisations do not confine themselves to lawyer members. It should be noted, however, that many of these national organisations tend to hold their meetings in London.

Continuing education and training

Some advisers will combine their practice with ongoing development by taking courses or qualifications, as discussed in chapter 2. Some advice practitioners (usually qualified lawyers) will be required to have continuing practice development (CPD) points obtained by attending or delivering training courses and will need to attend a minimum number of hours' training each year. Other advisers will attend short training courses or webinars in order to keep up to date. Training courses are also a useful way of meeting colleagues advising in similar fields and informally exchanging practice experience.

19.6 Using legal research for case preparation

The function of ensuring that research is up to date and accurate is to provide the best possible service to a client seeking advice. As we saw earlier, the adviser will carry out legal research prior to their first client interview. The following checklist of how and where legal research may be carried out is offered as final guidance on this topic:

Checklist: preparing to give legal advice

Topic
- What is the legal topic the client wants advice on?

Legal issue
- How do the facts provided by the client relate to the law and what is the relevant law applicable? For example, if my client has indicated that they are owed money what is the legal basis for their claim? Do they have a contract, for example, with the person they say owes them money?

Statute law
- What does the law say about these types of circumstance? Do I need to check out any statute or regulation to find this out?
- What does that statute or regulation say about this situation? Do I understand what it says or do I need to check this, perhaps by reference to a book or online?

Case-law
- Is there any case-law relevant to this situation? If so, how do the decided cases help my client?
- Do I need to check if there are any more recent cases than the ones I am thinking of – should I take a copy of what those cases say to the interview to refer to when I discuss this with my client?

Preparing to advise
- Am I properly prepared to advise on the legal aspects? Am I aware of the legal issues which are relevant to this claim so that I can ask relevant questions and then if necessary research the law in more depth once I have taken full details from my client in the interview?

The litigant in person

CHAPTER 20

The litigant in person: general advice

20.1   Definition of a 'litigant in person'

20.2   When an opponent is a litigant in person: protocol

20.3   Acting for yourself: survival tips for the litigant in person

20.1   Definition of a 'litigant in person'

'Access to justice is a right not a privilege.' These words open a guide prepared towards the end of 2012 by a group of circuit judges.[1] Concern was expressed at the beginning of the guide as to the growing number of individuals appearing in the civil courts without any legal representation and the difficulty that this clearly poses for that group in navigating themselves though the process of a court case. The guide is aimed at a litigant in person and provides legal and practical information and tips in pursuing or defending the multi-track civil cases, where the financial stakes can be very high.

The expression 'litigant in person' (LiP) has no legal definition. It is sometimes used interchangeably with the phrase 'self-represented litigant' (SRL). Both these descriptions mean the same thing: a person who conducts their own case in any criminal or civil court or any tribunal with no legal representation. The word litigant is based on the concept of 'litigation', where individuals use the court or tribunal system to resolve a legal dispute. There will also be individuals who will conduct legal matters themselves which do not involve litigation.[2] Examples might be proving a will and carrying out the wishes of the person who made the will as their legal executor, or buying and selling property. Given that this is a book aimed at advice centred around litigation, we will not discuss the other legal activities which individuals sometimes conduct without legal assistance, but will devote the final two chapters of the book to the LiP in the civil legal system.

Many people who are LiPs do not take on this role by choice. One reason offered by those providing guidance for the LiP is the substantial reduction in legal aid, and in some cases, the increased costs of litigating in tribunals or courts. In addition, many legal firms, especially smaller ones, have been forced to close or merge due to the loss of income from legal aid, which has reduced choice for potential clients. This malaise has also spread to some barristers' chambers where their income has derived from this source. Welfare benefits cuts and restrictions mean fewer people qualify for legal aid or fee remissions in court but cannot necessarily afford to pay. The result is something of a perfect storm as a result of which the perception in the courts is of increased numbers of LiPs. For the LiP much of the advice

---

1 *A handbook for litigants in person*, available online at the judiciary's website: www.judiciary.gov.uk.

2 This type of activity is usually referred to by solicitors as being 'non-contentious'.

and suggestions covered already in this book should hopefully be as relevant to them as to an adviser, aimed as they are at anyone who needs to use the legal system. That individual will not, however, have had the benefit of skilled and considered legal and practical advice to help them along the path of litigation. Furthermore, an LiP who is required to defend a claim already started against them may feel even more disadvantaged.

As with the guide referred to above, we will offer some form of map-reading of the process of litigation both for the LiP and an LiP's adviser opponent prior to the onset of a court or tribunal hearing and during the conduct of that hearing. Hopefully the precedents in appendix A will assist in the process of preparing claims or cases. Appendix E supplies an overview of some law in term of the types of legal matters with which an LiP may need to engage.

With some exceptions it will usually be less daunting to conduct litigation in person in the tribunal system. There, proceedings tend to be somewhat less formal and the process is one-sided, whereby the individual is asking the tribunal to make a decision based on their view of or representations about an administrative decision. One exception to this concerns appeals in an immigration and asylum tribunal where the law is often very complicated and the stakes (the individual's freedom to remain in the country) are high. In addition, as we saw earlier, the process of the employment tribunals is adversarial which means that they do run along similar lines to a court trial.

As a general reminder of the important matters which those using the court and tribunal system should bear in mind, the following points, already highlighted for the adviser in previous chapters and of equal importance for the LiP should be noted:

- **Is there a choice?** If you are served with forms or claims which mean that you are required to enter into a legal process, you may feel you have no choice but to defend these. Even in this situation there may be a choice. Is there, in truth, a defence or might you have to admit to the other party's case and let them know that? Whether claiming or defending, can you avoid litigation by opting for alternative dispute resolution (ADR), as discussed in chapter 16?
- **Financing the case:** Even if you are not paying for legal advice and representation because you are an LiP, are you fully aware of the costs or fees involved in going ahead? In particular are you aware of the costs which you might have to pay in many civil court claims if you lose the case, as outlined in section 17.3?

- **Time and stress:** Do you have the time set aside from your other commitments to devote to this litigation? Are you able to pace yourself and deal with the inevitable stress of conducting litigation with no professional support and guidance? We saw earlier, in chapter 5, that one of the primary functions of the adviser is to share the burden of a client's case, each aspect of which the LiP will be required to shoulder themselves.

- **Preparation:** We have already seen a number of aspects of preparation which advisers need to do as part of their function. The most important one for the LiP is to follow the exact manner in which the court or tribunal will require preparation for a hearing to be carried out. As an adjunct to that, are you prepared for the ongoing process of engaging in correspondence and drawing up any statements? Any legal process will expect neat and orderly preparation of the case, especially documents, and a focused oral representation at a hearing. Are you the type of individual who can function in this way?

- **Approach to the court and your opponent:** This involves prior consideration of the requirement to bow to the court's control of the process as well as dealing with an opponent or their representative whom you may have come to dislike. In addition, it will be necessary to follow a number of technical and tricky processes in order to come out unscathed at the other end. These features require a blend of self-control and a steep learning curve which you will need to be prepared to take on. You will be expected to focus on the issues before the court rather than your (perhaps very justifiable) sense of grievance. Some LiPs do achieve this in a highly commendable fashion, others less so, often at a great deal of personal and financial cost.

We will cover these points below and in the next chapter. First, we will give you an insight in to what your opponent might be thinking and how they need to approach an LiP.

20.2 When an opponent is a litigant in person: protocol

For the professional adviser faced with an opponent who is an LiP, the process of litigation is likely to be conducted in a more unpredictable and possibly slower fashion which can be time consuming and costly for your client. Some LiPs will display unfamiliarity with the legal process. They may not be able to communicate in an objective manner which the professional adviser is able to, with their distance from the emotions their client has brought to the case.

Sometimes an opponent LiP will ask for advice and help from their professional opponent. They may ask them what they should be doing next or what is likely to happen at court or they might ask for an explanation of the relevant law which the two parties are in dispute over. The same process can often be repeated at court and help sought also from the judge hearing the case. While these requests are usually put very reasonably, a fine balance needs to be exercised in terms of what assistance can or cannot be offered.

A legal adviser representing a client has primary obligations both to their client and to the court. Even when it might appear that time and cost might be saved by assisting the LiP on the opposing side, the adviser cannot act in a manner which gives their opponent any particular advantage over their own client. This means, first, not giving them privileged information.[3] Second, it means that they have no obligation to tell the LiP how they should conduct their own case, including any advice in that respect.

In the judiciary's guidance for the LiP referred to above, it is also confirmed that a judge hearing a case cannot give an LiP any advice or assistance in terms of their case, since the function of the judge is to sit as a neutral arbiter and decide on the dispute between the two parties in a fair and objective manner. There are some, fortunately rare, circumstances in which the LiP who is abusing the court's processes may be prevented from taking certain steps in that or other litigation, as we shall see in the next chapter. However, those instances relate more to where the LiP is simply not using the law in any meaningful way, rather than where they appear to be at sea in terms of the process they are engaged in. With regard to the latter, it is possible for others to offer some general pointers to the LiP.

Guidance offered to practising solicitors concerning the protocol of dealing with an LiP covers this aspect of assistance as well as others and will hopefully be useful to any adviser in this situation.[4] In summary, the advice is:

- If they themselves write a letter before claim to an unrepresented party, they should make it particularly clear that not acting in

---

3 That is, disclosing the contents of any advice or discussions between them and their client about the merits of their client's case or the way in which they have agreed that the adviser will conduct their case – see section 4.4 for guidance on what is confidential between an adviser and their client.

4 See the Law Society's Practice Direction arising out of the Solicitors Regulation Authority (SRA) Code of Conduct at para 11.7.

response to that letter may well incur a costs penalty at a later stage.

- If the LiP seeks information about what the procedures are or how to proceed, they can be referred to a source to find out that information, such as a website link.
- If the matter in dispute involves reference to case reports (usually called 'authorities' as they are meant to be an authority for the correctness of a point being made by a party), the representing solicitor should let the LiP have a copy of those authorities and should do so in plenty of time.
- If there is to be a fully contested hearing in court, the representing solicitor should be prepared to take responsibility for preparing court bundles and copies in readiness for the hearing.
- They should also make sure they keep the LiP opponent informed in good time of steps they are taking, either as required by the court or in order to safeguard their own client's interests.
- They should avoid using technical jargon.
- They should give the LiP ample opportunity to agree costs.

The same Law Society Practice Note from which these guidelines are drawn refers to a requirement on the part of the solicitor opponent not to use their professional status or knowledge in order to take unfair advantage of the opponent who is unrepresented. Although they must put their client's interests first, they cannot use their superior knowledge to gain any back-door advantages. An example of this might be using their knowledge of the court's processes to make surprise applications at a hearing. By the same token, they are guided not to engage in bullying, or misleading or deceitful behaviour with an unrepresented opponent. This will include making claims or demands which unbeknown to the LiP cannot be made in law.

The overall approach, therefore, for the LiP's opponent is that they need to be courteous, accessible and fair but have no obligation to do the LiP's job for them. Thus, the LiP will need as much help as possible from whatever source to get their own house in order.

20.3   Acting for yourself: survival tips for the litigant in person

Assuming that you have embarked on, or are firmly embedded into, some form of dispute or legal process, you will need to have all your wits about you to ensure you reach your intended goal, whatever that might be. In the next chapter we will offer guidance on the practical steps involved in preparing for and taking part in a court case or tribunal, whereby the territory is not your own and the other players in the process will have very different skills from yours and will be far more familiar with the processes. Knowing that to be the case, and that there are limitations on what standards an LiP may be able to achieve, the following tips are offered for survival and to assist in obtaining the correct mindset:

- **Identify the relevant law:** It will be essential to ensure that your claim or case does have a legal basis. An individual who perceives they may have been wronged by another may carry out a search on the internet to find out what the law says about such matters. Although this is a good starting point, it would be helpful to do some more detailed research. The sort of books referred to in chapter 19 as student guides, nutshells or crammers will provide a brief outline of some legal principles and, as long as they are up to date, they will hopefully provide a broad view of those being researched. If you have friends or relatives who are studying law, remember that they are not yet qualified. If you have friends or relatives who are practising lawyers, remember that they will not be insured to give you any legal advice no matter how 'off the cuff' and will therefore be very conflicted if you do approach them for any guidance or advice.

- **Know the relevant processes:** If you think you will end up going to a hearing, find out as much as you can about the court or tribunal and its processes well in advance of that hearing. HM Courts and Tribunals Service website[5] provides a good overview of the functions of courts and links to the tribunals they oversee. It would also be instructive to sit in on a hearing in that particular venue as a member of the public and observe what happens. It is best to ring the court in advance and make sure you will be allowed in as an observer and to ask what time you should arrive. You will also be allowed to make handwritten notes, but try to limit these to what the process is and not what evidence is given as this will relate to legal proceedings which cannot be published.

- **Start to keep a record:** As soon as you believe things are going wrong start to keep a record. This may form future evidence if your case does come to a hearing. There are many examples of situations this will apply to, from noting what you perceive to be a

---

5　See: www.justice.gov.uk/about/hmcts.

builder's poor work on your new house extension, to sexist abuse you are subjected to in the workplace, to potholes in your street causing danger to cyclists and cars. Keep these records in a neat and accessible form. If they are photographs, open an album, if they are emails, open a folder, and so on. You can also record conversations which may be used in evidence but be careful of causing offence to whoever you record. Note however, that with the large volume of paperwork it is now possible to generate, courts and tribunals are beginning to limit how much they are prepared to accept and read (or listen to) as part of a hearing. So, a store of 500 emails which you have amassed and think are all relevant will inevitably need to be filtered down at a later stage to a much smaller (and hopefully still relevant) collection.

- **Be careful about publicity:** Some people who feel aggrieved by the actions of another will want to publicise their opponent's alleged wrongdoing, perhaps to shame them into changing their ways. Social networking sites are visited, and blogs and Twitter feeds used. Apart from any rules the relevant platform may have about what content it will allow, there is more than one reason why this is not a good tactic. First, care has to be taken not to defame anyone. Anything published is capable of amounting to the basis for a claim of libel, and there have, for example, been successful claims made following Twitter feeds being publicised. Even if your opponent does not begin a libel action against you, you may receive a warning letter from their lawyer requiring you to withdraw your comments. Second, it will be important to think about the evidence which you may want to rely on for your claim or defence. You will not want either to disclose that to an opponent prematurely, or to find that a court tells you that your evidence cannot be used as it has been brought out in a way which will affect the conduct of a fair trial. If you do want publicity for whatever reason, contact your local newspaper. Decide if you want to do that before or after the case and why. Newspapers know what they are allowed to publish within the law.

- **Decide on a mode of communication with your opponent:** Even prior to claims or cases beginning, there will often be correspondence flowing between two opposing parties. If it is largely in the form of emails, do not copy lots of other people in, particularly not the court or tribunal you believe your case will be heard in. Courts and tribunals are rarely interested in seeing correspondence between two opponents arguing about the merits of their respective cases. In any event, they rarely read any documentation on the case they are hearing until just prior to the commencement of a hearing. Be careful about copying others into emails, keep the correspondence limited to whom you actually wish to address. If you think it helpful to send an email to someone other than the addressee, ask yourself why and then *forward* your sent email on to them (rather than copying them in to the original email).

- **Allow time for absolutely everything:** If you are going to embark on litigation it will take up a lot of your life for however long it lasts and you will need to find the time for it. By the same token, be wary of litigating 'on the move' and firing off texts and emails to various people wherever you are. As we saw earlier, you need to keep records. The process of litigation is serious and each and every communication should be carefully thought through before it is made.

- **Be flexible:** Be as flexible as you can not only in how you deal with any unforeseen developments in your case but also in terms of trying to agree costs or settle a claim. Keep as calm as you can in the face of fluctuations and hidden snags and try to deal with them in an equable manner. If your opponent's representative offers to settle a case or claim, don't assume that they have a 'hidden agenda' or are trying to trick you into 'giving in'. They are aware of the costs and risk of litigation, as they will have seen it at first hand before. They are also aware of the justice system's requirements to actively consider the use of ADR. So any offers or proposals they make will hopefully not be designed to put you into a corner, but to reach as reasonable and helpful a conclusion as possible. Don't be alarmed if such letters or emails headed 'Without Prejudice'[6] are also accompanied by robust statements of how weak your case is and how strong theirs is. Sometimes this is posturing; see it for what it is and focus on whether you do want to settle and on what basis.

- **Know your limitations:** Assuming you are not a trained or practising lawyer representing yourself, by definition as an LiP you will not have the background necessary to get yourself up to the standard of your opponent's legally-qualified representative. You will need to be realistic about this and not expect to achieve the standard of knowledge which they will have studied for many years to acquire and the practice familiarity which they will have attained

---

6 See sections 16.1, 16.2 and 16.5.

thereafter. They will be more familiar with the process and the law. You do not need to be cowed or overawed by this but you simply need to find your place. Remember you only have one case or hearing on your plate to deal with and they will have many. Furthermore, the sense of having achieved justice if you do succeed against your qualified opponent will be enormously gratifying.

CHAPTER 21

The litigant in person in court or tribunal

21.1 Gathering the facts and documents

Overview

If as a litigant in person (LiP) you do find yourself engaged in court or tribunal as a defendant or respondent, you may find that you have very little time to meet any deadline imposed by the relevant venue to put in your defence or response. Your first priority will have to be to meet that deadline. We will see below how time constraints are an integral part of preparation for hearings. Even if you are in this defensive position you will need to take the time to organise your thoughts and documents. This will be even more the case if you decide yourself to start a claim or application. As we have already seen, courts and tribunals will expect you to put your documents into a specific order and suggestions were made for the advocate preparing for a hearing as to the type of documents and the order they need to be in.[1]

Moving back in time, however, to when the problem arose, it will be necessary to look at the facts and documents side by side. People who go to tribunals are doing so because of a decision that was made by a government body or agency which they want to challenge as being wrong. Those who go to an employment tribunal do so because of some action taken against them or in respect of their rights in their workplace. So, first identify that decision or action. Who took it, how is it recorded in writing. If in a letter, when was it sent to you, what is the date both on the letter and, if you have kept it, the envelope it was in. This is probably your most important document. Start a paper file in a ring binder, and put a copy of that decision in as your first document. Start as you mean to go on. Your file should contain copies only and not originals. You should keep originals in a separate place and leave them completely unmarked. They should not be hole-punched or written on.

> - Identify letter or document which contains the decision or refers to the action you want to challenge.
> - Start a paper file in a ring binder.
> - Take a copy of that document – leave it completely unmarked.
> - Put that copy in as your first page.
> - Keep the original and all originals separate and in a safe place.

Starting with that document, you can then carry out the following two exercises. First, what do you say is wrong with that decision and what

---

1 See section 11.3.

is your story about the background to that decision. Start with the story and then lead up to your view of the decision you are unhappy about. You should write that story up on a computer, if possible. It will most likely later be adapted into a statement to be read by a court or tribunal so set it out in sequence. Start at the beginning of the story and move to the end. Use numbered paragraphs and page numbers for easy reading, both for you as you check it over and later for a tribunal or opponent.

- Start to write up your story – what happened to you – what was the background leading to the decision you are unhappy about.
- Put that story or statement onto a computer.
- Start at the beginning and keep it in sequence.
- Use short paragraphs, number them, use page numbers.
- Start a section in your ring binder called 'My Statement'.
- Put a paper copy of the statement in that section and update it as and when necessary.
- As you write it out you may need to refer to documents which you think are relevant – do so by describing what they are and when they are dated – see next paragraph.

Second, while you are writing up this story you will find that some things you say can be supported by documents, letters or emails which you sent or received. These will include documents sent or received by the government department you want to complain about if that what you are concerned with. Begin to collect these in strict date order, starting with the first in time. Set up a second section in your ring binder and insert these documents, all copied into strict date order. Later you will start to build up more sections, possibly court pleadings and notices or witness statements. At this preliminary stage if you have built up a file in this manner you will have made a good start.

You will, however, need to sort out what facts and documents are relevant. Many people amass documents which they believe to be relevant but which are not.

- Start to collect your documents.
- What are these – letters, emails, notices or other decisions?
- Are they relevant to the story – how do they help to show how the decision affected you or might not be correct?
- Does your statement refer to them by describing them and saying when they are dated?

- Put all these documents in strict date order starting with the earliest on top.
- Take copies of them all – keep the originals safe.
- Start a section in your ring binder called 'documents'.
- Put these documents in that section – add to them as and when necessary.

Example

To summarise and to illustrate this stage of preparation we will look at an example of someone who wishes to challenge a decision made by the Department for Work and Pensions (DWP) about entitlement to jobseeker's allowance (JSA). This is not a simple area of law and no advice on law will be a part of this illustration, which is provided only as a vehicle to show how people deal with decisions and prepare themselves for possible tribunal hearings.

The example offered is that of someone who is refused JSA because they left their job without 'good cause'. There is a letter from the employer sent to the DWP which states that they resigned and the DWP have written to the benefit applicant to state that this is not good cause. The applicant has been refused any entitlement to JSA.

What they should do

1) Find the letter which states they have been refused JSA. Copy and file it.
2) Write down exactly what happened when they decided to leave the job. This should be quite detailed in terms of what they did and said and what their employer did and said and describing how the job came to an end.
3) Collect relevant documents. These might be:
   - a copy of the form they sent to the DWP asking for JSA;
   - a copy of the letter refusing them JSA ('the decision letter' referred to above);
   - a copy of the letter they have received as sent to the DWP by the employer giving their reason as to why that person left the job;
   - copies of any letters passing between them and their employer prior to them leaving their job which refer to the reason why they left the job.

Again, it must be stressed that these documents are only examples in this particular scenario: there are many more complex rules surrounding welfare benefits. These documents will, nevertheless hopefully be of assistance in showing why the person did leave their job as well as going some way to show that they did so for a good reason and that they therefore should be awarded the benefit they are claiming. They all focus around the same issue – why did they leave their job? Note there is no suggestion that any law would need to be brought out as part of the background story. The law which the department is relying on has already been set out in their decision letter and contained within the reason given for the decision.

The initial story, therefore, in relation to an administrative reason or decision will usually focus on the reason for a refusal or denial of a right or benefit. The person affected by the decision will write down as a preliminary statement what they did and why they did it. They will refer to any relevant documents. At the end of that statement they will say that they believe the decision to be wrong and will leave the rest up to the tribunal. The judge or tribunal will decide, based on the additional information they receive from the person affected by the decision, if there is something wrong with the reasoning which they can put right.

21.2   Researching the law

An LiP is unlikely to be able to acquaint themselves with sufficient law in order to compete with a judge or legally-qualified opponent. However, at the very least, they should be able to feel confident that the claim or case they are making does have some basis in law and should have done some basic research as to how that law operates. They will not necessarily need to discuss the law in how they put their case, but to avoid a loss of face and indeed financial penalties it will be helpful to know what the legal basis of an appeal or claim is.

In appendix E some legal outlines are given of the types of claims or cases that individuals may find themselves conducting as an LiP. The choice of topics arises – largely these are the areas of law typically practised either by legal aid lawyers prior to the recent severe reductions in legal aid, or which continue to be practised by not-for-profit agencies, whose resources are now under considerable strain as a result of these reductions and their own funding limitations. Competition, therefore, for free or low cost advice in these areas of law is more fierce than ever before. It is therefore likely that in these areas in particular the courts and tribunals will see more LiPs in the foresee-able future. If your query relates to one of these areas of law, hopefully these notes will be a good starting point for you to understand how the law operates in these areas. These outlines are reproduced with the kind permission of the Bar Council who, like the judiciary, have recently drafted a guide for the litigant in person, which is available online.[2]

21.3 Drafting and preparing the case and dealing with your opponent

We have already referred to two guides for the LiP. Both of these pro-vide helpful advice in how to prepare a claim or case for a hearing in court or tribunal. They each set out guidelines for drawing up a claim against a builder who has not complied with the terms of the agree-ment entered into by the householder. Examples given in both relate to an adversarial approach where there are two parties in opposition, each seeking justice. Even where the process will only involve you challenging an administrative decision, that guidance is likely to be helpful in terms of how you express yourself. Some additional aspects of the process of entering into litigation are covered below.

Entering into the system

- **Forms:** Whether wishing to start off a process or defend a claim, the relevant jurisdiction will have specific forms for users to com-plete. These have been referred earlier in the book in some con-texts as 'pleadings'.[3] In First-tier Tribunals they will usually be called 'forms' or 'applications'. In the civil courts they will usu-ally be called 'statement of claim' or 'defence', but you will need to draft your statement into the relevant civil form. These will be available on the website of the court or tribunal and can usually be downloaded. Note that sometimes you will not be able to save what you put on to these forms, so as soon as you download the form, make a copy of it and in any event keep a backup of what you are drafting.

---

2 *A guide to representing yourself in court*, Bar Council, April 2013, available at: www.barcouncil.org.uk/instructing-a-barrister/representing-yourself-in-court.
3 See glossary in appendix F.

- **Applications:** As well as the core forms which set out the basis of a claim, application or defence, most First-tier Tribunals as well as the civil court system will allow for 'applications' to be made as well. These can vary from asking for documents to be provided to you to asking for more time or an adjournment of a hearing. Whatever you might want to do to change the course of or engage in the process of preparation for a hearing is likely to require you to make some sort of formal approach to that venue. Make sure you know what you need to do, if necessary by calling the relevant venue and asking the administrative staff what procedure you have to follow.

- **Drafting:** Drafting out what you want to claim or how you want to resist or defend a claim does not require you to set out the law. It does require you to set out the facts briefly as you understand them. However, because you have already satisfied yourself that you understand the relevant law to some extent, what you say will be underpinned by some legal basis. This may be as simple as a reference to a contract you entered into or an arrangement you made with someone to carry out a service for you, or what someone else did to cause you an injury or loss of money. Make sure that you therefore set out the relevant facts in short numbered paragraphs which lead you to challenge a decision or seek a remedy. Say in your own words as briefly as possible why you think the decision or action taken against you was wrong or what remedy you want. Note that some guidance in drafting is provided in appendix A which should hopefully be of assistance to both advisers and LiPs.

Engaging with the court or tribunal

As we saw in the previous chapter the system you have entered into will have its own procedures and processes. Make sure you keep up with the process and, overall, make sure you comply with time limits, as a failure to do so may prove to be very problematic. It may mean you cannot proceed further or that you are faced with an application to pay the legal costs wasted by another party as a result of your delay. Costs and how they operate are looked at in brief below and will vary from one jurisdiction to another.

Make sure you keep up with the process of preparation for any hearing as required and keep copies of letters, emails sent and received and notes of telephone calls made, including the date and time of the calls.

You may be required to go to the court or tribunal for a preliminary discussion with a judge which will normally be aimed at discussing what the main hearing is going to be asked to decide on and requiring you and or any opponent to make more preparations prior to that hearing. This can be anything from exchanging copies of each other's documents (or if you are in a First-tier Tribunal, putting your documents in order), to preparing statements, as well as agreeing to a time and date for the main hearing. These preliminary discussions will be fairly formal but will aim to make sure everyone is 'on the same page'. Although you will need to attend these discussions, you will not be expected to present your case or any evidence at them. Lawyers sometimes refer to the process of these preliminary stages as 'house-keeping' which is a useful description since it refers to them as a way of making sure everyone is ready for the main hearing. Take your file with you and a notebook and write down as far as you possibly can what the judge says you need to do to prepare for the hearing. If you don't understand what is being asked of you, say so. Note that if you don't get everything down on paper, the relevant venue will in any event be sending you a letter confirming the contents of that discussion and what you need to do next.

By this time you will have built up the correspondence in your ring binder file, and are likely to have a separate section now which contains copies of the applications or forms used to enter into the system and any orders or preliminary decisions made by the court or tribunal. Start to keep a note of how much time you have spent in preparation since the claim began. If you have lost any pay, for example, as a result of looking after your case, make a note of that too.

At some stage as part of preparing for a hearing (probably after the preliminary court discussion referred to above) you will be expected to re-order your documents in to a specific format required by the venue for a hearing. This is usually known as 'preparing a bundle'. However, as an LiP, if you have a legally qualified opponent they are likely to be expected to organise that bundle and send you a copy ready for the hearing. Some of the correspondence section is likely to be cut back into what is really relevant to the matters being decided by the judge.

- Start a section of your ring binder called 'court or tribunal papers'.
- Take a copy of your completed claim or application before you have send it off, as well as any formal response or defence you receive.
- Start to keep copies of any applications or orders you receive prior to the hearing.
- Keep all these copy documents in strict date order in that section with the earliest on top adding to them as you go along.
- Start a section in your ring binder called 'correspondence'. Keep a copy of any letters or emails you send out or receive and a note of phone conversations.
- Put these in strict date order with the earliest on top.
- Be prepared for this section to be 'pruned' down to what is really relevant for the purposes of the hearing, once the final bundle is drawn up.
- Keep a note of any money you spend on preparation, for example photocopying or travelling – keep receipts.

Dealing with an opponent

As we saw in the previous chapter, solicitors have their own guidance and advice about how to deal with an LiP. They should be courteous with you and while they will not be able to give you any legal advice or tell you how to conduct your own case, they will be able to give you some pointers concerning the procedures involved in preparing for a hearing. You may well find yourself in opposition to a legally-qualified or similarly experienced opponent in the civil court system or, if in a First-tier Tribunal, there may be a representative of the government body who made the decision involved in the process. The government's legal representative may also attend the final hearing in order to justify or explain the decision they have made which you are challenging.

Hopefully, you will be able to deal with that representative in as professional a manner as possible and remember that their job is to ensure they do the best for their client and also have a duty to the court to behave properly and fairly. Some lawyers in litigation do engage in a certain amount of 'posturing' in order to ensure a good outcome for a client, as sometimes portrayed in an exaggerated fashion in TV dramas. This may involve telling you that your case is unmeritorious or warning you that you may have to pay out in legal costs. While this may be a source of irritation for you as you attempt to carry on with a claim or case yourself, it should be seen in that context. By the same token, a reasonably worded call or letter suggesting to you that your case does indeed have less legal merit than you perhaps think it does, or that it could be in your best interests to reach a compromise, should be taken seriously and responded to with care and thought. Remember too that there is always the possibility that open correspondence may end up being shown to a judge at a final hearing, perhaps as part of an application for costs.

21.4 Conducting yourself in a hearing

If there has been no possibility of avoiding a hearing, then you will need to go along and do your part. Hopefully, by the time the hearing date arrives you will have a neat bundle of documents set out, either by an opponent with your co-operation, or by you yourself as required by the relevant tribunal. If you need to give evidence you should also have prepared a witness statement. That will be based on the story or statement you will have begun to prepare at a relatively early stage. It will be in a logical or sequential order to support the position you have already outlined in your claim application or appeal. If you also have other people as witnesses – individuals who saw what happened, for example – you will have asked them to prepare statements too and you will have ensured that they know where the hearing is taking place and that they will arrive in plenty of time. Just prior to the hearing, as though you might be revising for a test, you will have read over the bundle and fully familiarised yourself with it, including all the facts and documents you are relying on in order to ensure the judge sees the issue or dispute from your perspective.

At court or in tribunal you will be guided by the judge or chairman as to what will happen and in what order. You do not need to speak unless spoken to and you should not interrupt a judge no matter how mistaken you think their expressed views or statements are. Nor must you interrupt your opponent. The hearing must be conducted in as calm a fashion as possible. Some do's and don'ts:

- Do wait for guidance and instruction of how the procedure will be followed.
- Do try to address the panel or judge in the approved manner. See the list of titles in section 18.3. If you are in a tribunal or a small claims court and you can't remember what to call the judge it will be fairly safe to address them as Sir or Madam. Don't call them Your Lordship or Your Honour.

- Don't interrupt other people. You will always be given a chance to speak, even though you may need to wait for that chance.
- Don't react when you hear things that you disagree with or you think are untrue or incorrect, by pulling faces or making gestures or comments; try to keep a calm outlook at all times.
- If you are alone (and see below for where you might have a 'Mackenzie friend' with you) try to make notes of what is being said as far as you can. Note that the final decision will be sent to you, usually with full reasons for that decision supplied at the same time.
- If you are asked to give evidence, listen to how you need to do that. You may be asked to read out your witness statement, or you may be told that it has already been noted.
- If you are cross-examined or asked any questions by another party or by the judge or tribunal, listen very carefully and try to answer truthfully and succinctly. Don't answer a question with another question. You will have the chance to ask questions as well.
- If you are invited to ask questions of anyone there, make sure you have prepared these questions in advance. Try to make them short, see if you can elicit any information which might help your case or get another party to admit to any part of your case being correct.
- Don't turn your questions into a speech. The best questions are those which require a simple answer or admission of 'yes' or 'no'.
- You will be invited to make a speech or to sum up at the end of the process. Make sure you prepare that as much as possible in advance. It should focus on how you want the judge or panel to decide and refer to anything which you think might have come out that day which helps your case.
- You may have been handed some legal authorities or case reports by your opponent in advance (see section 20.2). Read those, but don't worry if you have no case reports you can refer to or any clear understanding of their relevance. The judge or tribunal will still have to address the law as part of their decision whether or not they are given any suggestions as to which law is most helpful or relevant.
- Finally, if you are given a decision there and then, whether it is in your favour or not, try to write it down and don't react other than to thank the judge or the tribunal for their decision.

Mackenzie friend

A Mackenzie friend is someone who can come to a hearing with an LiP but who is not their legal representative.[4] They may be someone you know who has studied some law or they may just be a friend or family member. Either way, their role is not to represent but to support. A Mackenzie friend will be recognised by most courts and all tribunals as being a person who can sit next to you, make notes for you of what is happening and, within reason, make whispered suggestions to you of how you can proceed. They are not allowed to address the court or tribunal at all and so they can take no part in the conduct of your case or hearing other than to give you private guidance. If you want someone to be your Mackenzie friend, contact the relevant court or tribunal in advance of the hearing (and your opponent if you have one). Tell them the name of the person and what their relationship is to you and ask them to confirm that they can attend with you as your Mackenzie friend. Once you have that approval, in advance of the hearing you can check over all the documents together and work through your preparation with them. You may also want to rehearse with them any final speech you might want to make or the wording of questions you may wish to raise during the course of the hearing. They will be a useful sounding board in advance and will hopefully be of great support and comfort to you during the hearing itself.

21.5 Final decision made

Decision against you: appeals and costs

At the end of a hearing, or some time after a case has been heard, there will be a decision made which may or may not go in your favour. Once you receive that decision, if it is unfavourable, think very carefully before you start to launch an appeal. Appeals from decisions of a court or tribunal to a higher court are complicated matters – they will always involve considerable consideration and drafting of legal principles and they can be very expensive to lose.

The decision may or may not include an order for costs against you. This depends on the venue, and it might also depend on whether

---

4 Mackenzie was involved in a divorce case in the UK in the 1970s and wished to be assisted by an Australian barrister who had no right of audience to speak on his behalf. The facility of someone being allowed to offer guidance and support but not to address the court was established in that case.

an application has been made for you to pay someone else's costs. Costs in civil court proceedings have been referred to at various points in this book. The simple rule of thumb is that a losing party will usually be required to pay the winning party's costs. This means the costs and fees they will have paid to their lawyers in order to get them to the end of the case. The civil rules allow for a number of circumstances to avoid this hefty penalty. Apart from settling out of court, which was discussed as part of negotiations and alternative dispute resolution (ADR) earlier[5] and would include coming to some arrangement about who pays costs, there are procedures requiring costs budgets to be agreed for some cases and also early resolution procedures as part of conducting the case. How all these various processes operate and which tribunals can make costs orders and for how much, are beyond the scope of this book. If you are involved in a civil claim and you receive letters or proposals about costs, make sure you read them carefully and understand them. If you do end up having to pay legal costs, the court or tribunal may give you time to do so; you will need to ask about this. The court may also assess your opponent's bill as a result of which you may end up paying less. All this needs to be factored into what is known as the risk of litigation.

An adjunct to the cautious approach which an LiP should take to the process of litigation is the power that the civil courts have to prevent some LiPs from carrying on with some claims or cases if they feel that they have no basis in law for doing so. The court will have formed a view that the court system cannot give them the remedy they seek or indeed any remedy.[6] These types of order are made in the civil courts, but some tribunals have similar powers. They can relate to one case that they are party to in that the LiP can be prevented from going any further with that case without the court's permission. A similar order can relate to their ability to conduct any further litigation, usually for a limited period of at least two years. These orders are fortunately the exception rather than the rule, but are worth knowing about and being aware of as they are only likely to be made once a judge has expressed their deep concern as to the merits of the case which the LiP wishes to continue with.

5 See section 15.5 and chapter 16.
6 See Civil Restraint Order: www.justice.gov.uk/courts/civil-restraint-orders.

Decision in your favour and costs

If you receive a decision in your favour, then you will hopefully feel a sense of achievement and justice having been done. You will also hopefully not feel the need to express your delight at the outcome in too extrovert a manner until you have left the court or tribunal room.

In relation to the costs position, you may, as a successful LiP, be able to recover some or all of your outlay in preparing for and attending a hearing, depending on the venue. It was suggested earlier that as an LiP you should start to keep a record of what it is costing you to conduct your own case. In the civil court system and in most tribunals you can take advantage of the Litigants in Person (Costs and Expenses) Act 1975 which allows you to recover sums you have spent in preparing for your case, including expenses or losses incurred as a result. Some tribunals limit the costs that can be recovered and/or operate a similar system under their own rules. The type of expenses or costs you are likely to recover as an LiP are as follows:

- travelling costs;
- stationery costs (stamps, envelopes, files, etc);
- any expenses paid out, such as child or other family care in order to allow you to attend the hearing;
- any loss of income as a result of attending a hearing, including a preliminary hearing.

Some courts allow an hourly rate for attending which is quite low but nevertheless worth claiming. Given that different courts and venues will operate a different approach to paying you, your best approach is to keep a record and to keep all receipts for expenses. At the end of a hearing before you are told the decision, ask if it is possible for you as an LiP to claim your costs and state that you have kept a record of your expenditure. This will be noted by the judge who will be able to factor it in to their decision if they feel it is appropriate. All in all, remember that litigation does not come cheap but that it should continue to be the entitlement of any citizen, with or without legal advice and representation, to access our justice system and to exercise their legal rights and obtain a proper and just outcome to their legal dispute.

APPENDICES

Precedents

CLIENT CARE LETTER
(see chapter 7)

Ms A Client
1 The Street
Anywhere Town
CU2 4IW

Date: xxx

Dear Ms Client

Re: Dry Cleaners Bill: Your Query

Thank you for contacting HelpULaw with your query. I am writing to confirm that we have arranged to meet you on Tuesday June X at X pm here in our offices. Please see the map attached for directions of how to get here and parking facilities.

I will have conduct of your case and am supervised by John Brown who is the team leader in our civil litigation team. Our offices are open from 9.30 to 5.30 from Monday to Friday. Please see our address and other contact details at the top of the page. You can also contact me directly during those hours on my email address and direct line as set out above.

HelpULaw is a charity which does not make a profit. We do however charge for some of our services at an hourly rate. The arrangement we will be able to offer you is the first 2 hours at £25 per hour plus VAT and thereafter a further charge of £20 per hour plus VAT up to a maximum of £160 plus VAT (£210 in total). This amount is limited to initial advice, letter of claim and if necessary issuing and preparing your case in the small claims court. If a hearing is necessary and you wish me to represent you at the hearing I estimate a further four hours' work at the rate of £20 per hour plus VAT. I estimate that I may need to carry out the maximum of ten hours' work on the preparation of your claim. If I need to spend any disbursements on your case, such as court fees for starting or continuing with a claim or enforcing a judgment, these will be payable in addition to our costs. I estimate that your case may take around six to eight months to complete.

We will keep all your matters confidential and will not disclose any information you provide to us except as required by law or as authorised by you.

I should be grateful if you would note that if you have any complaints about our service you can in the first instance send these in writing to our Director Max Green who will endeavour to deal with your complaint within 21 days. If you are still not satisfied with the outcome you may appeal to the Chairman of our Trustee Board Anne White care of our office address and she will inform you of our appeal procedures.

I confirm that you have supplied me with original documents confirming your identity in order for us to comply with the relevant money laundering rules.

I look forward to meeting you and should be most grateful if you would send or bring with you a signed copy of this letter enclosed herewith.

Yours sincerely

James Gray

ADVICE LETTER
(see chapter 15)

Ms A Client
1 The Street
Anywhere Town
CU2 4IW

Date: xxx

Dear Ms Client

Re: Your Query: Gary Reid t/a Kare-full Dry Cleaners

Many thanks for coming to see me yesterday with your query concerning the above service. As promised I am writing to you my advice to follow up what we discussed in our meeting.

Facts

You told me that you took a pair of damask curtains to Kare-full Dry Cleaners to be dry cleaned on X date. You have kept the pink slip issued to you that day. You were quoted a price of £50 by a male shop assistant to have the curtains cleaned. You do not know his name. Before agreeing to leave the curtains you asked the assistant when they would be ready for collection. He told you that they would be ready in around two weeks as they would have to be sent away for cleaning. You asked if they could be done any quicker than that as you wanted them cleaned in preparation for an important business meeting you were holding in your house the following week. Your recollection was that the assistant replied that 'usually we send these away to be cleaned but we can do them here if you like and they will be ready by Friday'. You then agreed to leave the curtains on the basis that they would be ready by Friday.

When you collected the curtains you paid the £50 in cash. You were handed them by the same shop assistant. He made no comment but simply took your money and gave you a receipt which you have kept. When you got home you saw immediately that the curtains had shrunk by approximately ten inches. The curtains were a year old and had been custom made for your living room windows and had cost £350. You have a photograph showing them in place prior to this incident as well as following the dry cleaning.

You returned to the shop first thing on Monday morning and spoke to the proprietor Mr Gary Reid. You showed Mr Reid the curtains and explained that they had shrunk. You asked him for compensation. Mr Reid looked at the curtains and said he was not to know if they had shrunk. He agreed that they had been cleaned on the premises. He said they would normally send curtains like that away to be cleaned and that you would have been told that. A heated conversation then ensued in which you denied that you had been warned as to the risk of having them cleaned on the premises and Mr Reid stating that you had. The shop assistant was also present at this discussion but your recollection was that he did not join in with it. You told Mr Reid that you wanted your £50 back as well as the cost of the curtains as they would need to be replaced. Mr Reid declined to pay you anything and invited you to leave his shop. You then left stating that you would get legal advice and take the matter further. You have had no contact with or from the shop since.

The law

The relevant law relates to your rights as a consumer. Under the Supply of Goods and Services Act 1982 you are entitled to receive a defined quality of service from someone who is carrying out that service as part of their business.

This Act states in Section 13 that the service provided must be carried out with reasonable care and skill. It also refers to a requirement to do the work within a reasonable time and for a reasonable price.

The Act does not specify what is meant by 'reasonable care and skill'. However in the case of a dry cleaner it would mean that an item should be returned keeping its original appearance and size and be cleaner than when it was left to be serviced. If the product has particular features such as a tendency to shrink this should be accommodated by the business as part of exercising their skill.

As a consumer you have also entered into a contract with the dry cleaners. Contracts have 'terms' both 'express' (as set out verbally or in writing) and 'implied' (not written down but nevertheless a part of the contract). The section of the Act I referred to above is what is known as an 'implied' term as it has been implied by law, or statute (ie The Supply of Goods and Services Act). So a consumer can rely on that implied term each time they contract with a business to carry out a service for them. The other terms I refer to above in relation to time and cost are also examples of terms implied by statute.

However there may also be express terms agreed between the parties. An example might be in relation to how the services are to be provided, either on site or at a factory. As part of those terms there may be a term relating to any risk acceptance by a party as to the level of care and skill that the business can offer. However this term would need to be carefully scrutinised as to whether it is in reality an attempt to deny a consumer their rights under section 13 which if it were the case might not be capable of being upheld by the courts.

Advice

In your case, the section 13 term would have applied. You entrusted the curtains to the shop and were entitled to rely on their ability to provide the service as professional dry cleaners to a reasonable standard as required by law. Even if they made a statement to you that they might not be able to guarantee a satisfactory outcome if they carried out the work on their premises, they have nevertheless in accepting the work bound themselves to carry it out to a reasonable standard. The issue is that the service was offered and you were entitled to expect that the curtains would not be damaged. The damage done is evidence that they have not performed the service to the required standards of reasonableness.

They will seek to avoid any liability by relying on the statement made by the shop assistant. Even if a court found that he did make that statement the shop should have tested the curtains before cleaning them on site and if they had any concerns they should have contacted you and declined to carry out the work on site. You would then have had the opportunity to take the curtains elsewhere. However to be absolutely sure that they have not carried out the service to the required standard of the exercise of reasonable skill and care it would be helpful to have the curtains tested with an expert. This person should be able to clarify the chemicals used in the cleaning process and supply advice as to whether these chemicals would have the damaging effect you experienced. This would be advisable should you decide to take the matter to court but would of course involve you in further expenditure.

There are therefore some evidential conflicts between you and the shop and Kare-full may be able to demonstrate to a court that it was an express term of the contract that you would accept any risk involved in having the curtains cleaned on site. For this reason and due to the inevitable risk of any litigation process I would on the facts known to me at present put your chances of success and of recovering the full amount you are seeking at no higher than 60 per cent.

When we met I advised you that your legal remedy would be to pursue the matter in the small claims court where you will seek compensation equivalent to the amount you paid for the cleaning bill as well as the cost of replacing the curtains. You are obtaining an estimate of that cost from the designer who supplied them for you and we will claim that amount. It is possible however that a court may reduce that sum to allow for a year's wear and tear, as I advised you in our interview. If you do issue a claim you will be required to pay an issue fee in the region of £50. If you are successful in your claim you will be awarded compensation equivalent to the cost of the dry cleaning service you paid for and in addition, if the court is satisfied that the curtains are no longer usable, the value of them as bought or replaced. Mr Reid will also have to pay your court fees. He will not be required to repay you any costs you have paid me for advice or representation nor the cost of any expert's fees as costs are not normally recoverable in the small claims court.

You would like me to correspond with Mr Reid and if necessary to issue a small claim against his business for the cost of the cleaning and the value of the curtains. However I have explained that you would need carefully to weigh up the costs in so doing when balanced with the advice I have given you about the value of your claim.

In any event it has been agreed that as a preliminary step you have instructed me to write to Kare-full on your behalf and set out the basis of your claim. This letter is usually referred to as a letter of claim. I will point out that they should not have carried out the work if they did not believe they could do so with reasonable care and skill, and that in accepting the work from you they were agreeing to be bound that statutory implied term. Once you give me the designer's cost estimate for replacement I will attach that to my letter as well as photographs of the curtains before and after the cleaning was carried out by Kare-full. I will ask you to check the contents of my draft letter before it is sent out.

Our initial meeting and the writing of this advice letter and the letter of claim letter is covered by the first two hours' work at the rate of £25 and if a swift settlement ensues as a result of the letter of claim I estimate no more than a further hour's work at the rate of £20. I will however keep you updated as to costs. I confirm that I am holding your money in the amount of £192 in respect of our costs.

You do not wish me to offer any form of resolution to them other than the full cost of the dry cleaning and the replacement cost. Depending on their reply however you may be prepared to settle for a lower sum, mainly to save yourself any further expense in relation to pursuing the matter further.

Please let me know if there are any queries arising from this letter.

Yours sincerely

James Gray

LETTER OF CLAIM
(see chapter 15)

Mr Gary Reid
t/a Kare-full Dry Cleaners
1 High Street
Anywhere Town
CU4 7LW

[Date]

My reference: JG/.Client/1123

Dear Mr Reid

Re Ms A Client: Dry Cleaning Curtains X Date

I should be grateful if you would note that I have been instructed by the above named in relation to a pair of damask curtains which she left with you for dry cleaning on X date and collected once cleaned on Y date.

You will recall that she paid £50 for the service and that when she returned to your shop the Monday after she collected the curtains, she explained to you that they had shrunk by approximately ten inches, a fact which you did not deny. She also told you that she would be unable to use them as they had been custom-made to fit her living room windows. I refer to the two photographs attached to this letter showing the curtains before and after cleaning. During that discussion you declined to accept any liability for the damage occasioned by the cleaning and indicated that she had been warned of the risk when she left the curtains with you.

I have advised my client that you owe her a duty under section 13 of the Supply of Goods and Services Act 1982 to carry out the service of dry cleaning her curtains exercising reasonable skill and care and that you have failed in that duty. The damage done to the curtains means that they are now unusable.

I am instructed that your shop assistant was told that my client required the curtains to be ready for collection in a matter of days. As a result he offered to have them ready by Friday of the same week. He told her that it was usual for you to send items like this away to be cleaned but that he would be able to clean them on site in order to have them ready by Friday. At no time did he point out to her any risk in cleaning the curtains on site. Even had he done so, he agreed to carry out the work. Your business was thereby accepting that it was bound by the implied term as to skill and care referred to in the above statute.

I also enclose an estimate by Ms Client's curtain designer showing that the cost of replacing the curtains will £450. I have advised her that were she to take this matter to the small claims court she would be successful in her claim. She would be awarded compensation of £50 being the cost of the dry cleaning together with compensation of the replacement cost of £450, totalling £500. She will also be awarded a reimbursement the return of her court issue fee by you.

I should be grateful if you would take this letter as my client's Letter of Claim and acknowledge it as such. She looks forward to receiving a full admission of liability and an agreement to pay her the sums claimed in this letter in order to save the further costs and expense which will be involved in taking this matter to the small claims court.

Please direct any response to this letter to me as Ms Client's legal adviser. If I do not receive any response or any satisfactory response within the next 21 days my client will have no option but to issue a claim in the small claims court in Anywhere County Court.

Yours faithfully.

James Gray
HelpULaw

STATEMENT OF CLAIM
(see chapters 11, 17 and 21)

IN THE ANYWHERE COUNTY COURT

STATEMENT OF CLAIM

1. The Claimant entered in an agreement with the Defendant business to provide her with a service, namely the dry cleaning of a pair of damask curtains on X date.

2. The Claimant collected the curtains on Y date. The curtains had shrunk by approximately ten inches as a result of the dry cleaning service carried out for the Claimant by the Defendant.

3. The Claimant is no longer able to use the curtains as they were custom made for her living room windows and are now too short.

4. The Claimant states that it was an implied term of the agreement that she entered into with the Defendant that the Defendant would carry out the service of dry cleaning her curtains with reasonable care and skill.

5. The Claimant further states that the Defendant has failed to comply with their duty and that as a result she has suffered loss and damage.

6. The loss and damage that the Claimant has suffered amounts to the cost of the dry cleaning which was £50 and the cost of replacing the curtains, which sum amounts to £450.

The Claimant relies on her rights under section 13 of the Supply of Goods and Service Act 1982 and seeks £500 by way of compensation from the Defendant, together with her fees incurred in issuing these proceedings.

Signed on behalf of the Claimant by James Gray, HelpULaw of
[Address]
dated X.

DEFENCE TO CLAIM
(see chapters 11, 17 and 21)

I am writing this as best as I can as I am trying to run a business. I have already received threats and threatening letters from this lady and her adviser.

I absolutely deny any liability for her alleged ruined curtains.

I agree that I have to carry out a good job on any dry cleaning job I accept. My assistant made it very clear to this lady that he could not guarantee what might happen if we cleaned the curtains on site as we always send away long curtains to a specialist cleaning service and it takes at least two weeks for them to come back.

This lady absolutely insisted she wanted the job done by Friday. She would not take no for an answer and said that she had left things with us before and it had always been fine in the past. Andre said that he could not guarantee a perfect job but we would take the job on as she was a good customer. She said that was OK, left the curtains and she collected them on the Friday. She made no complaint until the Monday and for all I know she may have washed them over the weekend and shrunk them herself. I believe we did a good job and that her curtains were cleaned properly. I cannot accept any responsibility for her allegations that we are responsible or that any damage has been done.

I can't afford to sully my reputation by giving in to such a flimsy and spurious claim and I hope that the judge will agree that her case is too full of holes and that I acted in a professional manner. I want her to pay all my legal costs as well.

Signed Mr G Reid
Kare-full Dry Cleaners
Address
date

LETTER TO LITIGANT IN PERSON
(see chapter 20)

Mr G Reid
Kare-full Cleaners
1 High Street
Anywhere Town
CU4 7LW

[Date]

My reference: JG/client /1123

Dear Mr Reid

Re: Ms A Client v Yourself: Case No 445566/14: Anywhere County Court

I refer to your Defence in the above case now received and discussed with my client. It is unfortunate that you were not able to reply to the letter of claim I sent you on X date and that proceedings have now been issued.

In relation to your Defence my client is unable to accept that she was warned of any risk when she left the curtains with you for cleaning. She also instructs me that when she collected the curtains on that Friday the shop was about to close. She did not take them out of their wrapping until Saturday evening when she discovered the shrinkage. She then came to see you with her complaint as soon as you opened the shop on Monday morning. I have advised her that her evidence on both these matters will be accepted by the court.

I should also be grateful if you would note that even were you to successfully defend her claim you will not be entitled to recover the costs of defending this case as costs are not usually recoverable in the small claims court.

I now attach a report obtained showing that the chemicals used on the curtains (which have never been cleaned before) would be likely to cause colour fading or shrinkage or both. Please acknowledge safe receipt.

I also attach a List of Documents as well as my client's witness statement and look forward to your confirmation that you agree the contents of the List. If you do I will prepare three copies of these documents ready for the hearing in two weeks. Please let me have any copy witness statements you have prepared.

Yours faithfully

James Gray

LIST OF DOCUMENTS
(see chapters 11 and 21)

IN THE ANYWHERE COUNTY COURT   CASE NO: 445566/14

BETWEEN:

MS A CLIENT

Claimant

and

MR G REID T/A KARE-FULL DRY CLEANERS

Defendant

LIST OF DOCUMENTS

No	Document	Date	Page
1.	Pink collection slip: Defendant	3.3.14	1
2.	Receipt for £50 paid: Claimant	7.6.14	2
3.	Photograph of damask curtains in situ at Claimant's home	25.2.13	3
4.	Ditto	9.3.14	4
5.	Invoice new curtains: Design-a-Hang	1.3.13	5
6.	Estimate to supply and fit new curtains: Design-a-Hang	15.3.14	6
7.	Report: ChemicalLabs Berkshire UK	12.4.14	7
8.	Letter of Claim: HelpULaw to Defendant	20.4.14	8

WITNESS STATEMENT
(see chapters 11, 17 and 21)

IN THE ANYWHERE COUNTY COURT   CASE NO: 445566/14

BETWEEN:

MS A CLIENT

Claimant

AND

MR G REID T/A KARE-FULL DRY CLEANERS

Defendant

WITNESS STATEMENT OF THE CLAIMANT

Ms A client of [ADDRESS] will say:

1. I am the Claimant in this matter and I make this statement believing the facts stated in it to be true.

2. I bought a new pair of green damask curtains for my living room in early 2013 as part of redecorations to my house. They were fitted and custom made by a local fabric designer called Design-a-Hang. I have kept the receipted invoice for £350 which is at page 5 of the bundle.

3. I am self-employed and make and sell soft toys. I work from home where I sometimes see business clients. Given that my income is unstable it is important for me to ensure that my meeting area in the living room looks professional when I see clients and hope to get new orders.

4. I had an important meeting in my home with a number of potential clients arranged for Tuesday March 11th. It had only been set up the previous week.

5. I wanted my furnishings to look good for the meeting and so I decided among other things that I would get the living room curtains cleaned.

6. Accordingly I went to my local dry cleaners, Kare-full, on the High Street on Tuesday 4th.

7. I had used the dry cleaners on a number of previous occasions before to have clothes cleaned and had been quite satisfied with their service.

8. When I went in with the curtains Mr Reid the proprietor was not in his usual place behind the counter. There was a young man there who did not appear to speak very good English.

9. I asked how much the curtains would cost to clean and he told me £50 as they were 'good quality curtains'. I felt that was a fair price.

10. I then asked when they would be ready for collection. The young man said about two weeks as they would have to send them away for cleaning.

11. I queried that as I had never been told before that items were not cleaned in the shop. I said 'Do you think I can have these back by Friday or even Monday at the latest as I need them for Monday evening?' The young man said 'Alright we can do that. Usually we send these away but if you like I can have them ready for you by Friday'. He did not say why the curtains should

be sent away and he did not say that there was any risk involved in cleaning them on site.

12. I therefore said that would be fine and I would be back on Friday to collect them. He gave me a pink collection slip (see page 1) and said 'no deposit you are good customer'.

13. I arrived five minutes before the shop was due to close on the Friday to collect my curtains. The same young man handed them over to me and I gave him the £50. I said 'All OK?' or words to that effect and he smiled and said 'Of course Madam, have good weekend'. I have kept the till receipt – see page 2.

14. As soon as I got home I had to go and visit an elderly relative who had been admitted to hospital out of London. I stayed overnight and did not return home again until the Saturday evening.

15. Later that evening I took the curtains out of their wrapping. I could see straight away that they had shrunk. The next day, with the help of Malcolm my neighbour I got them hung and they had shrunk by around ten inches. We took a photograph of them and then took them down. See page 4. I also found a marketing photograph I had had taken when the curtains were new the previous year and had kept – see page 3.

16. On Monday as soon as the shop opened I went in to Kare-full with the curtains. Mr Reid was in the shop and the same young man was sitting at the back. I told Mr Reid what had happened. He held up his hand and said 'Look lady I have got no proof that these curtains have shrunk'. I told him it was a fact and that I had photographs at home to prove it.

17. He then said that I might have washed them myself over the weekend and shrunk them. I said that was nonsense. I said I wanted a refund for the dry cleaning costs and I wanted him to pay for the cost of new curtains. He said that was not going to happen. He said we always send curtains like this away to be cleaned. I told him that the young man had said they could clean them on site and the young man just shrugged. He looked very nervous as though he might lose his job. Mr Reid then said he was busy and that I had better leave the shop, I said I would be taking the matter further and left.

18. My meeting went ahead as planned on the Tuesday but I had no curtains at the window and to me it looked cheap and embarrassing.

19. I have obtained an estimate from Design-a-Hang for supplying replacement curtains which will cost me £450. See page 6. I have also obtained a lab report which shows that Kare-full used the wrong chemicals to dry clean the curtains. I assume that this young man may have had something to do with all this as he may have been new and not understood the right way to deal with the customer or how to dry clean my curtains.

20. I pass the dry cleaning shop quite often on my way to the bread shop and I have never seen that young man again. I assume he has lost his job as a result of this incident.

I believe that the facts in this witness statement are true.

Signed

Dated

LETTER WITHOUT PREJUDICE
(see chapter 15)

To James Gray
Adviser
HelpULaw
Anywhere Town

Date
My reference

Dear Mr Gray

Ms A Client v Gary Reid t/a Kare-full Dry Cleaners

WITHOUT PREJUDICE

I refer to next week's hearing in the small claims court of your client's claim for £500 against Mr Gary Reid. Mr Reid has sought my advice on this and in order to avoid the time and possible expense of a hearing has asked me to make a proposal to settle your client's claim.

Mr Reid cannot accept any liability for any alleged damage to your client's curtains. He has interviewed all the staff on his premises involved in this transaction. The shop assistant gave your client a very clear warning of the risk she was taking in asking for the curtains to be cleaned on site. The machine operator nevertheless took great care to ensure that the temperature used and the chemicals used were of the right level for a job of this nature. Furthermore it is noted that she did not return with her complaint until two days had elapsed which calls into doubt whether it was my client's service which was responsible for the alleged shrinkage. Her expert evidence and photographs are therefore unlikely to assist her in showing that our client either caused the damage or fell below the necessary standard in carrying out this service.

Nevertheless in order to show good will and because she is a regular customer Mr Reid is prepared to refund to your client the £50 cost of the cleaning in full and final settlement of this dispute.

This offer remains open until 5 pm on Friday of this week.

I look forward to your response.

Yours faithfully

Karl Black
AllLawInc

LETTER TO CLIENT CONCLUDING CASE
(see chapters 12 and 15)

Ms A Client
1 The Street
Anywhere Town
CU2 4IW

Date: xxx

My Ref: AC/JG/112233

Dear Ms Client

Re: Yourself v Gary Reid t/a Kare-full Dry Cleaners

I refer to our recent discussions concerning a settlement of this case and our telephone conversation last night I am writing to confirm that you have now agreed to accept the sum of £250 in full and final settlement of your claim against Mr Reid.

As you know we reached this position having first of all received an offer of £50. There then ensued a number of calls and emails exchanged 'Without Prejudice' between myself and Mr Black concerning the respective risks and merits of each case. You have accepted my advice that a judge may uphold Kare-full's argument that you were warned of the risk of cleaning the curtains on site if you wished them to be done in a few days. It is also possible that if you were to succeed in your claim the judge would not award you the full replacement value of the curtains as compensation allowing for the fact that they were a year old when this incident occurred.

Factoring in that advice as well as that relating to the costs and risk associated with litigation, you authorised me to obtain a settlement for less than the £500 claimed but to include a sum towards the replacement costs as well as the dry cleaning costs.

While not conceding that you accepted any risk in leaving the curtains I was able to persuade Mr Reid's adviser that there is an element of risk in leaving the matter to be decided by a judge and that there are inherent difficulties with his client's defence in that he accepted the curtains for cleaning and has seen the report you obtained from ChemicalLabs. I also pointed out that further legal costs would be incurred by both parties should the matter proceed to a hearing.

His client has therefore agreed to go part way to meeting the cost of replacing your curtains up the amount of £200 to include the dry cleaning costs. He has also agreed to include a refund of your court issue fee of £50 on the basis that he did not respond to your letter of claim, thus bringing the total offered and accepted up to £250.

It has been agreed that you will be sent this sum by way of a cheque within 21 days to your home address. I have contacted the court and they are aware that the case has settled and will adjourn the hearing listed for next week for 28 days and await confirmation from me that your claim is to be withdrawn. You do not wish this agreement to be reflected in a court order and neither does Mr Reid to preserve your business reputations.

Please can you confirm agreement to the contents of this email by return so that I can finalise matters with the court and Mr Black.

I can also confirm that I estimate my time spent will be five hours totalling £126 and that I will be reimbursing you with the amount of £128 being held in anticipation of further costs.

Yours sincerely

James Gray

Useful organisations

Government departments and agencies

Department for Business, Innovation and Skills (formerly BERR, formerly DTI)
1 Victoria Street
London SW1H 0ET

Tel: 020 7215 5000
E-mail: enquiries@bis.gsi.gov.uk
Website: www.gov.uk/government/organisations/department-for-business-innovation-skills

Department for Communities and Local Government
Eland House
Bressenden Place
London SW1E 5DU

Tel: 0303 444 0000
E-mail: contactus@communities.gsi.gov.uk
Website: www.gov.uk/government/organisations/department-for-communities-and-local-government

Department for Education (formerly DFES)
Ministerial and Public Communications Division
Department for Education
Castle View House
East Lane
Runcorn WA7 2GJ

Tel: 0370 000 2288
Contact form: www.education.gov.uk/help/contactus
Website: www.gov.uk/government/organisations/department-for-education

Department of Health
Ministerial Correspondence and Public Enquiries Unit
Department of Health
Richmond House
79 Whitehall
London SW1A 2NS

Tel: 020 7210 4850
Textphone: 020 7210 5025
Contact form: www.info.doh.gov.uk/contactus.nsf/memo?openform
Website: https://www.gov.uk/government/organisations/department-of-health

Home Office
Direct communications unit
2 Marsham Street
London SW1P 4DF

Tel: 020 7035 4848
E-mail: public.enquiries@homeoffice.gsi.gov.uk
Website: www.gov.uk/government/organisations/home-office
See www.gov.uk/government/organisations/border-force for the Border
Force.

Ministry of Justice
102 Petty France
London SW1H 9AJ

Tel: 020 3334 3555
E-mail: general.queries@justice.gsi.gov.uk
Website: www.gov.uk/government/organisations/ministry-of-justice

Government agencies and legal services

Citizens Advice – consumer advice (formerly Consumer Direct)
3rd Floor North
200 Aldersgate Street
London EC1A 4HD

Citizens Advice consumer helpline: 08454 04 05 06
Website: www.adviceguide.org.uk/england/consumer_e.htm

Employment Appeal Tribunal
2nd Floor
Fleetbank House
26 Salisbury Square
London EC4Y 8AE

Tel: 020 7273 1041
Website: www.justice.gov.uk/tribunals/employment-appeals

Health and Safety Executive
Tel: 0300 3031 1747
Website: www.hse.gov.uk

HM Courts and Tribunals Service
5th Floor
Clive House
Petty France
London SW1H 9EX

Tel: 020 7189 2000
Website: www.gov.uk/government/organisations/hm-courts-and-tribunals-
service
See website for court telephone numbers and addresses.

Legal Aid Agency (formerly Legal Services Commission)
Website: www.gov.uk/government/organisations/legal-aid-agency
Civil legal advice: 0845 345 4345

National organisations

Advice Now
Website: www.advicenow.org.uk/

Advice Services Alliance (ASA)
Tavis House (Floor 7)
1–6 Tavistock Square
London WC1H 9NA

Tel: 07904 377460
Email: admin@asauk.org.uk
Website: http://asauk.org.uk/

Advice Services Alliance (ASA) – advice on alternative dispute resolution (ADR)
Website: http://asauk.org.uk/alternative-dispute-resolution/
This is not an ADR service but provides an overview of the options available.

AdviceUK
WB1
PO Box 70716
London EC1P 1GQ

Tel: 0300 777 0107 or 0300 777 0108
Website: www.adviceuk.org.uk/

Advisory, Conciliation and Arbitration Service (Acas)
Helpline: 08457 47 47 47
Helpline Online: www.acas.org.uk/index.aspx?articleid=1339
Website: www.acas.org.uk

Age UK
Tel: 0800 169 6565
Contact form: www.ageuk.org.uk/contact-us/
Website: www.ageuk.org.uk/

Bar Council
289–293 High Holborn
London WC1V 7HZ

Tel: 020 7242 0082
Website: www.barcouncil.org.uk/

Bar Pro Bono Unit
The National Pro Bono Centre
48 Chancery Lane
London WC1V 6JQ

Tel: 020 7611 9500
E-mail: enquiries@barprobono.org.uk

Contact form: www.barprobono.org.uk/new_contact_us.html
Website: www.barprobono.org.uk/

Chartered Institute of Legal Executives (CILEx) (formerly Institute of Legal Executives)
Kempston Manor
Kempston
Bedford MK42 7AB

Tel: 01234 841000
Website: http://www.cilex.org.uk/

Child Poverty Action Group
94 White Lion Street
London N1 9PF

Tel: 020 7837 7979
E-mail: info@cpag.org.uk
Website: www.cpag.org.uk/

Citizens Advice
Tel: 08444 111 444
Website: www.citizensadvice.org.uk/
Adviceguide: www.adviceguide.org.uk/england.htm
See website for details of bureaux and regional offices.

Coram Children's Legal Centre
Head office:
Riverside Office Centre
Century House North
North Station Road
Colchester CO1 1RE

London office:
48 Mecklenburgh Square
London WC1N 2QA

Advice line: 08088 020 008
Tel: 01206 714 650
E-mail: info@coramclc.org.uk
Website: www.childrenslegalcentre.com

DIAL Network – local disability information and advice
Tel: 0130 231 0123
Website: www.scope.org.uk/dial

Equality and Human Rights Commission
Hepline: 0808 800 0082
Website: www.equalityhumanrights.com/

Free Representation Unit
Ground Floor
60 Gray's Inn Road
London WC1X 8LU

Tel: 020 7611 9555
Contact form: www.thefru.org.uk/contact-us
Website: www.thefru.org.uk

Institute of Money Advisers (IMA)
4 Park Court
Park Cross Street
Leeds LS1 2QH

Tel: 0113 242 0048
Contact form: www.i-m-a.org.uk/contact-us
Website: www.i-m-a.org.uk

Joint Council for the Welfare of Immigrants
115 Old Street
London EC1V 9RT

Tel: 020 7251 8708
Website: www.jcwi.org.uk/

Law Society
113 Chancery Lane
London WC2A 1PL

Tel: 020 7242 1222
Contact form: www.lawsociety.org.uk/get-in-touch/
Website: www.lawsociety.org.uk/

Law Centres Network
Tel: 020 7749 9120
Contact form: www.lawcentres.org.uk/contact-us
Website: www.lawcentres.org.uk/

LawWorks (formerly Solicitors Pro Bono Group)
National Pro Bono Centre
48 Chancery Lane
London WC2A 1JF

Tel: 020 7092 3940
Website: www.lawworks.org.uk/

Money Advice Service
Holborn Centre
120 Holborn
London EC1N 2TD

Advice line: 0300 500 5000
Website: www.moneyadviceservice.org.uk

Refugee Council
Contact details: www.refugeecouncil.org.uk/contact
Website: https://www.refugeecouncil.org.uk
See website for regional and specific offices and advice line details.

Refugee Legal Centre
Website: www.refugee-legal-centre.org.uk
See website for regional and specific offices and advice line contact details.
RLC offer walk-in advice sessions.

Rights of Women
52–54 Featherstone Street
London EC1Y 8RT

Tel: 020 7251 6577
Contact information: www.rightsofwomen.org.uk/adviceline.php
Family law advice line: 020 7251 6577
Criminal law (including sexual violence) advice line: 020 7251 8887
E-mail: info@row.org.uk
Website: www.rightsofwomen.org.uk

Shelter
Helpline: 0808 800 4444
Website: http://england.shelter.org.uk
See website for Shelter Cymru, Scotland and NI.

Solicitors Regulation Authority (SRA)
Tel: 0870 606 2555
Contact form: www.sra.org.uk/contact-us
Website: www.sra.org.uk
See website for details of regional offices.
See www.sra.org.uk/solicitors/handbook/code/content.pagefor SRA Code of
Conduct.

Youth Access
1–2 Taylors Yard
67 Alderbrook Road
London SW12 8AD

Tel: 020 8772 9900
E-mail: admin@youthaccess.org.uk
Website: http://youthaccess.org.uk

Practitioner associations

Employment Lawyers' Association
Tel: 01895 256972
Contact form: www.elaweb.org.uk/forms/contactus
Website: www.elaweb.org.uk

Discrimination Law Association
Tel: 0845 478 6375
E-mail: info@discriminationlaw.org.uk
Website: www.discriminationlaw.org.uk

Housing Law Practitioners Association
Website: www.hlpa.org.uk

Immigration Law Practitioners' Association
Tel: 020 7251 8383
E-mail: info@ilpa.org.uk
Website: www.ilpa.org.uk

Resolution (formerly Solicitors Family Law Association)
Tel: 01689 820272
E-mail: info@resolution.org.uk
Website: www.resolution.org.uk

Resources for legal information

British and Irish Legal Information Institute (BAILII)
Website: www.bailii.org

legislation.gov.uk
Website: www.legislation.gov.uk

Rightsnet
Website: www.rightsnet.org.uk

Courses and training

General

Skills for Justice
Distington House
26 Atlas Way
Sheffield
S4 7QQ

Tel: 0114 261499
Website: www.sfjuk.com

The standards-setting body for the justice sector. The Skills for Justice legal advice toolkit is available for download.

Vocational training

Advice[UK]
WBI
PO Box 70716
London EC1P 1GQ

Tel: 0300 777 0107
E-mail: training@adviceuk.org.uk
Website: www.adviceuk.org.uk

The only advice sector based Advice NVQ Assessment Centre approved by City & Guilds.

Chartered Institute of Legal Executives (CILEX)
Kempston Manor
Kempston
Bedfordshire MK42 7AB

Tel: 01234 841 1000
E-mail: info@cilex.org.uk
Website: www.cilex.org.uk

Child Poverty Action Group
94 White Lion Street
London N1 9PF

Tel: 020 7837 7979
E-mail: info@cpag.org.uk
Website: www.cpag.org.uk/

Short courses in welfare rights training

Legal Action Group
3rd Floor
Universal House
88–94 Wentworth Street
London E1 7SA

Tel: 020 7833 2931
E-mail: lag@lag.org.uk
Website: www.lag.org.uk

One-day courses in areas of social welfare law

Rightsnet training
3rd Floor
Universal House
88–94 Wentworth Street
London E1 7SA

Tel: 020 7377 2748
E-mail: training@lasa.org.uk
Website: www.rightsnet.org.uk

One-day courses in welfare benefits

Legal advice qualifications

(Skills for Justice/Citizens Advice)
Website: www.sfjawards/portfolio-category/legal-services
or www.citizensadvice.org.uk

Academic courses

Birmingham City University
City North Campus
Birmingham
B42 2SU

Website: www.bcu.ac.uk

HND in legal studies

Peterborough Regional College
Park Crescent
Peterborough PE1 4DZ

Tel: 0845 872 8722
E-mail : info@peterborough.ac.uk
Website: www.peterborough.ac.uk

ILEX certificate/Professional Diploma in law and practice

Truro College
College Road
Truro
Cornwall TR1 3XX

Tel: 01872 267122
E-mail: heinfo@truro-penwith.ac.uk
Website: www.truro-penwith.ac.uk

Foundation Degree in law (FdSc Law) with business and advice based content (Full time: two years)

Staffordshire University
College Road
Stoke on Trent
Staffordshire ST4 2DE

Tel: 01782 294000
E-mail: admissions@staffs.ac.uk
Website: www.staffs.ac.uk

Various degree courses in advice (BA/MA) (Hons)

University of Wales
College Street
Lampeter
Ceredigion SA48 7 ED

Tel: 01570 422 351
Website: www.trinitysaintdavid.ac.uk

Certificate of Higher Education in Advocacy (community advocacy)

National Occupational Standards for Legal Advice[1]

These are be found in the Skills for Justice National Occupational Standards in the suite 'Legal Advice'. There are a number of 'generic' standards and also standards relating to advice-giving in all the key areas of social welfare law, including housing, education, welfare benefits and debt, immigration and asylum and employment law.

For the purposes of this book a table is provided of the generic standards most relevant to the topics covered. Each of these standards is also reproduced in this appendix.

Thereafter a full list is provided of the standards in the Legal Advice suite which existed at the time of publication and prior to any changes which may have come about as a result of the standards review commenced in 2013.

Table of Generic Standards

STANDARD	RELEVANT CHAPTER
SFJGA6: Develop and manage interviews with clients	Chapter 9
SFJIA1: Provide legal advice to clients	Chapter 10
SFJIA2: Manage legal advice cases	Chapter 12
SFJHA5: Manage personal caseload	Chapters 8 and 12
SFJDA3: Act on behalf of clients in informal proceedings	Chapter 11
SFJDA7: Prepare cases for representation in formal proceedings	Chapter 16
SFJDA4: Represent clients in formal proceedings	Chapter 16
SFJAB3: Facilitate communication using interpreters	Chapter 6

Here each of these is reproduced from the NOS Skills for Justice website.

[1] See http://nos.ukces.org.uk.

SFJGA6
Develop and manage interviews with clients

Overview

This standard is about establishing a supportive working relationship with clients and helping them to explain their needs in interviews. You will need to be able to make clients feel at ease and also be able to explore any additional information about clients, which may be important in providing appropriate help. You must also be able to recognise when there is a need to take immediate action and follow appropriate processes for doing so. You may also have to cope with clients who are abusive or violent and must know how to do this safely.

There are three elements

1   Enable clients to explore their problems and concerns
2   Manage interview processes
3   Bring interviews to an end

SFJGA6
Develop and manage interviews with clients

Performance criteria	**Enable clients to explore their problems and concerns**

You must be able to:	P1	create an environment where clients feel comfortable to express their problems and concerns
	P2	establish with clients whether other services provide them with advice and support, and:
	P2.1	address any related issues in line organisational procedures
	P3	identify clients circumstances, responsibilities and priorities in line with organisational requirements
	P4	provide clients with opportunities to explore their issues in line with their needs
	P5	establish the nature and scope of issues raised by clients in line with information provided
	P6	summarise clients' issues in line with their requirements, and:
	P6.1	check your understanding
	P7	identify situations where immediate action is required to assist clients in line with their needs and:
	P7.1	take appropriate action in line with organisational requirements
	P8	identify where clients may be excluded from receiving services in line with organisational requirements

Manage interview processes

You must be able to:	P9	provide suitable opportunities for clients to contribute to discussions in interviews in line with organisational requirements
	P10	encourage clients to provide additional information in line with their situation or needs
	P11	respond to clients at each stage during interviews in line with their immediate needs
	P12	provide suitable feedback to reassure clients of continued attention during interviews
	P13	provide reassurance to clients when they display signs of increased stress during interviews
	P14	identify problems with maintaining interactions during interviews, and:

SFJGA6

Develop and manage interviews with clients

P14.1   take appropriate action to address problems

P15   follow organisational health and safety and risk-assessment procedures when managing interviews

P16   respond to difficult or challenging clients in line with organisational requirements, and in ways that:

P16.1   sustain interviews

P16.2   minimise difficult behaviour

P17   end interviews safely in line with organisational requirements

Bring interviews to an end

You must be able to:

P18   provide opportunities for clients to end interviews in line with their needs

P19   manage tensions between time, resources and clients' needs

P20   provide assurance to clients that their decisions will be respected after interviews

P21   summarise discussions and outcomes of interviews in line with clients' requirements, and:

P21.1   check client's understanding

P22   identify opportunities for providing further support to clients in line with organisational requirements

P23   record interview outcomes and agreed actions in line with organisational requirements

SFJGA6
Develop and manage interviews with clients

Knowledge and understanding

You need to know and understand:

K1 the types of atmosphere and environment that are appropriate to different clients

K2 what situations could make clients feel uncomfortable and how to minimise them

K3 organisational procedures for when clients are receiving advice and support from another agency and why it is important to establish this

K4 why it is important to recognise clients' circumstances and priorities

K5 ways of providing opportunities to clients for exploring issues

K6 issues that may occur and how they should be explored

K7 ways of establishing the nature and scope of different issues

K8 how to summarise issues

K9 situations that require immediate action and how to deal with them

K10 reasons why clients may be excluded from services and organisational procedures for addressing this

K11 reasons why clients may not be eligible to receive services

K12 how to provide opportunities for clients to contribute to interviews

K13 the type of information that should be obtained from clients

K14 why it is important to respond to clients at regular intervals

K15 what type of indications of reassurance are appropriate for clients

K16 organisational guidelines and procedures for providing client responses

K17 how to recognise the signs of increased stress in clients and what the significance of this may be

K18 types of problems that could occur and how to address them

K19 why it is important to address problems

K20 organisational health and safety and risk-assessment procedures related to different interview procedures

K21 ways that clients may display difficult or challenging behaviour and ways of minimising this

K22 organisational procedures for ending interviews with abusive or violent clients

K23 the relevant national, local, professional and organisational requirements relating to:

SFJGA6

Develop and manage interviews with clients

K23.1	equal opportunities
K23.2	discrimination
K23.3	health and safety
K23.4	security
K23.5	confidentiality
K23.6	data protection
K23.7	conflicts of interest

K24 the importance of complying with national, local, professional and organisational requirements

K25 how clients might signal their desire to end interviews

K26 how much time and resources are available for interviews

K27 types of tensions that could emerge with clients

K28 why it is important to assure clients their decisions will be respected

K29 how to summarise interview outcomes and agreed actions

K30 what further support might be available to clients

K31 organisational procedures for ending interviews with abusive or violent clients

K32 organisational systems and procedures for recording referrals and why it is important to follow them

SFJGA6
Develop and manage interviews with clients

Additional Information

Skills

The skills you will need to enable you to deliver the service effectively are:

1   questioning
2   active listening
3   presenting information
4   summarising
5   reviewing/reflecting
6   prioritising
7   negotiating
8   decision making
9   challenging
10   time management
11   interviewing
12   assessing risk
13   assertiveness
14   recording and storing information

SFJGA6
Develop and manage interviews with clients

Developed by	Skills for Justice
Version number	3
Date approved	November 2013
Indicative review date	November 2018
Validity	Current
Status	Original
Originating organisation	Skills for Justice
Original URN	SFJ GA6
Relevant occupations	Legal Advisers; Legal Associate Professionals
Suite	Legal Advice
Key words	confidentiality; data protection; feedback; interviewing clients; working relationship with clients; interviews; risk assessment; tensions

SFJIA1
Provide legal advice to clients

Overview

This standard is about working directly with clients to establish their needs and expectations of services, researching information which is relevant to their situations and providing them with appropriate and accurate legal advice.

SFJIA1
Provide legal advice to clients

Performance criteria

You must be able to:

P1 explain to clients the services that you can offer in line with their requirements

P2 check that clients' understanding of legal advice services is consistent with information you have provided

P3 agree with clients where situations require immediate action in line with their requirements, and:

  P3.1 take steps to implement this

P4 agree next steps with clients in line with their requirements

P5 agree further actions with clients in line with their requirements, including:

  P5.1 procedures

  P5.2 responsibilities

  P5.3 time limits

P6 analyse available client information to assign relevance to their case in line with your professional judgement

P7 review sources of information to assess applicability to clients' situations

P8 check that information obtained enables you to advise clients

P9 analyse information received from clients and the research process to formulate options in line with clients' needs

P10 present clients with information and possible options for action in line with organisational requirements

P11 advise clients on the implications of possible options in line with organisational requirements

P12 check clients' understanding of the advice offered in line with organisational requirements

P13 open client case files in line with organisational procedures

P14 design an action plan with clients in line with organisational processes, and:

  P14.1 agree roles and responsibilities for progressing actions

P15 progress actions on behalf of clients in line with agreed timescales

P16 evaluate case progress against milestones and outcomes in line with organisational procedures

SFJIA1

Provide legal advice to clients

P17   progress case outcomes to conclusion in line with organisational
requirements
P18   record client details and agreed actions in line with organisational
requirements

SFJIA1
Provide legal advice to clients

Knowledge and understanding

You need to know and understand:

K1   the importance of discussing service provision with clients, including any limitations of the service

K2   situations that require immediate action, and the organisational procedures to follow

K3   actions that may be required from you and clients and why these are important

K4   organisational systems and procedures for working with clients, and why it is important to follow these

K5   the importance of checking clients' understanding

K6   the importance of agreeing with clients the time limits, responsibilities and procedures for actions

K7   the types of client information that may be available about cases and why it is important to review this

K8   relevant national, local, professional and organisational requirements relating to:

K8.1   equal opportunities

K8.2   discrimination

K8.3   health and safety

K8.4   security

K8.5   confidentiality

K8.6   data protection

K8.7   conflicts of interest

K9   the importance of complying with national, local, professional and organisational requirements

K10   organisational procedures for recording and storing client details

K11   information sources when researching, including:

K10.1   relevant legislation

K10.2   case law

K10.3   national and local policies and practice

K10.4   internal and external colleagues

K12   the importance of checking that information is accurate and up to date and how to do this

SFJIA1

Provide legal advice to clients

K13 the importance of obtaining appropriate information and ways of doing this

K14 the importance of considering organisational procedures and timescales for research

K15 the importance of advising on the implications of possible options for action

K16 different ways and formats for providing advice that promote clients' understanding

SFJIA1
Provide legal advice to clients

Additional Information

Skills

The skills you will need to enable you to deliver the service effectively are:

1   questioning
2   active listening
3   negotiating
4   summarising
5   checking understanding
6   decision making
7   planning
8   problem solving
9   presenting information
10   recording and storing information
11   research
12   analysing
13   time management
14   persuading

SFJIA1
Provide legal advice to clients

Developed by	Skills for Justice
Version number	2
Date approved	November 2013
Indicative review date	November 2018
Validity	Current
Status	Original
Originating organisation	Skills for Justice
Original URN	SFJ IA1
Relevant occupations	Legal Advisers; Legal Associate Professionals
Suite	Legal Advice
Key words	Analyse clients needs; accurate advice; research needs; research information; advise; assess; explore

SFJIA2
Manage legal advice cases

Overview	This standard involves managing an ongoing case for a client. It may involve briefing someone outside the organisation to carry out some part of the case (e.g. a barrister, solicitor or expert witness) but it will be your overall responsibility to ensure that the case moves forward.

There are three elements

1   Establish case files
2   Progress cases
3   Close cases

SFJIA2
Manage legal advice cases

Performance criteria	**Establish case files**

You must be able to:

P1 open client case files in line with organisational requirements
P2 agree with clients the potential case outcomes and milestones
P3 determine the method of funding cases
P4 advise clients about any cost implications for them
P5 explain to clients the organisational systems and procedures for managing cases in line with organisational requirements
P6 record client details and agreed actions in line with organisational requirements

Progress cases

You must be able to:

P7 progress agreed actions on behalf of clients in line with agreed timescales
P8 brief other individuals required to progress cases with details and responsibilities
P9 inform clients about progress against milestones and outcomes in line with organisational requirements
P10 meet all deadlines and key dates for cases
P11 maintain case files to ensure they are accurate and up to date in line with organisational requirements
P12 evaluate case progress against milestones and outcomes in line with organisational requirements

Close cases

You must be able to:

P13 review how cases progressed against milestones and desired outcomes in line with organisational requirements
P14 evaluate the performance of externally instructed individuals for future reference in line with organisational requirements
P15 inform clients about actions they can take to progress cases towards closure in line organisational requirements
P16 explain reasons and procedures for closing cases to clients

SFJIA2

Manage legal advice cases

P17   check that clients' understanding of reasons for closing cases is
consistent with information you have provided

P18   agree with clients arrangements for case closure

P19   perform closure tasks for cases in line with organisational requirements

SFJIA2

Manage legal advice cases

Knowledge and understanding

You need to know and understand:

K1 organisational procedures for opening and maintaining client case files

K2 why it is important to establish and agree the desired case outcomes and milestones

K3 different funding sources for cases and how to access them

K4 organisational systems and procedures for working with clients

K5 the importance of checking client's understanding

K6 the relevant national, local, professional and organisational requirements relating to:

K6.1 equal opportunities

K6.2 discrimination

K6.3 health and safety

K6.4 security

K6.5 confidentiality

K6.6 data protection

K6.7 conflicts of interest

K7 the importance of complying with national, local, professional and organisational requirements

K8 organisational procedures for recording and storing client and case details

K9 actions that should be taken to progress cases

K10 why it is important to consult with and inform clients at each stage of the case

K11 who might need to be briefed about cases and what information they will require

K12 the importance of

K12.1 meeting all deadlines and key dates

K12.2 accurately maintaining case files

K12.3 reviewing and evaluating case milestones and outcomes

K13 why it is important to review case progress and ways of doing this

K14 why it is important to consider any opinions and rulings and how to use them to decide further actions

K15 the importance of evaluating the performance of externally instructed

SFJIA2

Manage legal advice cases

individuals and how to do this

K16 the importance of keeping clients informed about the progress of cases, including plans for conclusion

SFJIA2

Manage legal advice cases

Additional Information

Skills | The skills you will need to enable you to deliver the service effectively are:

1   presenting information
2   active listening
3   questioning
4   oral and written presentation
5   negotiating
6   problem solving
7   summarising
8   checking understanding
9   time management
10   resource management
11   decision making
12   recording and storing information

SFJIA2
Manage legal advice cases

Developed by	Skills for Justice
Version number	3
Date approved	November 2013
Indicative review date	November 2018
Validity	Current
Status	Original
Originating organisation	Skills for Justice
Original URN	SFJ IA2
Relevant occupations	Legal Advisers; Legal Associate Professionals
Suite	Legal Advice
Key words	Managing ongoing cases; briefing; responsibility; support; prepare; casework

SFJHA5
Manage personal caseload

Overview

This Unit is for you if you are responsible for managing your own caseload of clients. Caseload management is an important part of ensuring that all cases are dealt with appropriately to achieve the outcomes required by the client within the timescales required by the service.

There are three elements
1   Record and maintain case notes
2   Review personal caseload
3   Establish priorities for dealing with personal caseload

SFJHA5
Manage personal caseload

Performance criteria	**Record and maintain case notes**
You must be able to:	P1 record all key information about each case
	P2 record all actions being undertaken for clients
	P3 ensure case notes are accurate and an appropriate amount of detail is included
	P4 ensure case notes are structured in a way that provides a clear case history
	P5 ensure case notes are legible and clear
	P6 use relevant documentation and systems to record the case notes
	P7 comply with all relevant legislation, codes of practice, guidelines and ethical requirements

Review personal caseload

You must be able to:

P8   review all relevant information on the personal caseload
P9   monitor the progress in achieving the required outcomes for the cases
P10   identify any obstacles in achieving the required outcomes for the cases
P11   identify any factors that might affect the structure or content of the caseload
P12   identify any improvements that can be made to the management of the cases
P13   exchange information on the cases according to the procedures of the service
P14   record the information on the cases in the appropriate systems
P15   comply with all relevant legislation, codes of practice, guidelines and ethical requirements

Establish priorities for dealing with personal caseload

You must be able to:

P16   establish criteria for setting priorities for cases
P17   assess cases against the specified criteria
P18   identify any immediate action required to meet deadlines
P19   specify clearly the cases that require highest priority
P20   inform all relevant people of the need to prioritise specific cases
P21   ensure high-priority cases are implemented and assigned the appropriate resources
P22   monitor the effect of the priorities on the entire caseload
P23   ensure all cases receive the appropriate attention within the timescales established by the service
P24   provide a clear rationale for the priorities

SFJHA5
Manage personal caseload

Knowledge and understanding	**Record and maintain case notes**

You need to know and understand:

K1 what types of information should be recorded about cases
K2 why it is important to record what is happening
K3 how to confirm that case notes are accurate
K4 how much detail should be included for different types of case
K5 how case notes should be structured
K6 why it is important that case notes are legible and clear
K7 what the systems are for recording case notes and the procedures relating to the use of these
K8 why it is important to use the systems
K9 the relevant national, local, professional and organisational requirements that relate to equal opportunities, discrimination, health and safety, security, confidentiality and data protection
K10 why it is important to comply with different requirements
K11 what the consequences are of not complying with different requirements
K12 how to obtain information on the requirements

Review personal caseload

You need to know and understand:

K13 the types of information on personal caseloads that should be reviewed
K14 how often information on personal caseloads should be reviewed
K15 how many cases can be managed
K16 how to monitor the progress of cases
K17 what type of obstacles could occur in achieving the required outcomes for the cases
K18 how the obstacles can be overcome
K19 the factors that can affect the quantity of cases being managed
K20 what types of improvements could be identified to the management of cases
K21 what types of information are involved in different types of case
K22 who should be provided with information on cases
K23 who should provide information on cases
K24 what the systems are for recording case information and the procedures relating to the use of these
K25 why it is important to use the systems
K26 the relevant national, local, professional, and organisational requirements that relate to equal opportunities, discrimination, health and safety, security, confidentiality and data protection
K27 why it is important to comply with different requirements
K28 what the consequences are of not complying with different requirements
K29 how to obtain information on the requirements

Establish priorities for dealing with personal caseload

SFJHA5
Manage personal caseload

You need to know and   K30   what types of criteria could be used for setting priorities
understand: K31   how to agree on the priority criteria
                          K32   how to match cases against the priority criteria
                          K33   what deadlines can occur
                          K34   what the consequences are of not meeting the deadlines
                          K35   how to specify the highest priorities
                          K36   who should be informed of the priorities
                          K37   who is responsible for implementing cases
                          K38   which resources should be assigned to implementing different types of
                                case
                          K39   what types of effect or distortion the priorities could have
                          K40   what timescales are required by the service for different types of case
                          K41   why it is important to provide a clear rationale for priorities

SFJHA5
Manage personal caseload

Additional Information

Skills

The skills you will need to enable you to deliver the service effectively are:

Record and maintain case notes
analysing
prioritising
decision making
problem solving
presenting information
recording and storing information
time management

Review personal caseload
analysing
prioritising
decision making
problem solving
evaluation
presenting information
recording and storing information
time management

Establish priorities for dealing with personal caseload
analysing
prioritising
decision making
problem solving
evaluation
presenting information
recording and storing information
time management

SFJHA5
Manage personal caseload

Developed by	Skills for Justice
Version number	2
Date approved	July 2009
Indicative review date	July 2011
Validity	Current
Status	Tailored
Originating organisation	ENTO
Original URN	AG14
Relevant occupations	Public Services; Public Service and Other Associate Professionals; Paralegal
Suite	Legal Advice; Providing Legal Services
Key words	Record cases, maintain cases, establish priorities; Legal Services

SFJDA3
Act on behalf of clients in informal proceedings

Overview	This standard is about representing or acting on behalf of clients. This will involve representing clients' interests in situations other than formal proceedings where the clients are either unable to represent themselves or where the most successful outcome will be achieved by this course of action.

There are five elements

1 Explore and analyse the nature of clients' needs
2 Research information relevant to clients' situations
3 Prepare to act on behalf of clients
4 Represent clients in informal proceedings
5 Review cases in informal proceedings

SFJDA3

Act on behalf of clients in informal proceedings

Performance criteria	**Explore and analyse the nature of client's needs**

You must be able to:	P1	explain accurately the service you can offer, and:
	P1.1	check client's understanding
	P2	agree with clients the nature of their advice needs and expectations in line with organisational requirements
	P3	analyse available client information to determine their case
	P4	agree with clients where a situation requires immediate action, and:
	P4.1	take steps to implement this in line with organisational requirements
	P5	agree next steps with clients in line with organisational requirements
	P6	explain the organisation's systems and procedures for working with clients, and:
	P6.1	check clients' understanding
	P7	agree with clients the procedures, responsibilities and time limits for further actions
	P8	record clients' details and agreed actions in line with organisational requirements

Research information relevant to clients' situation

You must be able to:	P9	review sources of information relevant to clients' cases
	P10	check information obtained is accurate and up to date in line with organisational requirements
	P11	check that information obtained is appropriate to enable you to advise clients
	P12	analyse information received from clients and the research process to formulate options that could meet clients' needs

Prepare to act on behalf of clients

You must be able to:	P14	review all relevant information on the needs of clients in line with organisational requirements
	P15	manage and agree with clients their desired outcomes in line with

SFJDA3

Act on behalf of clients in informal proceedings

organisational requirements

P16 advise clients as to any additional information that might be required to support the representation

P17 obtain authority to act on behalf of clients

P18 agree with clients who should be contacted to pursue their interests

P19 identify with clients the points to be addressed in the representation which support the desired outcomes

P20 identify time limits appropriate to clients cases in line with organisational requirements

P21 record details of the representations in line with organisational requirements

Represent clients in informal proceedings

You must be able to:

P22 ensure all relevant people, documentation, and associated materials are available for representation

P23 provide correct information to all relevant people according to the agreed timescales

P24 check with appropriate parties that oral and written representations are clear and effective

P25 comply with relevant protocols relating to representing clients in informal settings

P26 represent clients' interests in a way that emphasises the key points and how they affect clients

P27 address the issues represented by others by offering constructive suggestions for their resolution

P28 address problems with representations by taking appropriate actions in line with organisational requirements

P29 review the results of representations with clients to agree next steps

Review cases in informal proceedings

You must be able to:

P30 review the outcome of cases with clients to ensure they understand the implications

P31 confirm with other parties their agreement to the outcomes of cases in

SFJDA3

Act on behalf of clients in informal proceedings

line with organisational requirements

P32 review the possible consequences of the outcomes of cases with clients

P33 assess with clients whether the process of representation should be continued in line with organisational requirements

P34 agree any further actions with clients in line with organisational requirements

P35 record details of cases in line with organisational requirements

SFJDA3

Act on behalf of clients in informal proceedings

Knowledge and understanding

You need to know and understand:

K1 the importance of discussing service provision with clients, including any limitations of the service

K2 the importance of reviewing the types of client information about cases that may be available

K3 the types of situations that require immediate action and organisational procedures for doing so

K4 the types of actions that may be required from you and clients and why these are important

K5 organisational systems and procedures for working with clients, and why it is important to follow these

K6 the importance of checking clients' understanding

K7 the importance of agreeing with clients the timescales and procedures for closing the case

K8 the relevant national, local, professional and organisational requirements relating to:

K8.1 equal opportunities

K8.2 discrimination

K8.3 health and safety

K8.4 security

K8.5 confidentiality

K8.6 data protection

K8.7 conflicts of interest

K9 the importance of complying with national, local, professional and organisational requirements

K10 organisational procedures for recording and storing clients' details

K11 the range of information sources for accessing:

K11.1 case notes

K11.2 relevant legislation

K11.3 case law

K12 the importance of checking that information is accurate

K13 how to check that information is up to date and accurate

K14 the importance of checking that you have obtained appropriate

SFJDA3
Act on behalf of clients in informal proceedings

information and ways of doing this

K15 how to analyse information to identify options

K16 the options that may be available to clients

K17 how to obtain accurate information on the needs of clients

K18 how to check the relevance of the information

K19 how to obtain authority to act for clients

K20 the importance of time limits relating to cases and permitted action when they have been exceeded

K21 the possible results of the representation and why it is important to discuss these with clients

K22 systems and procedures for recording representation and why it is important to use them

K23 what and who should be available at different stages of representation

K24 what type of information is required and who requires it

K25 relevant protocols relating to representation in particular settings

K26 the information that should be included in the representation and how to present it

K27 the types of issues or problems that could emerge and how they have been resolved previously

K28 the importance of identifying and addressing problems

K29 what further actions are available to clients

K30 outcomes of cases that might require explanation to clients, and why this is important

K31 types of agreement that should be obtained from other parties

K32 consequences that are likely to result from different outcomes

K33 the range of options available that would allow the process of representation to continue

K34 types of further action available in different proceedings

K35 organisational systems and procedures for recording referrals and why it is important to follow them

SFJDA3

Act on behalf of clients in informal proceedings

Additional Information

Skills   The skills you will need to enable you to deliver the service effectively are:

1   questioning
2   active listening
3   negotiating skills
4   decision making
5   problem solving
6   presenting information orally and in written form
7   recording and storing information
8   analytical
9   time management
10   research

SFJDA3

Act on behalf of clients in informal proceedings

Developed by	Skills for Justice
Version number	3
Date approved	November 2013
Indicative review date	November 2018
Validity	Current
Status	Original
Originating organisation	Skills for Justice
Original URN	SFJ DA3
Relevant occupations	Legal Advisers; Legal Associate Professionals
Suite	Legal Advice
Key words	Representation; clients interests; review cases; informal; representative; cases; mediation

SFJDA7
Prepare cases for representation in formal proceedings

Overview	This standard is about preparing cases and clients for formal proceedings. You will need to understand the legislation involved in any case and the codes of practice, procedural rules and ethical requirements governing the preparation of cases for formal proceedings in courts or tribunals. An important part of your role will be helping clients to understand and be prepared for their role in formal proceedings. Before embarking on research or preparation for any case you should consider whether formal legal proceedings are the best option available. You should also have taken into consideration your own skills and limitations and that of others in your organisation.

There are three elements

1   Research information relevant to cases
2   Prepare cases for formal proceedings
3   Prepare clients for formal proceedings

SFJDA7
Prepare cases for representation in formal proceedings

Performance criteria	**Research information relevant to cases**

You must be able to:	P1	access sources of information relevant to clients' cases in line with organisational requirements
	P2	identify evidence relevant to clients' cases which promotes clients' desired outcomes
	P3	identify statutory and case law which is relevant to cases
	P4	analyse and interpret the relevant law in line with clients' desired outcomes
	P5	establish the rules and precedents relating to the relevant areas of law
	P6	assess the strength of relevant evidence in relation to cases
	P7	identify options available to progress clients' cases in line with organisational requirements

Prepare cases for formal proceedings

You must be able to:	P8	prepare clients issues for presentation using the prescribed format
	P9	assess the strength of evidence in relation to cases
	P10	prepare arguments for cases which promote clients' desired outcomes
	P11	evaluate the relative merits of different arguments
	P12	draft legal documents in line with organisational requirements
	P13	ensure all relevant documents are collated, labelled and presented in the required format, and made available for disclosure
	P14	comply with all due dates under internal and external procedural rules
	P15	check courts and tribunals have received all required documents
	P16	respond to requests from other parties within agreed timescales
	P17	request information from other parties in line with case requirements
	P18	coordinate lay witnesses in line with organisational requirements
	P19	instruct relevant expert witnesses in line with organisational requirements
	P20	prepare questioning for examination of witnesses at hearings

Prepare clients for formal proceedings

You must be able to:	P21	explain to clients the roles and responsibilities of those involved in the

SFJDA7

Prepare cases for representation in formal proceedings

formal proceedings

P22 describe the potential outcomes of the proposed proceedings to clients in line with organisational requirements

P23 outline costs and potential risks and implications of proposed proceedings to clients in line with organisational requirements

P24 describe accurately to clients the stages and timescales of formal proceedings

P25 check clients' availability for formal proceedings

P26 advise clients on the nature of the arguments that will be used in cases

P27 confirm the understanding of clients and;

P25.1 secure their agreement to cases proceeding

P28 prepare clients to be witnessed in courts or tribunals

P29 provide clients with additional information they may require in line with organisational requirements

SFJDA7
Prepare cases for representation in formal proceedings

Knowledge and understanding

You need to know and understand:

K1 the range of information sources, relevant legislation, case law, national and local policies and practice and internal and external colleagues that can be consulted when preparing cases

K2 what factors within clients' case notes are relevant to the case

K3 how to interpret relevant legislation and case law

K4 how to identify and comply with the rules, precedents and ethics relating to the relevant areas of law

K5 how to assess the strength of evidence and evaluate its relevance to cases

K6 how to identify and prioritise the options available

K7 who the relevant witnesses and experts are and how to identify them

K8 the practice and policy of your organisation on representation and the types of cases they take on

K9 funding criteria of your organisation for accepting cases

K10 the kinds of evidence and documents that courts and tribunals will require and the format required

K11 how to assess the strength of evidence and its relative merit in cases

K12 which issues cases will rely on

K13 the prescribed format for putting cases together

K14 when a skeleton argument is required by courts or tribunals

K15 how to develop themes for presentation of cases

K16 the rules of evidence

K17 the principles and procedures that apply to drafting legal documents

K18 the timescales and due dates to be observed under procedural rules

K19 the importance of checking that required documents have been received by the court or tribunal

K20 the types of requests that may be made by other parties and the agreed timescales for response

K21 how to instruct expert witnesses

K22 the relevant legislation, codes of practice, procedural rules and ethical requirements for representation, and why it is important to comply with these

SFJDA7

Prepare cases for representation in formal proceedings

K23 what is involved in different types of formal proceedings

K24 the roles and responsibilities of different organisations and people

K25 how to estimate the costs of proceedings

K26 the potential risks and implications for clients from different outcomes

K27 the stages and timescales of different types of formal proceedings

K28 when clients need to be involved in formal proceedings

K29 the types of legal arguments that could occur

K30 who is involved in reaching final judgements and decisions in formal proceedings

K31 how to confirm clients' understanding

K32 the importance of securing clients' agreement

K33 what documents and procedures should be completed for formal proceedings

K34 when it is appropriate to prepare witnesses and how to do this

K35 the types of additional information that might be required by clients

SFJDA7
Prepare cases for representation in formal proceedings

Additional Information

Skills   The skills you will need to enable you to deliver the service effectively are:

1   questioning
2   active listening
3   research
4   analytical
5   prioritising
6   presenting information
7   evaluating information
8   negotiating
9   drafting legal documents

SFJDA7
Prepare cases for representation in formal proceedings

Developed by	Skills for Justice
Version number	3
Date approved	November 2013
Indicative review date	November 2018
Validity	Current
Status	Original
Originating organisation	Skills for Justice
Original URN	SFJ DA7
Relevant occupations	Legal Advisers; Legal Associate Professionals
Suite	Legal Advice
Key words	Responsible; preparing cases; understand legislation; research; evaluate; evidence; merits; arguments

SFJDA4
Represent clients in formal proceedings

Overview

This standard is about presenting cases in formal proceedings in courts or tribunals. As part of this responsibility you will need to consider your own skills and limitations and whether clients should be referred.

There are two elements

1   Present cases for clients in formal proceedings

2   Review cases in formal proceedings

SFJDA4
Represent clients in formal proceedings

Performance criteria	**Present cases for clients in formal proceedings**

You must be able to:	P1	check all relevant people, documentation and associated materials are available for cases
	P2	present cases in a structured way relevant to the type of proceedings in line with organisational requirements
	P3	select lines of questioning consistent with court rules
	P4	adapt prepared cases in response to cases presented by other parties
	P5	identify inconsistencies and contradictions in the evidence relating to clients, witnesses and third parties
	P6	counter the arguments of opposing parties in line with clients' desired outcomes
	P7	identify issues with formal proceedings in line with court rules, and:
		P7.1 take appropriate action to address them
	P8	explain to clients the progress of proceedings based on the evidence and arguments presented

Review cases in formal proceedings

You must be able to:	P9	review the conduct and outcome of cases with clients in line with organisational requirements
	P10	clarify issues outstanding from the outcomes of cases in line with organisational requirements
	P11	review the consequences of cases with clients in line with organisational requirements
	P12	advise clients on the merits of continuing the proceedings or appealing by considering anticipated outcomes
	P13	agree further actions and responsibilities with clients in line with organisational requirements
	P14	record details of cases in line with organisational requirements

SFJDA4
Represent clients in formal proceedings

Knowledge and understanding

You need to know and understand:

K1 the documentation and who should be available at different stages of the case

K2 the standard of proof required at hearings

K3 where the burden of proof lies for different cases

K4 what your legal responsibilities are when presenting in formal proceedings

K5 what information should be provided and who should receive it

K6 the relevant procedures for disclosing information in different types of formal proceedings

K7 the demeanour and relationship relevant to different courts and tribunals

K8 the structures, rules and procedures that apply to the presentation of cases in different formal proceedings

K9 how to present cases in different types of formal proceedings

K10 the rules concerning the use of witnesses

K11 how to adapt a prepared case and the kinds of issues that may be raised by other parties

K12 the appropriate responses to different issues that could be raised

K13 the rules and procedures that affect the way in which you can adapt cases

K14 the range of other parties who may raise issues and bring evidence in different types of proceedings

K15 the types of errors or contradictions that may occur in evidence

K16 how to counter or use arguments effectively

K17 the types of problems and issues that can occur in different proceedings

K18 the range of action and procedures appropriate to addressing problems or issues in different types of formal proceedings

K19 the organisation's practice and policies on formal representation

K20 the relevant national, local, professional and organisational requirements relating to:

K20.1 equal opportunities

K20.2 discrimination

K20.3 health and safety

SFJDA4

Represent clients in formal proceedings

K20.4   security

K20.5   confidentiality

K20.6   data protection

K20.7   conflicts of interest

K21   the importance of complying with national, local, professional and organisational requirements

K22   the types of conduct and outcomes that may require explanation to clients

K23   the types of issue that may need to be clarified

K24   the types of consequences that are likely to result from different outcomes

K25   the range of options available that would allow the proceedings to continue

K26   the types of further action available in different proceedings

K27   what systems and procedures should be used to record details of formal proceedings and the importance of following them

SFJDA4
Represent clients in formal proceedings

Additional Information

Skills   The skills you will need to enable you to deliver the service effectively are:

1   questioning
2   active listening
3   analysis of information
4   prioritising
5   decision making
6   negotiating
7   relating facts to law
8   pleading cases
9   presenting information oral and written
10 planning
11 problem solving

SFJDA4
Represent clients in formal proceedings

Developed by	Skills for Justice
Version number	3
Date approved	November 2013
Indicative review date	November 2018
Validity	Current
Status	Original
Originating organisation	Skills for Justice
Original URN	SFJ DA4
Relevant occupations	Legal Advisers; Legal Associate Professionals
Suite	Legal Advice
Key words	Present cases; review cases; courts; tribunals; represent; on behalf of; formal hearings

SFJAB3
Facilitate communication using interpreters

Overview

This standard is about communicating with clients with the help of interpreters to assist the communication process. Interpreters may be involved in directly assisting you to communicate with clients in a way that facilitates understanding. The standard is generic and is designed to include working with interpreters in a range of languages, including British Sign Language. It is important to note that it is not the role of interpreters to explain anything to clients.

The standard is not about the functions performed by interpreters. There are National Occupational Standards for interpreting. The standard is about the functions and actions that you need to help interpreters to do their job effectively.

There are three elements

1   Establish and agree the communication support needs of clients
2   Contract with, and brief, interpreters
3   Facilitate communication through interpreters

SFJAB3

Facilitate communication using interpreters

Performance criteria	**Establish and agree the communication support needs of clients**

You must be able to:

P1   identify communication support needs of clients in line with organisational requirements

P2   establish whether communication support is best met through interpreters, and:

      P2.1   agree this with relevant others

P3   access sources of interpreters in line with client needs

P4   establish any costs involved in contracting with interpreters in line with organisational requirements

P5   access any sources of funding available to support working with interpreters following appropriate application processes

Contract with, and brief, interpreters

You must be able to:

P6   make initial contact with interpreters to establish their suitability for cases based on client needs

P7   provide suitable opportunities for clients to establish rapport with interpreters

P8   provide interpreters with appropriate information about the nature of the service you can offer clients

P9   evaluate whether the physical environment is conducive to the interpreting process

P10 agree working arrangements with interpreters in line with organisational requirements

P11 agree cultural and ethical considerations with clients and interpreters in line with organisational requirements

Facilitate communication through interpreters

You must be able to:

P12 use language appropriate to clients' needs

P13 encourage interpreters to query aspects of interchanges they are unclear about

P14 address clients rather than interpreters whilst performing your duties

SFJAB3

Facilitate communication using interpreters

P15   assess clients' continued satisfaction with the communication process according to their reactions during interchanges

P16   identify opportunities for providing further support for clients in line with organisational requirements

P17   record interactions and agreed outcomes in line with organisational requirements

SFJAB3

Facilitate communication using interpreters

Knowledge and understanding

You need to know and understand:

K1	how to establish the communication support needs of clients
K2	different kinds of communication needs and ways of meeting them
K3	when it may be appropriate or necessary to use more than one interpreter
K4	ways of communicating with clients informally to establish their communication needs
K5	how to access sources of qualified public services interpreters
K6	why it is important to establish any charges that interpreters will make before contracting with them
K7	how to access sources of funding that may be available to support the use of interpreters
K8	what needs to be considered when establishing the suitability of interpreters
K9	why it is important to enable clients to meet with interpreters before contracting
K10	what kind of information you need to provide for interpreters and why this is important
K11	what needs to be considered when setting up the physical environment for the interpreting process
K12	organisational procedures for contracting with interpreters
K13	ethical and cultural considerations for communicating with clients using interpreters, and;
K11.1	why it is important to agree these with clients and interpreters
K14	why it is important to use clear and unambiguous language when working with interpreters
K15	why it is important to encourage interpreters to ask for clarification
K16	why it is important to address clients directly rather than interpreters
K17	ways of assessing clients' satisfaction with the interpretation service
K18	the importance of assessing clients' satisfaction with the interpretation service
K19	why interpreters may need rest periods and how to arrange these
K20	what further support may be available to clients

SFJAB3

Facilitate communication using interpreters

K21   organisational systems and procedures for recording interactions and outcomes

K22   why organisational procedures are important

SFJAB3

Facilitate communication using interpreters

Additional Information

Skills   The skills to enable you to deliver the service effectively are:

1   questioning
2   active listening
3   presenting information
4   non-verbal communication
5   summarising
6   reviewing/reflecting
7   prioritising
8   reviewing
9   negotiating
10   decision making
11   recording and storing information
12   interviewing

SFJAB3

Facilitate communication using interpreters

Developed by	Skills for Justice
Version number	3
Date approved	November 2013
Indicative review date	November 2018
Validity	Current
Status	Original
Originating organisation	Skills for Justice
Original URN	SFJ AB3
Relevant occupations	Legal Advisers; Legal Associate Professionals
Suite	Legal Advice
Key words	Assist communication; process; agree needs; support; interpreter; language; communication;

A Guide to Representing Yourself in Court, The Bar Council, April 2013[1]

This Guide is not legal advice. It is intended to help you to find your way around a difficult and complex system. All information was correct at the time of writing (April 2013). Please try to get some professional advice wherever you can.

Section 4: Areas of law

This Section of the Guide gives you more detailed information about seven different areas of law which will be dramatically affected by the Government changes to who can get legal aid. It is likely that only one of the seven areas will be useful to you, so go straight to that area, and ignore the others.

Contents

Personal injury law

What is a personal injury?

A personal injury can be a physical or psychological injury, disease or illness. If you have suffered a personal injury that you believe to have been caused by another person or an organisation you may be able to recover compensation.

The most common forms of personal injury claims stem from the following types of accident or incident:

- Road traffic accidents
- Slipping and tripping accidents

---

1 This is an extract from section 4 of *A Guide to Representing Yourself in Court*, 2013. It has been reproduced with the permission of The Bar Council. The guide can be downloaded at: www.barcouncil.org.uk/media/203109/srl_guide_final_for_online_use.pdf.

- Accidents at work
- An injury or illness sustained by a victim in the course of a crime, and
- An injury caused by errors in receiving medical treatment.

Before starting a claim

If you think you may have a personal injury claim you may ultimately need to go to court to resolve it. However, the courts expect that the parties in a personal injury case will have attempted to resolve the problem between themselves before starting legal proceedings.

A court will expect those involved (called 'parties') in a personal injury dispute to have followed the correct procedures (the 'pre-action protocol') for personal injury claims. That protocol can be found at: www.justice.gov. uk/courts/procedure-rules/civil/protocol/prot_pic.

If you have been involved in a road traffic accident and the value of your claim is not expected to be more than £10,000, you must use the following protocol: www.justice. gov.uk/courts/procedure-rules/civil/protocol/prot_rta. This protocol is known as the 'portal' and from the end of July 2013 it will apply to personal injury claims against employers and claims where public authorities may be liable for personal injury. For example, in 'slipping and tripping' accidents. The value of claims that the portal will deal with will rise to £25,000 from the end of July 2013.

If you have suffered injury or illness as a victim of crime you may be able to apply to the Criminal Injuries Compensation Authority. Details of the compensation scheme which it operates may be found at www.justice. gov. uk/victims-and-witnesses/cica.

Letter before Claim

Broadly speaking, before starting a claim you should send two copies of a letter to the prospective defendant giving a summary of the facts on which the claim is based, together with an indication of the nature of any injuries suffered and of any financial loss incurred. You should try to give an estimate of the value of your claim, or to put it another way, the amount of compensation you think you are due (See the paragraph on 'Valuing the Claim' below).

The prospective defendant should then respond within 21 days identifying who their insurer is. They will then have up to three months to investigate the allegation that has been made.

The defendant (or their insurer) must reply after no more than three months, stating whether they admit that they are at fault for causing your injury or illness (that is whether they are liable for it) or whether they deny that they are at fault.

If the prospective defendant denies that they are at fault they need to enclose documents relevant to the allegation made along with their letter of reply. If the prospective defendant admits that they are at fault but states that the claimant contributed to the incident then the claimant should write back in response stating whether they accept they contributed or if not, and if not, why not, before issuing proceedings (starting legal action).

If matters cannot be resolved at this stage then it may be necessary for a claim to be started or 'issued' so that the court can provide resolution.

You must be careful before you proceed to start a claim – bringing legal proceedings can be very expensive even if you are representing yourself. You may, depending on the outcome of the case, be ordered to pay the legal costs of the other side in a dispute. Legal costs can become very substantial and can be more than the value of the claim itself in some cases.

Experts

It is standard practice in personal injury claims for the claimant, and often the defendant, to obtain evidence from an expert to help the court in deciding the outcome of a claim.

Usually this expert will be a medical expert who will be able to set out what injury or illness the claimant has suffered and whether or not they are likely to recover fully from it. They may also be able to say how the injury or illness was caused.

There may also be a need to obtain evidence from an expert to help the court decide who was at fault for the incident. For example, in a road traffic accident it may be helpful to instruct an engineer who specialises in vehicle damage to look at the damage to both vehicles to see whether it supports one driver's version of events over another's. If you have suffered from an accident at work involving machinery, it may be helpful to have evidence from an expert to say whether the machine was faulty or whether there was some other reason for the accident.

If you think you might need to instruct an expert the following websites may help you identify the correct type: www.expertwitness.co.uk and www.thelawpages.com.

It is likely that you will have to pay any expert you instruct, so you need to think carefully about whether one is necessary, and how much they will charge. As mentioned above, in personal injury cases the court will expect to see some medical evidence setting out the nature of the injury or illness. If you cannot afford to instruct an expert to do that you should obtain as much information from your NHS GP as to the nature of your injury or illness and the steps that have been taken to help you recover from it.

You may also have to give the prospective defendant access to your relevant medical records so be prepared to ask for them from your GP's practice.

Starting a claim – which court?

Personal injury claims are heard in either the County Court or the High Court. Proceedings must not be started in the High Court unless the value of the claim is £50,000 or more. Refer to Section 2 of this Guide for a table that outlines types of case and the relevant court.

Procedure

Personal injury claims are governed by what are known as the Civil Procedure Rules ('CPR'). These rules can be found at the following website: www.justice.gov.uk/ courts/procedure-rules/civil/rules. The rules set out the key aspects of bringing and defending a personal injury claim.

CPR Part 7 sets out the procedure for starting or issuing a claim. If you wish to bring a personal injury claim you need to use 'Form N1' which can be found at this website: www.justice.gov.uk/courtfinder/forms/n001-eng.pdf. The claim form should:

- Identify the full name of each party to proceedings and state whether they are the claimant or defendant
- State the claimant's date of birth
- Contain a concise description of the nature of the claim
- State why the claimant believes the defendant is at fault
- Give brief details of the claimant's personal injuries, and
- Include the claimant's estimate of the value of the claim and any interest accruing on it.

The claim form must also include the report of a medical practitioner if the claimant is relying upon it and it must include a document known as a 'Schedule of Details of Past and Future Expenses and Losses', which outlines your predicted past and future loss of earnings and expenses such as the cost of replacing damaged clothing or taxis to and from hospital.

The claim form should contain the 'Particulars of Claim', which is the document setting out the claimant's case (the legal and factual reasons why the defendant is liable for the claimant's injury or illness). If it is not included with the claim form it should be sent to or 'served' on the defendant within 14 days of the defendant having received the claim form.

The Particulars of Claim, if not included in the claim form, should also contain the above information so that the defendant can understand the allegations which are made against him or her.

Finally, the claim form should contain what is known as a Statement of Truth signed by the claimant. The claimant must believe its contents to be true. The Statement of Truth should state as follows:

"I believe that the facts stated in this claim form are true."

Valuing the claim – understanding the 'Schedule of Past and Future Expenses and Losses'

Whether you are in the pre-action protocol stage or whether you wish to issue a claim you will need to work out what you think you should be paid by way of compensation, and set out your various losses in a clear list.

In a personal injury claim the main type of losses include the following:

Compensation for pain, suffering and loss of amenity

The court may award you damages for the pain, suffering and loss of amenity that has been caused by your injury or illness if you can prove that it has been caused by the defendant. It can be difficult to estimate exactly how much you will receive for this type of compensation but the judge will consider the guidelines given by the Judicial College to come up with a fair figure. These guidelines are known as the 'Judicial College Guidelines for the Assessment of General Damages in Personal Injury Cases'. The current guidelines are in the 11th Edition. You may be able to find a copy at your local library. Otherwise you may be able to purchase them online or in a legal bookshop.

Loss of income

The injury or illness that you have sustained may have caused you to take time off work or may have caused you to give up your job if you felt unable to continue in employment because of your injury. As a consequence you may have lost out on income that you otherwise would have received. You may be able to recover that 'lost' income if you can prove that it was due to the injury or illness that you suffered.

You need to work out how much lost income you have suffered at the time you send your pre-action letter or issue your claim, and have the figure to hand at the trial.

If you think that loss will be ongoing into the future you may need to work out how long you think that will be for, or whether you will have been disadvantaged in obtaining other employment because of your injury.

Miscellaneous

There may be other types of loss that you have sustained as a result of the incident that caused your injury or illness.

If you think that you have suffered such a loss, you should include it in the schedule that you put together. Examples might be: damaged clothing, or if you have paid for a holiday but missed it because of the accident.

Defending a claim

If a claim has been issued and served on you, you can either accept the claim against you or defend all or part of it. If you wish to defend all or part of the claim you must file a 'defence' at court.

A 'defence' is a document that sets out why you say you are not liable or not at fault when the claimant has stated that you are. In a personal injury case the defence should state why the incident that caused the injury or illness was not your fault. You can also challenge the amount of compensation that the claimant says they are owed.

If you fail to file a defence within 14 days of service of the claim form, or within 28 days if you have filed an Acknowledgement of Service (the form that is sent with the claim form), the claimant may obtain default (or automatic) judgment against you. This means you may be fully liable.

You must also include a Statement of Truth in your defence similar to that set out above for a claim form.

Procedure in trial

Once the court has received the claim form and the defence it will send out 'directions' (instructions). The directions may include requiring the parties to fill in what are known as Allocation Questionnaires. Once those questionnaires have been received the court will allocate the claim to a particular 'track'. The tracks in personal injury claims are as follows:

- **Small Claims Track** – where the claim for personal injury compensation is less than £1,000
- **Fast Track** – where the claim for personal injury compensation does not exceed £25,000, and
- **Multi-Track** – for all other claims.

A judge may also require both parties to come to a court Hearing to investigate the issues in the case. This Hearing may be called a 'directions' Hearing or a 'case management' Hearing and is not the same as a trial. If you are in any doubt as to the type of Hearing you are to attend, carefully read the Order notifying you of the Hearing, which the court will have sent to you and, if necessary, contact the court to clarify exactly what they expect to do at that Hearing and what you need to do to prepare for it.

In any event it is very important that both parties comply with any dates that are given by the court. If they do not, the claim or the defence may not be allowed to proceed and the other party will have won. The aim of the directions given by the court are to enable both parties to be ready for the trial, where the issues they do not agree upon will be dealt with.

If you are not sure about some of the terminology in the directions given by the court you may wish to check the Civil Procedure Rules to see if they may help explain what is being requested. You can also write to the judge to ask them to explain what is meant by a certain direction or Order.

Trial

Once you have been given the date for the trial of the case you will need to make sure that you have all you need in time for it. Make sure you comply with any directions given by the court to prepare for the trial. You will need to have all of your relevant evidence ready to be given at trial, including evidence from an expert (this may be a written statement or letter), and you will need to have an up to date Schedule of Past and Future Expenses and Losses. See Section 3 for further help on preparing for trial.

Further help

Personal injury cases can be complex both in terms of deciding whether someone else has caused your injury or illness and in trying to work out how much compensation you are owed. Further assistance can be obtained from the Citizens Advice Bureau (www.adviceguide.org.uk/ england/law_e/ law_legal_system_e/law_personal_ injury_e.htm).

Remember, going to court should be a last resort and can be a very stressful, expensive and complicated process. If you lose you may have to fund the other party's legal costs (which can be very high) as well as any compensation that the court Orders you to pay. If you can, you should try to resolve your problem before you get to that stage.

Employment Tribunals

If you have a legal problem to do with employment, read this section of the Guide. It will take you through some key steps involved in Employment Tribunals, which is where you will need to take most cases involving employment issues, if you go to court.

An Employment Tribunal is led by an employment judge, who is a lawyer specialising in employment law issues. The employment judge will sit alone in many cases, but in some cases (such as discrimination) will be joined by 'lay members'; people who do not have a legal background, but are experienced in dealing with workplace disputes, and have received specific Tribunal training. You should call the employment judge and the lay members 'Sir' or 'Madam'.

Remember that any and all documents you are bringing with you to court need to be available as copies for each member of the Tribunal; one copy for the witness stand, and one copy for the other party.

Types of Tribunal Hearing

Procedural Hearings

This is a Hearing which simply acts to lay out how the case will be conducted. In some cases, for example, a procedural Hearing will consider:

- 'Directions' in order to prepare the case for a full Hearing (for example, the date for disclosure of documents and exchange of witness statements), and
- Individual issues such as whether a claim has been brought in time, whether the person bringing the claim (the 'claimant') is an employee, or whether the claimant is disabled within the meaning of the Equality Act.

These Hearings are usually held before an employment judge only. It is important to concentrate your preparation and any documents on the specific issues that the Tribunal has said that it will be considering: do not try to argue the full case. You may find it helpful to spend some time looking at the websites set out below, to help you to understand the key factors that the Tribunal will take into account, and to prepare accordingly.

Full Hearings

Employment Tribunals are relatively informal and all parties remain seated throughout, except witnesses when asked to stand to give the oath, who then sit down for the remainder of their evidence. Whilst more informal than some other courts, it is still important to be polite and respectful throughout.

Types of employment claims

There are many different issues that a Tribunal can consider, and this Guide cannot hope to be comprehensive. At the end of this section there is a link to some websites that provide further information. You should consider carefully what types of claim you may be able to bring. All claims have a time limit within which they must be brought. Those time limits tend to be strictly kept to. Failure to comply with the time limit will prevent a Tribunal from considering your claim. It is essential that you check the time limit for bringing any claims, and act promptly.

Most common types of claim

Unfair dismissal

There are two basic types of unfair dismissal claim. The first is where your employer has dismissed you and you believe it is unfair. In this type of case, you will need to be able to explain what you believe made your dismissal unfair. Common complaints include the decision to dismiss was not fair or genuine, or that the process followed was unfair in some regard.

The second is known as 'constructive unfair dismissal', and this is where you have resigned because you believe that your employer has seriously breached your contract (a common complaint is that the employer's conduct has led to a breakdown in trust and confidence resulting in the employee not feeling that they can continue to work there). In this type of case, you need to be able to set out exactly what your employer did that breached your contract.

Wages claims

A number of disputes can arise in relation to wages and pay: holiday pay, redundancy pay, bonuses and ordinary pay can all lead to disagreements. If you think you have not been paid correctly, then you will need to set out carefully the reasons why you believe you are owed money, and how much you believe is owed. Be sure to set out your calculations clearly and provide any documents to support them, such as diary records, pay slips or rotas. A Tribunal might be able to consider such claims under two headings:

- An unauthorised deduction from wages claim, or
- A breach of a contract claim (this type of claim can only be brought after termination of an employee's employment, and the amount of an award is capped).

Discrimination

Discrimination claims are some of the most complex claims that can be brought in a Tribunal. Discrimination claims are based on conduct which is linked to a 'protected characteristic', not simply conduct that is negative or unfair. Protected characteristics include: race, religion or belief, age, gender, sexual orientation, disability, gender reassignment, marriage and civil partnership, pregnancy and maternity. In bringing a discrimination claim, you need to be able to explain:

- The protected characteristic you rely on. For example, if you are bringing a race claim, state what your race is
- What your employer has done which you believe is unfair, and
- Why you think that conduct is linked to your protected characteristic.

It will greatly assist you if you can spend some time researching the different types of discrimination claim, and focus your evidence and arguments accordingly.

Types of discrimination claim

Direct discrimination claims are where you believe that the conduct was because of your protected characteristic: someone without your characteristic would not have been treated in this way. For example: "I was not promoted because I am a Muslim, my colleague who is not Muslim was promoted".

Indirect discrimination claims are where you believe that a rule (known as a 'provision, criterion or practice') puts you and others with your protected characteristic at a disadvantage. For example, bonuses are based on full-time work, most women in your company work part-time and therefore do not qualify for bonuses.

Harassment is where someone subjects you to unwanted conduct related to your protected characteristic with the purpose or effect of violating your dignity or creating an intimidating, hostile, degrading, humiliating or offensive environment for you. For example, anyone who makes a mistake in the office is called 'gay', which offends homosexuals.

Victimisation is where you have done something to protect your discrimination rights, like raising a grievance (where you have a concern, problem or complaint at work that you take up with your employer), or bringing a claim, and you are treated less favourably because you have done so. For example, you raise a grievance saying that you think you have been bullied because you are 18, and following that grievance you are no longer invited to office social events.

Particular claims arise in respect of **disability discrimination**. If you are bringing a disability discrimination claim, and your employer does not accept that you are disabled, you should remember that it is not normally sufficient simply to say that you have a physical or mental impairment (like depression). You must prove that that impairment has a significant and long-term impact on your ability to carry out normal day-to-day activities. If you are found to be disabled, your employer has an obligation to make reasonable adjustments for your condition, and not treat you unfairly because of anything arising from your disability.

If you succeed in your claim, the Tribunal then need to consider what you might win in terms of compensation.

You will be asked to state what you believe you are owed in a 'Schedule of Loss', which is what lawyers call the document where you set out how much compensation you want to get if you win your case. There are rules about what can be claimed and the limits on how much the Tribunal can award, which can be found on the Employment Tribunal website.

Further information

Some useful sources of information on employment Tribunals and employment claims are:

- ACAS: www.acas.org.uk. In addition to providing mediation services, ACAS has a number of useful Guides and can assist you in understanding your employment rights
- The Employment Tribunal website: www. employmentTribunals.gov.uk. This contains forms and guidance
- The Government website, www.gov.uk, which has information about various different types of employment claims, and
- The Equality and Human Rights Commission: www.equalityhumanrights.com. This website has considerable guidance on bringing discrimination claims, and also contains links to the statutory Code of Practice that Tribunals may consider as part of a discrimination claim.

Immigration Tribunals

This Section looks at appeals against decisions by the UK immigration authorities, many of which are heard by the Immigration and Asylum Chamber of the First-tier Tribunal, which we will call the 'Immigration Tribunal' in this Section. We will refer to the immigration authorities as the UK Border Agency or 'UKBA'.

This Section primarily deals with immigration cases which are **not** eligible for legal aid. If you are still eligible for legal aid, you should speak to an immigration solicitor, who should be able to assist you. Asylum cases are likely to be eligible for legal aid.

In immigration appeals, the UKBA is often referred to as the 'respondent', and someone who is bringing an appeal is called an 'appellant'. In a case where someone is applying to visit or stay with a family member in the UK, that family member is often referred to as the 'sponsor'.

How it begins

You must be told in writing about any immigration decision by the UKBA. A 'Notice of Decision' (the document which tells you that your application has been refused) should tell you whether you have a right of appeal to the Immigration Tribunal, and what the time limit for appealing is. The reasons for the decision should also be included, either in the notice of decision or in a separate letter.

Some decisions cannot be appealed to the Immigration Tribunal, and if that is the case, the notice of decision should say so. In those cases it may be possible to bring a claim for judicial review in the High Court (see the Section on 'Public Law and Judicial Review' for more information).

This Section only deals with decisions that you can appeal against in an Immigration Tribunal.

If you are appealing against a decision made while you are in the UK, you have ten working days to send your appeal to the Tribunal after you receive the notice of decision, unless you are in immigration detention, in which case you must appeal within five working days. If you are outside the UK and are appealing against a refusal to grant you a visa to come here, you have 28 days to appeal. If you do not appeal in time, you should explain why in the appeal form and ask the Tribunal to allow you to appeal even though you are late.

You must return the appeal forms with a copy of the decision which you are appealing against. When completing the form it is not necessary to explain everything you would like to tell the Tribunal, just give an outline of what you are appealing against and why you think the decision was wrong.

You will have to pay a fee to bring your appeal, unless you fall into certain exceptions. Exceptions include appeals against deportation or removal from the UK, people getting legal aid, and people being paid some types of asylum support by the UKBA. Otherwise you can apply to have the fee remitted or reduced if you cannot pay. Detailed guidance on whether you have to pay a fee and how to pay it is available at: www.justice.gov.uk/downloads/Tribunals/immigration-and-asylum/ lower/online-fees-guidance.pdf.

If the Tribunal allows your appeal, it may order the UKBA to refund all or part of your fee.

You will also be asked to say whether you want a Hearing of your appeal (whether you would like to come to the Tribunal and speak to a judge about your case) or whether you would like it to be dealt with on the papers, that is to say, without a Hearing. Although the fee is lower if you ask for an appeal on the papers, your appeal is usually more likely to succeed if you ask for a Hearing.

When the Tribunal receives the appeal forms from you, it will set a date for a Hearing. For appeals by people in the UK, this is usually within a few weeks. For people outside the UK, there is a longer process, allowing time for UKBA to send copies of all the papers to the Tribunal from the Consulate abroad – in those cases it often takes several months before the Tribunal sets a Hearing date.

It is extremely unusual for an appellant who is outside the UK to be allowed to come to the UK to attend their own appeal Hearing, and in most cases it will be their sponsor, if they have one, who comes to the Tribunal. What this Section says about coming to the Tribunal applies to sponsors of people outside the UK as well as to appellants themselves.

Before the Hearing

When a date has been set, the Tribunal will send out a notice of Hearing telling you and the UKBA when and where you (or your sponsor) need to come to the Tribunal.

Before the Hearing, the UKBA has to make copies of all the papers which it looked at when making its decision. This includes any application form which you filled in, the notes of any interview which you went to and any letters or evidence which you sent in, as well as the decision and the reasons for it. In a deportation case for someone who has been convicted of an offence, this should also include details of the offence and the sentence passed. The papers should be put together and sent to the Immigration Tribunal and to you. This is called the 'respondent's bundle'. If you think there are any papers missing from this, for instance if you sent some evidence to the UKBA and it has not been included in the respondent's bundle, you should contact the Tribunal as soon as possible.

In many cases the Tribunal will hold a pre-Hearing review, in which a judge looks at the papers in the case and decides what you or the UKBA need to do before the final Hearing. You may be asked to fill in a questionnaire, in which you may be asked to confirm things like whether you have a representative, whether you are ready to go ahead with the appeal and what arrangements need to be made for the Hearing (for instance, whether you need an interpreter or whether you have a disability).

In some cases, the Immigration Tribunal may also arrange a Case Management and Review Hearing at which you and a representative of the UKBA will be asked to come to the Tribunal to discuss preparations for the Hearing. This usually only happens in more complicated cases or if the UKBA has failed to do something which the Tribunal told it to do.

The Tribunal may send out 'directions' (court Orders) telling you and the UKBA when to send in any documents and saying what else needs to be done before the final Hearing of the appeal. Usually the deadline for sending in documents is one week before the final Hearing. Copies of any documents you send in should also be sent to the UKBA. You must keep copies for yourself. The addresses where you have to send the documents will be on the Notice of Hearing or the directions.

In all cases you will need to use the time between the decision and the date of the final Hearing to prepare your case. This will include putting together documents which support your case and sending them to the Tribunal. Some suggestions are made below about what you may need to think about in different types of case.

If you have any witnesses, who may be able to give helpful information to the Tribunal, you should tell the Tribunal in advance and they should provide a letter or written statement saying what it is that they would like to say to the Tribunal.

On the day of the Hearing

Most appeals in the Immigration Tribunal are heard by a single judge, who will be a lawyer. In deportation cases the judge usually hears the case with a lay member, i.e. a member of the Tribunal who is not a lawyer. Some important or complicated cases are heard by panels of two or three judges. You should be told in advance if your appeal will be heard by more than one person.

You should call the judge and any lay members 'sir' or 'madam'. The judge will usually introduce themselves and explain to you what is going to happen.

The UKBA is usually represented by a Home Office Presenting Officer or 'HOPO'. This person is a civil servant and is not usually a lawyer. They will not usually be the person who made the decision which you are appealing against and sometimes they may not know very much about your case.

Hearings are usually in public, which means that anyone can come into the room. If for any reason you want your case to be heard in private so that only the judge and the HOPO know about it, then you should ask the judge.

Timings

At the moment almost all Immigration Tribunal Hearings are listed to start at 10:00am. You should make sure that you arrive at the Tribunal in good time before 10:00am, but this does not automatically mean that your Hearing will start at that time. The judge will often have several appeals to hear on the same day and will decide which order the appeals will be dealt with. It is usually a good idea to prepare to spend the whole day at the Tribunal, but if there is some reason why you need to leave early, you must tell the judge as soon as possible.

Documents

If you have documents which you want to show the Tribunal and which are not in the respondent's bundle and which you have not sent in already, you should give them to the judge as soon as possible upon arrival. You should bring three copies of these documents; one for the judge, one for the UKBA representative and one for yourself.

To assist you with preparing your case you should read the paragraphs in Section 2 entitled: 'Preparation is key'; 'Convincing the judge'; and 'Evidence', as well as the whole of Section 3, with the exception of 'Cross-examining witnesses', 'When judgment is given' and 'Costs', which are not relevant to immigration cases.

There is guidance on the Tribunal website about how judges should deal with cases where the appellant does not have a representative: www.justice.gov. uk/ downloads/Tribunals/immigration-and-asylum/ lower/GuideNoteNo5. pdf. This is written for judges but may be useful to you in understanding what the judge can and cannot do to make the Hearing easier for you.

Interpreters for non-English speakers

There will be an interpreter if you need one, as long as you have asked for one in advance. The judge should give you and the interpreter a chance to talk to each other before you begin to make sure that you both speak the same language and that you understand each other. If you are not completely happy with the interpreter, it is very important to say so. If you do not understand something which the judge or the HOPO says to you, or if you say something which is not properly interpreted into English, then the appeal can go badly wrong. Judges will usually be sympathetic to requests to change the interpreter if they believe that there may be a genuine problem.

Evidence

The Hearing will begin with evidence from you. This is called 'evidence-in-chief'. You will not be asked to give your evidence on oath. You will simply be asked to confirm that what you are saying is true. If possible, you should have written down what you want to say to the judge in a letter or statement and have sent it in before the Hearing. In that case you can usually just tell the judge that what you have said in writing is true, unless there is something new or something important which you have forgotten to say in writing that you would like to add. The judge may ask you questions to make sure that they understand you properly and that you only talk about what is really important in the case.

Cross-examination

Once you have given your evidence, the HOPO will have the chance to ask you questions. This is called cross-examination. The type of questions will depend on what reasons the UKBA have for not accepting your appeal. For instance, if the UKBA think you are not telling the truth about something, they will say so and give you the chance to explain. If it is just a matter of whether you have enough money to support yourself, for example, they will ask you questions about that.

Section 2 of this Guide talks about how to give your evidence, but you should remember that when there is an interpreter, you need to speak especially slowly and carefully, so that the interpreter understands you and has time to interpret what you say into English.

If you have any witnesses, they should be waiting outside while you give your evidence. You should make sure that the judge knows they are there. They will then be called into the Hearing room one by one, and the same process of questioning applies.

Submissions

After the evidence has been heard from you and any witnesses, each side will make submissions. Normally the HOPO will be asked to go first, and they will explain to the judge why the UKBA thinks your appeal should fail. You should not interrupt during the HOPO's submissions, even if you disagree strongly with what they are saying.

After the HOPO's submissions, you have the chance to make submissions explaining why you think that your appeal should succeed, and replying to anything the HOPO has said. Try to stay polite and calm, even if you do not like the things which have been said about you or your case by the HOPO. If the judge says anything or asks you any questions during your submissions, you should listen very carefully as he or she may be giving you an idea of what they think and what your submissions should focus on.

At the end of submissions, the Hearing is over. Sometimes the judge will tell you immediately what the result of the appeal is, but in most cases they will reserve their decision, meaning that they are going to think some more about it before making their decision. Do not worry if that happens in your case.

In every case, the judge has to write down the reasons for the decision in a judgment or 'determination'. This will be sent to you by post, usually about two to three weeks after the Hearing.

When putting together your own evidence, remember that the judge will have no prior knowledge of your case. Present your evidence in a logical and direct way.

After the decision

If your appeal is allowed, that will generally mean that the UKBA has to do what you asked it to do, such as grant a visa, or allow you to stay in the UK. However, the UKBA can appeal in certain circumstances. In some cases the effect of the Tribunal's determination may simply be that the UKBA has to make another decision because the previous one was not lawful.

Both sides have the right to appeal against the Tribunal's decision to the 'Immigration and Asylum Chamber of the Upper Tribunal'. This can only be done on a point of law, which means you believe the judge got the law wrong when he or she decided your case. You cannot appeal (and nor can the UKBA) simply because you do not agree with the decision which has been reached. Appeal forms will be sent out with the determination and the time limits are strict. Again, see the section on Public law and Judicial Review for more information about challenges.

Types of Immigration Hearing

There are many different kinds of immigration appeal, and this Guide cannot hope to cover absolutely everything.

This section focuses on some types of case where you are less likely to have a lawyer. Legal aid will still be available for asylum cases, and as asylum is a particularly complicated area of the law, you should try to find yourself a solicitor. There is a Best Practice Guide for asylum appeals, aimed at lawyers, at www.ein.org.uk/bpg/contents.

Deportation cases

'Deportation' has a special meaning in immigration law and usually refers to someone whose presence in the UK is considered to be against the public interest. The most common example is someone being forced to leave the UK because they have committed a criminal offence. Apart from asylum cases, the main basis on which deportation can be resisted is if it would interfere disproportionately with your family life, under Article 8 of the European Convention on Human Rights. In particular, that arises if you have a spouse, partner or children who are British or have the right to live in the UK. You will need to ask any adult family members to come to the Tribunal to speak about their relationship with you. It is particularly important to show that, if you are deported, any children you have will be negatively affected, as the Tribunal has to take the interests of children very seriously.

It may also help if you can show that you have lived in the UK for a long time, or if you have health difficulties, although these factors by themselves may not be enough to stop you being deported, especially if the offence is a serious one. In such cases it is also particularly important that you try to show that you have behaved well in prison or after being released, so that the judge can have confidence that you will not commit any more offences.

Applications to stay with partners or other family members

In these cases it is important that you try to understand the Immigration Rules (see below) concerning family applications, and that you make sure you understand exactly why your application has been refused. It is also important that your partner or other family member(s) should come to the Tribunal with you to give evidence and that you provide the Tribunal with as much financial information as you can.

EU applications

Special rules apply to citizens of the European Union (or European Economic Area), including in deportation cases, meaning that it is often harder for them to be deported even if they have committed offences. Special rules also apply to the partners and other close family members of EU citizens, as long as the EU citizens are working in the UK or exercising their rights under EU law in other ways. Unlike for non-EU applications, there are no strict financial rules for applications by people to be allowed to stay with family members who are EU citizens, so you are not required to provide the same level of financial information. This means that you do not need to be earning a particular amount of money, or to have a particular level of savings, or to show bank accounts for a particular period of time, whereas if you are applying as the partner or family member of someone from a non-EU country, you generally do have to give detailed information about their earnings and/or savings. The rules are very rigid and the application is likely to be turned down if the rules are not met.

Student applications

Refusals by the UKBA to allow people to stay as students often concern whether the college or university has provided the right documents. You should make sure you understand what documents are needed and you should speak with your educational institution about this. You may also need to provide detailed financial information, if there is a dispute about your financial situation. In other cases you may need to prove that you are genuinely coming to study and not to work. In these kinds of case, the Tribunal can only consider evidence about the situation at the date of the UKBA decision; it cannot normally take account of any changes, for example in your financial position, after the date of the decision. The UK Council for International Student Affairs (UKCISA) has guidance on immigration for students and their families at: www. ukcisa. org.uk/student/immigration.php.

Bail

If you are in Immigration Detention (being held by the authorities), you may be able to make a bail application for yourself. This means asking a judge to order your release. Bail Hearings are usually arranged at only a few days' notice and the procedures are even less formal than in other cases. There is a comprehensive Guide on bail, aimed at helping detainees to run their own bail Hearings, published by the charity Bail for Immigration Detainees (BID), at: www.biduk.org/10/how-to-get-out-of- detention/how-to-get-out-of-detention.html.

Further information

In addition to the websites mentioned above, other useful sources of information on immigration law include:

- The Immigration Rules and UKBA policies, found on the UKBA website: www.ukba.homeoffice.gov.uk/ policyandlaw/
- The Tribunal's website: www.justice.gov.uk/Tribunals/ immigration-asylum
- The website of the Immigration Law Practitioners Association (ILPA): www.ilpa.org.uk, which includes information sheets and updates on recent developments, aimed at non-lawyers
- The Electronic Immigration Network: www.ein.org.uk. This has a lot of information about various aspects of immigration and asylum law (some pages are members- only)
- The Legal Action Group, which has published a handbook, *Foreign National Prisoners: Law and Practice*, that includes useful sections on immigration law, especially asylum, human rights and deportation, and
- The Joint Council for the Welfare of Immigrants (JCWI), which is expected to be issuing a new edition of its very accessible *Immigration, Nationality and Refugee Law Handbook* (in 2013).

Family law

Family law is the area of civil and public law which deals with a broad range of family-related legal issues and domestic relations, such as divorce, adoption, property settlements and taking children into care. However, this section is limited in scope to deal only with the legal problems associated with the termination of relationships (that is, divorce or separation) which can frequently result in court Hearings that help to settle disputes over the separating couple's finances, and the living arrangements for their children. Property settlements are covered in the next section of this Guide.

What is your case?

If you are involved in care proceedings (also known as public law cases, which are brought about when a local authority believes that a child's welfare is endangered) public funding is still available, so you should see a solicitor who specialises in care work as a first step.

Legal aid is generally not available in private law matters involving children (disputes between parents or other individuals about the upbringing of children), and in financial disputes between married couples or those in civil partnerships. In these cases you are expected and encouraged by the court to have considered negotiation or mediation before issuing (beginning) proceedings. This is the process of the parties involved trying to agree an outcome outside of court. However, if that is not possible, as a final resort, you can ask the court for help. The courts will come to a decision on your case and make an Order, which you will have to follow, and will be made with the best interest of the child in mind. When making any decision about the upbringing of a child, the court's paramount consideration is always the child's welfare.

If you have a child or children with someone you are not married to, the courts can also help. For example, it is possible to claim for Financial Provision under section 15 and schedule 1 of the Children Act 1989 for financial support provided by the other parent of the child in question.

If you are a victim of domestic abuse (including violence, threats of violence or other physical or verbal abuse) you may be able to get public funding for your case. Also, some solicitors offer short, free advice sessions and they will be able to advise you on what you can and should do.

If you are co-habiting with your partner (living together, but are not married or in a civil partnership) in a jointly owned property, or a property owned by your partner that you believe you have a right to a share of, you may have a claim under Trust Law. See the next section in this Guide for further information.

Private law children applications

Most of the relevant law is contained in sections 1–14 of the Children Act 1989 (CA 1989), so it is advisable that you read as much of it as you can before you begin to prepare for your case.

First, find out if you have 'parental responsibility' for the child or children in question. Parental responsibility means all the rights and duties you have as a parent. See the Children Act sections 2–4 for more information. If you are the mother you have parental responsibility automatically. If you are the father you are deemed to have parental responsibility if you were married to the mother when the child was born, if the birth was after 1 December 2003 and you are registered on the birth certificate, or if you have entered into a 'parental responsibility agreement' with the mother of the child. If you do not have parental responsibility you are able to apply to the court for an Order granting it to you.

Orders under the Children Act 1989, section 8

In a private law child application, the court's decision will be in the form of an Order (these are mandatory instructions from the court that you must abide by). The most common Orders are those under Children Act 1989, section 8. When making a section 8 Order the court will take the child's wishes and feelings into consideration, and the older the child is, the more weight their wishes usually carry. Tempting as it may be, the courts do not appreciate parents (or others) discussing court cases with children or trying to influence their views. You must not do this. The most common Orders are outlined below.

Residence Orders

These specify who a child is to live with. It can be more than one person, which is referred to by lawyers as 'shared residence', and is an outcome the courts increasingly favour, as they see it in the best interest of the child to spend time with both parents, where at all possible.

Contact Orders

This is an Order which requires the person the child lives with, to make the child available for contact with the other person named in the Order (often the non-resident parent). Parents and relatives do not have a right to contact with the child if they are not named on the Order. However, unless there is a good reason why it is not in the child's best interests, the starting point from the court's perspective will be that a child benefits most from having a relationship with both parents. If a Contact Order is made and the child is not made available for contact, the court can enforce the Order and penalties may apply for non compliance.

Prohibited Steps Order

This prohibits the person named in the Order from doing certain actions without permission from the court, for example, removing the child from the other parent or from the jurisdiction (the geographical area covered by the court's legal reach; in this case, England and Wales).

Specific Issue Order

This Order gives 'directions' (mandatory instructions) about a particular element of the child's upbringing, for example, which school they must attend.

Procedure – what happens at the Hearing?

You should follow the Family Procedure Rules 2010 (www. justice.gov.uk/courts/procedure-rules/family), as they outline the steps you will need to take during a Hearing. If you are lost at any point, do not be afraid to ask the judge about any 'directions' made in court, as it is very important that you understand fully what is expected of you and what is going on if you are unsure.

At the first hearing (known as the First Hearing Dispute Resolution Appointment: FHDRA) you may be seen by a Children and Family Court Advisory and Support Service Officer, often called 'CAFCASS' officers, who will try to assist you and the other party in coming to an agreement about some or all of the issues. The CAFCASS officer will tell the court the outcome of the meeting and make recommendations for next steps towards the most positive outcome. For example, you might be ordered to attend a short course for separated parents (SPIP). There is a useful 'Practice Direction' about the first hearing at: www. justice.gov.uk/courts/procedure-rules/family/practice_directions/pd_part_12b#IDAKUXXC.

If the court feels more information (including about the child's wishes and feelings) is needed at this stage, it may ask that a report is carried out by a CAFCASS officer (or a social worker). This is called a 'section 7 report'. The person writing the report will come and talk to you, the other party and the child, and the report will make further recommendations to the court about the Orders it might consider making. If the parties cannot agree what should happen, the court will make the decision at a final hearing at which the parties, and sometimes the CAFCASS officer, give evidence. The court does not have to follow the report but has to have a good reason not to.

Financial Remedies (formerly called 'Ancillary Relief')

Financial Remedies is what lawyers call the process where the court looks to determine how fairly to distribute assets between former spouses or civil partners following a divorce or dissolution of the civil partnership. Here the court can also decide whether or not there should be ongoing maintenance payments. Financial Remedies applications only apply to married couples or those in a civil partnership who are in the process of getting, or have got, a divorce. However, if you are unmarried but have children together you still may be able to make a claim against the other parent for Financial Provision under Schedule 1 of the Children Act 1989.

Dividing assets fairly

The court has to work out what the parties' financial resources are and then divide them fairly by way of an Order. The Orders the court can make are set out in the Matrimonial Causes Act 1973 (MCA 1973) sections 23–25, so it is a good idea to read this. The court can make these Orders any time after they have made the first Order in divorce proceedings (called a 'grant of Decree Nisi' by lawyers), but they cannot take effect until after a divorce that has been granted (called 'Decree Absolute').

There is one exception to be aware of: an 'Order for Maintenance pending suit' (maintenance refers to the periodical payments to be made by one party to the other). An Order for Maintenance pending suit can be made by the court any time after the process to get a divorce has begun, and the payments can be ordered to continue for any period of time until a decision, called a Final Order, has been made about the case (i.e. whether a divorce has gone through or not).

Some Orders cannot be made once a party re-marries unless an application has been brought beforehand. This means it is important to have applied for Financial Provision before a divorce is finalised.

The most common Financial Provision Orders are:

- The sale of property and division of proceeds (dividing the money made from the sale).
- Transfer of the family home to one party, in some cases with the other party retaining an interest in the property which can be realised at some time in the future, frequently when the youngest child reaches 18 or leaves full-time education.
- Payment of a lump sum by one party to the other.
- Maintenance payments by one party to the other for a specified period or for as long as both parties are alive.
- A pension sharing Order (where the court orders a pension to be shared).

The court looks at how the separating couple can mostly fairly share any assets by looking at the 'Sharing Principle' (which looks at the right to share assets that have built up during the marriage), the individual needs of both and any children, and potential compensation that either or both party could claim. 'Sharing' and 'needs' are considered to be the most important, although quantifying 'needs' can be very hard. Note, that the court cannot order one party to pay the other's debts other than by payment of a lump sum or through maintenance.

To understand more about how the court decides how to fairly divide any assets, you should refer to MCA 1973 section 25. Whilst the court tries to divide the assets fairly, remember that this does not necessarily mean in equal shares. It is also important to remember that the court will consider 'bad behaviour' only in exceptional circumstances, for example gambling away significant levels of matrimonial assets. Also, if a party gives away or moves assets in order to avoid an Order, the court can reverse or prevent the transaction to prevent this (see MCA section 37).

If the parties have a child, then the child's welfare is the court's first consideration and ensuring the child is securely housed is a priority. This can have implications for who the court grants property to.

Child support

Child support is not usually dealt with by the court. If the child or children live with you and your former spouse (wife or husband) is not paying child maintenance (financial support), you should consider applying through the Child Support Agency.

It is very important to comply with court deadlines, but if you are struggling, make a formal application.

Procedure – what happens at the Hearing?

Procedure is mainly outlined by the Family Procedure Rules 2010. Again, do not be afraid to ask the judge about any 'directions' made in court as the judge understands that you will not have done this before.

Before the first Hearing, known as the First Appointment, you have to complete, file at Court and serve (send, to the other party) a form called: 'Form E', which you can find here: www.justice.gov.uk/forms/hmcts. On Form E you will have to set out your financial position: your assets (including all property you own), income (from all sources), liabilities and income needs. Make sure you include a copy of Form E in your 'bundle' (the papers you will take to court).

The First Appointment is your chance to ask for any further information from the other party that you think is relevant. For example, if you think there are assets or income that have not been disclosed, now is your time to mention it. Put your questions and requests into a "Request for Further Information and Documents" and file and serve it together with a short chronology (timeline) of events and a list of the issues you consider to be relevant in your case. You must do this at least 14 days before the Hearing. The judge will decide what information each party needs to provide, and will tell you when you should submit it by, and how. The judge may also decide if expert evidence is required, for example valuation evidence in relation to properties or businesses (understanding the value of a property).

At the First Appointment the court will list the case (arrange a date) for a Financial Dispute Resolution Hearing (FDR), which is a court appointment used for settlement of financial matters in divorce cases. At least seven days (although this can change, so do check) before this Hearing you will need to have written to the other party saying what you would accept by settlement and then have filed a copy of this document at court. At the hearing the judge will expect each party to briefly set out their case, and then the judge will advise on an appropriate settlement. The judge cannot force you to settle, but he or she will encourage and assist you to do so. If you do reach an agreement the judge will approve it. It will then be made into an Order by the Court. If your case does not settle at FDR it will be listed for a Final Hearing for the judge to hear further evidence and then make a Final Order.

Further information

For further information, family barrister, Lucy Reed, has published a book: Family Courts without a Lawyer, which is specifically designed to help people involved in disputes with a former partner over money or children and do not have a lawyer to represent themselves in court.

Property ownership in relationship breakdowns

Where there is an argument about the ownership and/or occupation of a property when a relationship breaks down between an unmarried couple, the parties can ask the court to help them reach a solution. The power of the court to do so is contained in the Trusts of Land and Trustees Act 1996, sometimes referred to by lawyers as 'TOLATA'. The law in this area is complex and if possible legal advice should be sought.

It is important however, to consider whether a negotiated agreement can be reached before taking the matter to court. Assistance is available through mediation, when a qualified third party will assist you in trying to reach a settlement. For more information on mediation, visit: www.familymediationcouncil.org.uk or www. civilmediation.justice.gov.uk.

In English property law there are two elements relating to the ownership of property. First, there is the legal interest (the property owner registered at the Land Registry), and second, the beneficial interest (when somebody is entitled to a portion of ownership, but is not the registered legal owner). The legal owner may be holding some of the beneficial interest on behalf of (or for the benefit of) another person.

In a case of joint legal ownership, where the precise details of the two elements are fully recorded in writing, this will determine the ownership. For properties purchased after 1998, refer to the Land Registry's Form TR1 (www. landregistry.gov.uk/public/forms/completing-form-tr1). If the position is not clear from the written documentation, there will be arguments as to how much each party owns. Where the property is held in one party's name only, the non-owner will have to persuade the court that it was intended that they have some beneficial interest in the property. Where there are children who need to be housed, the 'Schedule 1 of the Children Act 1989' (www.legislation.gov.uk/ukpga/1989/41/contents) may provide a remedy to help secure a home during their dependency.

If your case is taken to court, there are a number of key documents that will assist your case, and it is advisable to secure them at an early stage. They include:

- Any documents relating to the purchase of the property
- The title deeds and Land Registry documents (post 1998, the TR1 Form)
- Any documentation relating to a mortgage on the property, and
- A short chronology of events and discussions relating to the purchase and running of the property.

This section is very concise, and more information can be found here: www. advicenow.org.uk/living-together/ and here: www.landregistry.gov.uk.

Public law and Judicial Review

Challenges to Government decisions, actions and failures to act

This Section will give you more information about how you would go about challenging a decision, action or failures to act by a Government Department, or some other public body, like a local authority. This is known as 'public law'. In this area, it is a very good idea to seek some legal advice at an early stage (see Section 1). These cases are complicated and you can be at risk of paying the other party's costs if you lose. You may want to consult a specialist public law solicitors' firm or, using public access (for information visit: www.barcouncil.org.uk/publicaccess), a specialist barrister. They may even be able to represent you on a 'no win, no fee' basis or with legal aid funding. If not, they may at least be able to give you some advice to set you off on the right track.

There are very short time limits which you will have to stick to if you want to bring a claim. This is particularly the case in judicial review, which is explained later in this section. Please make sure you are fully aware of these and start your case as early as possible so that you do not miss any deadlines.

Which Court or Tribunal?

You have to bring your challenge in the right Court or Tribunal. More and more challenges to decisions of public bodies are now heard by the 'First-tier Tribunal'. This is the name given to a large family of Tribunals that hear lots of different kinds of cases. Each type of case has its own specialist Tribunal with judges who are expert in that area. If your case can be heard by the First-tier Tribunal you are obliged to bring it there. If not, you may be able to bring your case to the High Court.

Therefore, your first task is to work out whether you can bring a claim before the First-tier Tribunal.

The First-tier Tribunal is split into six different parts, known as Chambers. Within those six Chambers are a number of Tribunals which specialise in particular types of case. The most important ones are:

Chamber	Type of Tribunal	Type of case
General Regulatory Chamber	Charity	Appeals against and applications for review of decisions of the Charity Commission in relation to the registration and functioning of charities.
	Consumer Credit	Appeals against decisions of the Office of Fair Trading in relation to consumer credit matters.
	Environment	Appeals against sanctions and regulatory action taken by the Environment Agency and Natural England.
	Estate Agents	Appeals against decisions of the Office of Fair Trading in relation to estate agents and their duties.
	Food	Appeals against certain types of decisions made by the Food Standards Agency and other food industry regulators.
	Gambling	Appeals against regulatory decisions of the Gambling Commission in relation to gambling licences.
	Immigration Services	Appeals against decisions of the Immigration Services Commissioner about the regulation of the provision of immigration services.
	Information Rights	Appeals against decision notices of the Information Commissioner under the Freedom of Information Act 2000 and the Environmental Information Regulations 2004.
	Transport	Appeals about approved driving instructors, trainee driving instructors and providers of driving training.
Health Education and Social Care Chamber	Care Standards	Appeals against decisions relating to the registration of individuals wishing to work with children or vulnerable adults, or provide health and social care.
	Mental Health	Appeals, applications and references in all types of decisions and actions which relate to the mental health of an individual under the Mental Health Act 1983.

Chamber	Type of Tribunal	Type of case
	Special Educational Needs & Disability	Appeals against decisions of local education authorities in relation to assessments and statements of special education needs, as well as disability discrimination claims against schools.
	Primary Health Lists	Appeals against decisions of Primary Care Trusts about lists of medical, dental and ophthalmic practitioners.
Immigration and Asylum Chamber	Immigration and Asylum	Appeals against decisions relating to your immigration status or an application for asylum. See Section 4.
Social Entitlement Chamber	Asylum Support	Appeals against decisions of the UK Border Agency about the social support arrangements for asylum seekers.
	Criminal Injuries Compensation	Appeals against decisions of the Criminal Injuries Compensation Authority.
	Social Security and Child Support	Appeals against decisions of the Secretary of State for Work and Pensions, HMRC and local authorities about entitlement to all types of welfare benefits and tax credits.
Tax Chamber	Tax	Appeals from all types of decision made by HM Revenue and Customs about any type of tax or national insurance payments.
War Pensions and Armed Forces Compensation Chamber	War Pensions and Armed Forces Compensation	Appeals about war pensions, compensation given to former members of the armed forces and the assessment of disability for that compensation.

If your problem seems to fall into one of the areas covered by one of these Tribunals, it does not necessarily mean you can bring a claim there. For example, you may only be allowed to challenge specific types of decision or action in a Tribunal, or you may only be allowed to challenge the decision or action for particular reasons, which do not apply to your problem. You need to look at the relevant Tribunal rules to find out exactly which kinds of case you can bring in each Tribunal. The rules can be found at www.justice.gov. uk/Tribunals/rules. There is also a lot of helpful information on the Tribunals website: www. justice.gov.uk/Tribunals.

What to do if you can bring a case in a Tribunal

If you cannot bring a case in a Tribunal, skip this section, and go to the next section, entitled: What to do if you cannot bring a case in a Tribunal: Judicial Review, which discusses how to challenge a Government decision in the High Court.

Work out how to bring your claim

Tribunals are intended to be more informal and less complicated than courts. The idea is that anyone should be able to represent themselves in a Tribunal, without the need for a lawyer to help them. However, each of the different Chambers of the First-tier Tribunal has procedural rules which you should follow and some of them can be complicated. It is always sensible to check the rules carefully to make sure you understand what the Tribunal will expect of you.

The rules can be found at www.justice.gov.uk/Tribunals/ rules. Make sure you have found the correct form for bringing a claim. Then follow the rules carefully for how to bring your claim.

Time limits

When you look at the rules, pay close attention to any time limits. The length of time you have to make your challenge will depend upon the type of case it is. Make sure you check the relevant rules or the Tribunal's website to see how many days you have. If you are late, you will have to apply to the Tribunal to ask for permission to bring your case. Your application may be refused and then you will have missed your opportunity.

The Hearing

Usually, any Hearing you have in a Tribunal will be heard by a Tribunal judge. A Tribunal judge is a lawyer. In some types of Tribunal, the judge will also sit with non- legal professionals who have specialist knowledge, such as doctors or chartered surveyors. Each member of the Tribunal will be able to vote on the decision in your case.

In the Tribunals, you do not stand up when you are speaking. The room will feel a little less formal than other courts, although people still wear smart clothes.

Costs

Different Chambers of the First-tier Tribunal have slightly different rules on when you might have to pay for the cost of the lawyers representing the other party if you lose your case. Under most of the rules, a Tribunal will not require you to pay costs unless you have acted unreasonably, but you should always check this. In the Social Entitlement Chamber and War Pensions and Armed Forces Compensation Chamber, you will never have to pay for the other party's costs.

Appeals to the Upper Tribunal

If you lose your case in the First-tier Tribunal (FTT) you can appeal to the Upper Tribunal. There are four different Chambers of the Upper Tribunal.

Chamber	Appeals from the FTT	Other types of case
Administrative Appeals Chamber	General Regulatory Chamber	Appeals against decisions of the Traffic Commissioners.
	Health Education and Social Care Chamber	Appeals against decisions of the Independent Safeguarding Authority.
	Social Entitlement Chamber	
	War Pensions and Armed Forces Compensation Chamber	
Immigration and Asylum Chamber	Immigration and Asylum Chamber	
Lands Chamber	(None currently)	Land compensation claims.
		Appeals from Leasehold Valuation Tribunals and Residential Property Tribunals. Appeals concerning land value.
Tax and Chancery Chamber	Tax Chamber	References from decisions of the Financial Services Authority (not an appeal).
	General Regulatory Chamber (charity cases only)	References from decisions of the Pensions Regulator (not an appeal).

However, you can only appeal to the Upper Tribunal in certain circumstances. It must be an appeal on a 'point of law'. This means you can only go to the Upper Tribunal if you are arguing that the judge got the law wrong when he decided your case. You cannot usually appeal to the Upper Tribunal just because you think the decision was wrong or because the judge did not believe you.

Because you can only appeal a 'point of law', you must ask for permission to carry on with your case if you have lost. You should first ask the judge of the First-tier Tribunal if you can appeal their decision, explaining why you think they have got the law wrong. If they refuse, then you can ask a judge of the Upper Tribunal to give you permission.

The amount of time you have to appeal a decision can be different depending on which Chamber of the First-tier Tribunal your case was in. You should check the rules of that Chamber and of the Chamber of the Upper Tribunal that your appeal would be heard by.

As with the First-tier Tribunal, each of the different Chambers of the Upper Tribunal has procedural rules that you should follow. Usually, the rules of the Upper Tribunal will be very similar to those of the First-tier Tribunal Cham-

ber that you have appealed from. The rules can be found at www.justice.gov.
uk/Tribunals/rules.

Further information about the Tribunals

You can find a lot of helpful information for free through the Tribunals' websites at www.justice.gov.uk/Tribunals.

If you need more detail on what the procedural rules mean, your local library may be able to help you get hold of a copy of *The New Tribunals Handbook* (by Blakeley, Knight and Love) or *Tribunal Practice and Procedure* (by Edward Jacobs).

What to do if you cannot bring a case in a Tribunal: Judicial Review

If you cannot bring a case in a Tribunal, you may be able to challenge a decision, action or failure to act in the High Court, by a procedure called a 'Judicial Review'. There are also similar challenges in the High Court by what are called 'Statutory Appeals'. These cover specialist areas like planning appeals and public procurement challenges, and are beyond the scope of this Guide.

Limits on your right to bring a Judicial Review

There are a number of important limits to note regarding when you can bring a Judicial Review challenge.

You can only bring Judicial Review proceedings if you do not have a reasonably convenient alternative remedy. This is why you cannot go to the High Court if you have the option of going to the First-tier Tribunal (or if you have a Statutory Appeal).

There are **very strict time limits** in Judicial Review cases. You have to bring your challenge within three months of the decision that you are challenging. You are also required to bring it 'promptly' within those three months. This means you have to bring the claim as quickly as you can within the three month period. You may be able to get time extended if you fail to meet the time limit, but only for 'good reason', for example, extreme ill-health.

You have to have some kind of interest in the decision that you want to challenge. Lawyers call this having 'standing'. This means that if a decision is made that affects somebody who has nothing to do with you, you may not be allowed to challenge it. If it affects you or a member of your family directly, you will be able to challenge it. You may also be able to bring a challenge if it is considered to be in the public interest that you do so. If you are bringing a human rights challenge, then the rules are stricter. You have to be a direct victim of the human rights breach.

Decisions can you challenge via Judicial Review

You can only judicially review the decisions of public bodies, and only when they are acting in their public capacities. You may be able to bring human rights challenges to a private body exercising a public function. There is no complete list of what is or is not a public body (or what counts as a public capacity of such bodies). But broadly speaking, it includes decisions by:

- Government Ministers, departments and agencies
- Public regulatory bodies
- Local and health authorities

- Chief constables and prison governors
- Some Tribunals (but only if you cannot appeal to a higher Tribunal or court)• Magistrates, coroners and county courts (but only if you cannot appeal to a higher Tribunal or court), and
- School Governor Boards (but not independent schools).

Grounds for challenging a decision or action using Judicial Review

Judicial Review can only be used to challenge decisions on the grounds that they were made in an unlawful way. The High Court will not decide whether the public body has made a "good" decision or not. Instead, it will consider whether the decision was **outside the legal powers of the decision-maker**. Lawyers say that what the decision maker did was 'ultra vires'. This simply means that the decision was beyond the powers of the decision maker. This may be because it was:

- **Based on an error of law.** This could be any situation where the decision-maker has misunderstood or misapplied the law. For example, the decision-maker might have refused to do something because they thought they had no legal power to do it, when in fact they did have the power to do it.
- **Done for an improper purpose.** What is a proper purpose will depend on the situation, and the court will consider this in the given circumstances.
- **Taken when the decision-maker had not taken into account relevant matters or had taken into account irrelevant matters.** The court will look at the situation and consider what the decision-maker should have taken into account in the given circumstances.
- **Affected by unlawful limits placed on the exercise of the decision-maker's discretion.** Sometimes the law will give a decision-maker a lot of freedom to make a particular decision. If the decision-maker then creates excessively strict rules for themselves about how to make the decision they may be found to have improperly limited their freedom to take the decision. In other words, they may have created an excessively strict policy that has limited their ability to be flexible. Lawyers call this "fettering their discretion".
- **Irrational.** The court can reverse a decision if it is so unreasonable that no reasonable public authority would ever take it. This is a roundabout way of saying that the decision was extremely unreasonable, to the point that it was absurd or perverse. This is a much higher standard than simply saying that the decision was wrong or not reasonable.
- **Made in breach of your legitimate expectations.** If you were clearly promised something (or given such a strong signal that it almost added up to a promise), it may be unfair for a decision-maker to go back on that promise without sufficient justification, or without giving you a Hearing first.
- **Based on an unfair process.** This might mean that you were not given a fair opportunity to explain your arguments to the public body. It also might mean that the decision-maker was in some way biased. It might mean the public body should have given you reasons for its decision, but failed to do so.

- **Contrary to the Human Rights Act 1998**. You should look at the Human Rights Act. The organisation Liberty also provides some helpful information and an advice line about the Act: www.yourrights.org.uk/get-advice/.

What you can get from Judicial Review

Even if you win your case, the court will not necessarily give you any remedy at all. The court has the freedom to decide, and will consider factors such as whether you acted promptly, whether you acted in good faith and whether you have been harmed by the decision.

If you win your case, the court may award six different kinds of remedy. These are:

- **Quashing Order**: A quashing Order overturns or undoes a decision that has already been made.
- **Prohibiting Order**: This stops a public body from taking an unlawful decision or action it has not yet taken.
- **Injunctions**: This is also a restraining Order, which, for example, stops a person from acting in a public office in which they have no legal right to act. The court may also grant an 'interim injunction'. This is a temporary Order requiring a public body to do something or not to do something until a final decision has been made in your case. There are detailed rules as to when an interim injunction is appropriate.
- **Mandatory Order**: This makes a public body do something that the law says it has to do. Normally, if the public body is ordered to make a decision, it will still be free to decide whatever it likes, as long as the decision is taken lawfully.
- **Declarations**: The court can state what the law is or what the parties have a right to.
- **Damages**: Damages may be awarded where a public body has breached your human rights. Otherwise, the court will not normally give you any compensation if you win your case, unless you have some other entitlement to damages.

It is important to remember that the court will not normally make the public body's decision for it, even if you win your judicial review. Very often, after a Judicial Review, the public body will have to retake the decision and you may still not get what you want. They will just be obliged to follow a fairer process the second time round.

What you can lose from Judicial Review

If you lose your case, you will usually have to pay the public body's 'reasonable' costs of defending the claim. These can be very high. This is one of the reasons why it is so important to try to seek specialist advice about your case at an early stage if you can. At every stage throughout your claim, think about the costs that the public body will be spending. This may affect your decision to keep fighting at the next stage.

If it is in the general public interest that you bring a claim, you should apply to the court for a Protective Costs Order. This is an Order given by the court at the beginning of the case that even if you lose you will not have to pay the public body's costs above a certain level.

What to do before bringing your Judicial Review claim

If (but only if) you have time before the three month time limit (and the requirement of promptness) runs out, you should write to the public body, following the format set out in the 'Pre action protocol': www.dca.gov.uk/ civil/procrules_fin/contents/protocols/prot_jrv.htm. This is called writing a Letter before Claim.

The letter should:

- Explain in detail what you say the public body has done wrong
- Ask for detailed reasons for the decision or (if you have them) a response to your letter within a time limit, usually 14 days, and
- Threaten Judicial Review if you are not sent reasons or if the reasons do not satisfy you that the decision or action was lawful.

This Letter before Claim may encourage the public body to do the right thing before you get to court. If time is short, it is still a good idea to make telephone contact with the public body.

How to bring your claim

Claims for Judicial Review are made in several stages.

The application

First, you make your written application to the court. This includes paying a court fee. As with any application to a court, you need to explain your case in clear, simple terms. Specifically, you must identify: what decision or action you are challenging; the date of that decision or action; your grounds for challenging it; whether the case is urgent and if so any relevant time limits; and if necessary any application for temporary relief (like an interim injunction) pending final determination of your claim (the final decision made). The application is made on form N461 (found under www.justice.gov.uk/ courts/procedure- rules/civil/forms), and is often accompanied by written evidence.

The first permission stage

This allows the court to filter out cases that should not be allowed to go to a full Hearing because they are so unlikely to succeed. A judge will read all the papers sent in by both parties and decide whether your case will be allowed to go ahead. You will not be given permission to have a full Hearing if the judge decides that you do not have an arguable case or that for some other reason, the case cannot succeed, for example, you have not met the time limit. You will be told the result by post. If you are unsuccessful, the judge will give short reasons for why that is so. Sometimes, the judge does not decide but refers the case to the second permission stage.

The second permission stage

If you are refused permission, you may decide that it is time to stop. You should consider carefully why you were denied permission and whether you accept that the reasons given were correct. If you still wish to carry on, you have a right to a Hearing in court to try to persuade a judge in person that you should be granted permission. The Hearings are usually quite short, often around half an hour.

The third permission stage

If you are still not granted permission, you might try to appeal the Court of Appeal. However, you should think hard about doing this. It is unlikely to succeed and will increase the public body's costs substantially, which you may well end up having to pay.

Full Hearing

If you are given permission, you will need to pay another fee within seven days of being given permission. There will be more exchanges of written evidence. Then, when all parties are ready, and when the court has time available, the case will be listed for a full Hearing so the court can listen to the arguments on both sides. Full Hearings in the High Court are very formal. You stand when you speak and when the judge enters and leaves the room. Barristers will be wearing wigs and gowns. Try not to feel intimidated. Nobody expects you to speak or look like a lawyer. Just explain the case as simply and as clearly as you can.

Claimants currently wait between six months and one year for a case to go to a full Hearing, although urgent cases can be heard within 24 hours if necessary. However, the first 'permission' stage of the proceedings may only take a few weeks. Often, if you are granted permission, public bodies will compromise and deal with your concerns to avoid the case going to court.

Further information about Judicial Review

A charity called the Public Law Project provides a lot of useful resources on how to bring a Judicial Review claim: www.publiclawproject.org.uk/Advice-General.html.

A number of specialist solicitors' firms also provide short Guides to the process. For example:

- www.deightonpierceglynn.co.uk/resources/pdf/ Judicial_Review_Procedure.pdf
- www.leighday.co.uk/LeighDay/media/LeighDay/ documents/JR-Quicky-and-Easy-Guide.pdf?ext=.pdf
- www.bevanbrittan.com/articles/Pages/ GuidetoJudicialReviewincivilmatters.aspx

There are lots of books about Judicial Review. Most of them are difficult to understand if you are not a lawyer, however we recommend *Judicial Review: A Practical Guide* (by Southey, Weston and Bunting). There is also a chapter on Judicial Review that might be helpful in *The New Tribunals Handbook* (by Blakeley, Knight and Love). You can also find more if you Google: "Guide to Judicial Review".

Housing law

Housing law covers a wide range of issues, from homelessness and Possession Proceedings (when another party reclaims your property), all the way through to grants used to adapt properties for disabled persons.

Certain areas of housing law are still within the scope of legal aid (for example, certain Possession Proceedings and assistance for the homeless) so you should always check first with a solicitor whether legal aid might be available.

There is also a range of excellent, free, resources on housing law available on the internet, in particular, provided by the housing and homelessness charity, Shelter, (www.shelter.org.uk). The Legal Action Group also publishes law books on housing aimed at non-lawyers (for example, '*Defending Possession Proceedings*', and '*Repairs: tenants' rights*').

This Section only deals with two of the most common areas of disputes about housing, Possession Proceedings (which is explained below) and cases of disrepair to rental property. In some circumstances you may still be able to get legal aid for these sorts of cases, so you should always check.

Possession Proceedings

If you fall behind with your rent or mortgage repayments, your landlord or lender can start court action to get back whatever money you owe them. These are called Possession Proceedings and can lead to you losing your home. In this case the landlord or lender is the 'claimant'. If a claim is brought against you, this is called a Possession Claim.

There is a range of different kinds of claims regarding possession which can be brought against people occupying residential property, depending on the nature of what is called their 'right to occupy' a property. The most common types are discussed below. There are three pieces of advice which apply regardless of what sort of claim you are facing:

1. You should always try to attend the Possession Hearing, where your case will be initially discussed. Judges have lots of experience in dealing with possession claims and, in many cases, have relatively generous powers to allow you to stay in your home. If you are not present and therefore not able to explain your circumstances to the judge, then it is very likely that an Order will be made against you.

2. In some courts, there may be a 'duty solicitor' present who is paid (not by you) to assist those facing Possession Hearings each day. If you do not attend court, you cannot make use of this service.

3. Try to seek advice about your case as early on as possible. Legal aid is still available for most Possession Proceedings. There are also many advice agencies (such as the Citizens Advice Bureau) which have a great deal of experience in helping people to stay in their homes. It is often possible to reach a negotiated agreement before any Possession Hearing, particularly where the claimant is a social landlord (for example, a landlord who is renting out council or housing association owned property).

Mortgage possession claims against an owner / occupier

If you are behind with your mortgage repayments, your lender may issue proceedings (the legal way for saying a case against you will begin) against you, seeking an Order for Possession of your home, which is a court Order that might lead to your home being taken from you. In most cases the crucial issue is whether you are likely to be able to repay the amount you are behind by within what is known as a 'reasonable' period of time, which can be as long as the remaining term of your mortgage. You need to be able to explain to the judge why you fell behind in your repayments (this is called falling 'into arrears') and how you plan to pay the lender back, and at the same time meeting the normal monthly instalments. For example, if you have lost your job and been out of work for six months, but have now found work, and can manage as a result to pay £50 per month off the arrears, on top of the normal monthly mortgage instalments. You should, if possible, bring evidence to support your explanation (such as the letter offering you a new job, wage slips, etc).

If the judge is satisfied that you are able to repay the arrears within a reasonable period of time he or she can either:

- Adjourn (end) the case on the condition that you pay your normal monthly instalments plus a portion off the arrears each month, or
- Make a Possession Order that will be suspended so long as you pay your normal monthly instalments plus a portion off the arrears each month. The second Order is more common. It means that although according to the law the lender is given the right to repossess your home, they cannot exercise that right if you keep making the payments which the Possession Order sets out.

If you are not able to repay the arrears within a reasonable period of time, you should seek debt advice from a specialist debt advisor (see the Bankruptcy and Debt section in this Guide). For example, it may be in your best interest to seek to sell the property to repay the mortgage.

Mortgage Possession claims against the tenant of a borrower

If you are renting your home from a landlord who has a mortgage on the property, and if the landlord has stopped paying the mortgage, the mortgage lender may take steps to repossess the property from the landlord, as described above.

Except in relatively rare cases (for example, if your tenancy pre-dates the mortgage), it is unlikely that you will have a substantive defence to the claim for possession from the mortgage lenders. You do, however, have a right to apply to the court to be given up to two months in order to make arrangements to leave the property before the possession occurs. Many mortgage companies will consent to giving you this time once your application is made. The court will normally make it a condition that you pay your rent directly to the mortgage company during these two months.

Private sector Possession Claims

If you are the tenant of a private sector landlord (an individual who owns a property and rents to an individual), then it is likely that you have an 'assured shorthold tenancy', which means that your tenancy has a limited amount of security. However, it is possible that you have another form of tenancy (for example, a 'fully assured tenancy' or a 'Rent Act 1977 tenancy'). If you are unsure about your tenancy status you should seek advice from a solicitor or the Citizens Advice Bureau. You should also read up on your type of tenancy to ensure you understand it.

There are two different routes which a landlord might use to try to evict you (essentially, remove you from living in the property) under an assured shorthold tenancy. The first is to serve a notice under section 21 of the Housing Act 1988. This entitles the landlord to a Possession Order so long as he has given you the required amount of notice (usually two months). So long as the notice is valid then the court **must** make a Possession Order, and you will be forced to move out. There are certain limited restrictions on when a landlord can use a section 21 notice (for example the landlord would have been required to protect the deposit you paid in accordance with the rules of a tenancy deposit scheme), but these are likely to be fact- specific and are not covered in this Guide. If you are given a notice under section 21 of the Housing Act 1988 and do not wish to leave the property, you should seek advice from a solicitor, the Citizens Advice Bureau or a similar advice centre. Be aware that advice from a solicitor will incur costs.

Be sensible about the arguments you make: if you argue bad points that are difficult to comprehend or stretch the truth, you will have a harder job convincing the judge.

The second option is for the landlord to serve a notice under section 8 of the Housing Act 1988. This will refer to one or more 'grounds' for possession, that is, reasons for eviction.

The most common are grounds 8, 10 and 11 (all of which relate to rent arrears), so you should try to read them. In the case of grounds 10 and 11, the court will need to be satisfied that:

- The ground is 'made out' (which means the facts alleged in the notice are proved to be true)
- It is reasonable to make an Order for Possession, and
- It is reasonable to make an immediate Order for Possession, as opposed to an Order which is suspended on terms (dependent upon you keeping to certain conditions), such as, payment of future rent and arrears.

In the case of ground 8, however, once the ground is made out, the court has no choice but to make an Order. You must check the notice carefully to see what ground(s) are referred to and, again, seek immediate advice as to what can be done to avoid a Possession Order being granted.

Tenants of local authorities

Local authorities can operate a range of tenancies including secure tenancies, non-secure tenancies, flexible tenancies, introductory tenancies, demoted tenancies and family intervention tenancies. You should look up these terms on the internet. The most common kind of Possession Proceedings involves a Secure Tenancy, where the authority is seeking possession because you have not paid your rent. The other types of tenancy are more complex and are beyond the scope of this Guide.

The process for evicting a tenant starts with the service of a 'Notice Seeking Possession', this means you are given a notice which will set out the nature of the claim against you (for example, not having paid your rent). You should immediately contact your housing officer to discuss the notice. In many cases, you can usually reach an agreement with the housing officer to let you remedy the problem without the need for further court action.

If you cannot reach an agreement outside of court with the local authority, they can issue Possession Proceedings, but in order to make a Possession Order, the court must be satisfied:

- That a ground for possession is made out (for example, ground 1 regarding rent arrears)
- That it is reasonable to grant an Order for possession, and
- That it is reasonable to make an outright Order instead of one which is suspended subject to certain terms being met (such as repayment of any arrears).

In many cases, if you can explain to the judge why the problem arose (for example, problems with renewing a housing benefit claim or temporary unemployment) and make proposals to resolve whatever the problem is, the judge will be prepared to make a Suspended Possession Order, meaning that you cannot be evicted so long as you keep to the terms of the suspension.

Tenants of housing associations

Housing associations usually have either assured shorthold tenancies or fully assured tenancies. If you have an assured shorthold tenancy, then please refer to the 'Private sector Possession Claims' heading, above. In the case of a fully assured tenancy, the procedure is similar to that set out for local authorities (explained above).

Disrepair

Your landlord owes you certain obligations with regards to the physical condition of the property. These are sometimes set out in the tenancy agreement. In any event, regardless of what the tenancy agreement says, the obligations in section 11 of the Landlord and Tenant Act 1985 are implied as part of that agreement. The landlord is under an obligation to ensure that the structure and exterior of the property is in good repair. There is also an obligation to ensure that things like the pipes for supplying water and gas are in good working order.

It is important that any problems are raised with the landlord as soon as you become aware of them. You should also keep a record of each complaint in a diary, setting out who you spoke to, what you told them, etc. If your landlord does not carry out the repairs within a reasonable period of time, then you must send him or her a formal letter before legal action can begin, setting out the nature of your complaint (what you feel the disrepair is) and what repair works you require to be done which you feel have not been, even though you have asked. At this stage, you should also make a note of any compensation you think you are entitled to as a result, which you can calculate by looking at how much your rent is, and what percentage of it you feel you should not have had to paid because of the level of disrepair – the third bullet point below gives an example of how you can calculate this).

If the landlord still does not respond, you may wish to issue proceedings in the County Court. You will need to prove that:

- There is some disrepair to something that the landlord is obliged to repair. In some cases, this will be obvious (for example, a photo of a hole in the wall), but in most disrepair cases, it is necessary to obtain a report from a surveyor or environmental health consultant, which can incur significant costs to you.

- The landlord has been given notice of the disrepair and has failed to rectify it. This is why it is important to keep records of things like who you complained to, and
- You have suffered loss and damage. This can take the form of damage to items (for example, clothes damaged by water penetration), additional living costs (such as increased heating bills because the property was damp, or take-away food bills because it wasn't safe to cook), and loss of enjoyment of the property (this is generally easiest to explain as a proportion of the rent; so if the rent is £1,000 per month, but the kitchen and bathroom were uninhabitable owing to disrepair, then you might seek 'damages' (compensation) of £600 per month, representing the difference between the rental value of the property and the actual value, given its condition).

If the works are still not carried out then you should also seek to achieve an injunction requiring the landlord to do them.

In certain circumstances, disrepair claims are still eligible for legal aid. In addition, many solicitors undertake disrepair cases on a 'no win, no fee' basis, however, you should always be clear before entering any such arrangement, what fee you will be expected to pay should you win the case.

Bankruptcy and debt law

If you cannot repay the debts that you owe, you may be made bankrupt. This is a formal process administered by the court, and will mean that (with some exceptions) your existing debts are wiped out, but your assets are taken away to meet those debts.

The most common situations in which you can be made bankrupt are at the request of someone to whom you owe money (called a 'creditor's petition') and at your own request (a 'debtor's petition').

When a Bankruptcy Order (an Order from the court, making you officially bankrupt) is made, a person, called the 'Official Receiver', who is a public servant, or in some cases a 'trustee', is appointed to collect the money and other things you own (but not the basics you need for everyday life) and to pay your creditors. For example, if you own your home, the Official Receiver / trustee might sell it. During your bankruptcy, there will be some limits on what you can do ('bankruptcy restrictions'), for example you cannot be a company director and you may need to tell certain people that you are bankrupt. For the year after you are made bankrupt, the Official Receiver / trustee has the right to claim certain income that you earn to pay your existing debts. However, after the expiry of that period, you are discharged (released) from your state of bankruptcy which will mean that you are free, with some exceptions, from your old debts.

For some, bankruptcy represents the only way that they will free themselves from debts which they will never be able to repay. However, it is not the easy answer to debt problems. If you own your home, bankruptcy will normally mean that you lose it, which means that your family may be forced to move. In addition, a Bankruptcy Order will seriously impact your ability to raise money in the future, and former bankrupts can find it impossible to get a mortgage, credit card or unsecured loan, or sometimes even to open a bank account.

Bankruptcy is a very technical area of law, and procedure is important. Judges understand that it is difficult, and will try very hard to help people representing themselves in court. Help is available, both for a fee and for free, for example, from your local Citizens Advice Bureau, www.gov.uk/bankruptcy, the National Debtline (www. nationaldebtline.co.uk) or StepChange (www.stepchange. org). Some organisations will offer to help you without an upfront fee (sometimes they advertise on the radio or the internet), but if you do speak to such companies, you should **always** ask whether there will be further fees at a later date.

If you are facing any type of debt problem, it is very important that you get help at an early stage. Many people with debt problems put their head in the sand and seek help at the last minute, when it may be too late to sort things out.

Debtor's petitions – bankruptcy at your own request

Bankruptcy should be a last resort. You should first consider asking those who you owe money to for some time to pay them back. In addition, there are various formal mechanisms for ring-fencing your debts such as 'Debt Relief Orders' and individual voluntary arrangements.

If you are still struggling with your debts, you can ask the court to 'declare you bankrupt'. You can get the forms that you need from: www.gov.uk/bankruptcy/applying-for- bankruptcy. Many people complete the process on their own, but get some, often free, advice along the way. It is very important that you complete the form accurately and truthfully, because inaccurate or untruthful answers can have very serious consequences. If you are made bankrupt, the trustee will look very carefully at anything you did with your assets in the years leading up to the bankruptcy, in particular if you have recently paid off debts to friends or family, or given money or assets away.

Creditor's petitions – at the request of someone you owe money

The process is relatively complicated so you should try to get help if you can. There are in essence two stages if a creditor wants to make you bankrupt.

1. In the first stage, the creditor must show that you are unable to pay your debts. There are two ways a creditor can show this:
   a. If they send you a 'Statutory Demand' (an official letter telling you how much you owe and giving you 21 days to pay), and you do not pay or have the demand 'set aside' (see below), or
   b. If they obtain a court Order against you specifying the amount of the debt and they are unable to get you to pay. Some creditors do both and obtain a court Order first and then serve a Statutory Demand.
2. Once the creditor has completed the first stage, the second stage is that the creditor can start a 'Bankruptcy Petition' at court (this is a request to the court to make you bankrupt).

Legal problems can be very emotionally draining. Try to remain calm and be civil with the other party and respectful of the judge and all others present in court.

The Statutory Demand

If the creditor has served you with a Statutory Demand, you are entitled to go to the Bankruptcy Court to ask to have it set aside, if:

- The creditor owes you an equal or higher amount of money
- You have substantial grounds for saying that the debt is not due (if you agree that part of the debt is due, you should pay that part)
- The creditor holds enough security (for example, a charge over your house; although the creditor can choose to give up this security if they wish), or
- There are other important grounds that mean the demand should be set aside.

If you have a defence to the debt (a reason why you have debts, but do not have to pay the amount claimed), then you should apply to set aside the Statutory Demand. It is always far better to run a defence at the Statutory Demand stage rather than the Bankruptcy Petition stage. If you fight at the Statutory Demand stage and lose, you have a short period in which to pay the debt before the creditor can start a Bankruptcy Petition. Once the Bankruptcy Petition starts, a notice will be placed on the Land Registry in relation to any property you own. This means that if you fight and lose at the Bankruptcy Petition stage, you might find it very difficult to raise finance to pay the debt.

Decide what your position is in the very beginning: if, for example, you ask for time to pay, it is difficult to say later on that you dispute the debt. Be sensible about the arguments you make: if you argue bad points, the creditor's costs will increase and that will increase the debt that you have to pay. In many bankruptcy cases, the legal costs exceed the value of the debt, so if you fight a debt that you could afford to pay and you lose, you could find yourself facing a Costs Order you are unable to pay. Try to look at the case objectively and critically. For example, you may have run up large credit card debts because of personal problems. That does not mean that you do not have to pay the debt, but you could try explaining the situation to the credit card company and asking for time to pay. The court will usually give you time to pay if you feel you can, and if you do not have a good defence, it is usually better to try to negotiate time to pay than to argue bad points and lose.

If you choose to apply to the court, you should do so within **18 days** of being served with the demand. The Statutory Demand will tell you how you can apply to the court. If possible, though, you should try to speak to your creditor first to try to come to some agreement.

If the Statutory Demand is based on a court Order (for example, a County Court judgment or Magistrates' Court liability Order for council tax), the Bankruptcy Court will not hear arguments about whether there was a defence to the underlying debt. In those circumstances you should apply to the appropriate court (not the Bankruptcy Court) to set aside or appeal the underlying court Order, and you should get advice on whether to apply to set aside the Statutory Demand. The Bankruptcy Court may allow you time to pursue an appeal or an application to set aside the Order, but it will usually need to see some evidence that you are taking the appropriate steps, and be advised of progress. Be prepared to show the court copies of the documents relating to your application or appeal and to advise the Bankruptcy Court of any future Hearing dates.

The Bankruptcy Petition

A creditor can present a petition only if:

- You owe a definite amount payable either now or sometime in the future
- You owe £750 or more
- You cannot pay the debt, and
- You have not applied to set aside a statutory demand sent to you in connection with the debt.

If you have not applied to set aside the statutory demand, the creditor can present the Bankruptcy Petition 21 days after the Statutory Demand is served on you.

If the creditor moves on to the second stage (Bankruptcy Petition), you can still defend the claim and the grounds of defence are essentially the same (although there are some procedural defences too). Again, if the claim is based on a court Order, and you have a defence, you should apply to set aside or appeal that court Order. If you have previously applied to set aside the Statutory Demand and lost, you cannot run the same points in defence of the Bankruptcy Petition.

Hearings of applications to set aside Statutory Demands and Bankruptcy Petition Hearings

Applications to set aside Statutory Demands and disputed Bankruptcy Petitions are generally dealt with by the courts in the same way. You will be permitted to attend court to make representations to the judge but the judge will expect all of the evidence to be given to the court, in writing, in advance of the Hearing. There are two main forms of evidence that the court will consider: **underlying documents** (such as letters, emails, bank statements, agreements) and **witness statements** in which those involved in the dispute set out their version of events. Each side can decide what evidence they want to put in and you should think carefully about who had first-hand experience of the issues in dispute and who could support your case. You should also try very hard to pull together the relevant documents and this may mean trying to get copies from other people if they are not in your possession. All of this work must be done well in advance of the Hearing.

In an application to set aside a Statutory Demand, you will need to give the court what you can when you issue the application, but given you should lodge the application within 18 days of being served with the demand, it can be very difficult to get everything together in that time period. The court will normally in those cases give you a further opportunity to put more evidence in. In a Bankruptcy Petition case, the judge will set a timetable for the parties to prepare their evidence. In both types of cases, the court will expect you, at the time that you give it to the court, to send your evidence to the creditor. The creditor will also have to send their evidence to you.

It is very important to remember that the Bankruptcy Court does not hear oral evidence from witnesses and so, if you have a point to make based on the facts, you should do this in a witness statement (i.e. written, not spoken). Remember, as the first sections of this Guide note, you have to have given the court and the other party copies of all your documents in advance, as the court will not normally be willing to hear your version of the facts for the first time, in court.

In cases where there is a dispute over whether the Statutory Demand or the Bankruptcy Petition was served (given or sent to you), the practice is slightly different. In those cases, you should still raise your defence and send your written evidence to the court in advance, however, at the Hearing, the court will want to hear oral evidence on the question of service (from you and the person who claims to have served you). In these circumstances, the court will allow for both of you to be cross-examined on your evidence at the Hearing.

Be cautious about taking points on the service of the Statutory Demand or the Bankruptcy Petition. Both are meant to be personally served but there are a number of circumstances in which the creditor will be permitted to serve the document by another method (such as post). It is possible that the creditor complied with the court rules on service even though the document may not have come to your attention. If you are thinking about challenging service, it is worth remembering that it is very common for service to be disputed and judges generally take a lot of persuasion that a person was not served. In addition, raising a dispute over service is likely to increase the costs, and you will have to bear those costs if you are unsuccessful in persuading the court that you were not served. You should also remember that errors in service (and other procedural errors) can usually be corrected so generally the only advantage in taking procedural points is that you delay the pursuit of the creditor's claim.

Payment of the debt

Even if you think that you have a good defence to a creditor's claim against you, you should always think carefully about whether it makes sense to try to reach an agreement with the creditor. You should also be aware that there are cost consequences of disputing the creditor's claim at court. If you apply to set aside a Statutory Demand or dispute the creditor's Bankruptcy Petition and are unsuccessful then the court is likely to order that you pay the creditor's legal costs. These can run into thousands or even tens of thousands of pounds. In some cases, the legal costs will far exceed the value of the underlying debt. This may mean that whilst you may have been in a position to pay the underlying debt, you cannot afford to pay the legal costs as well. A failure to pay legal costs ordered by the court can itself be used as a basis for a Bankruptcy Order so you should think very carefully about the merits of your position before disputing the creditor's claim at court.

In cases where the level of the creditor's claim is close to the £750 threshold, you could pay part of the debt to reduce the debt below that level as that will then mean that the creditor cannot bring a Bankruptcy Petition against you.

Once a Bankruptcy Order is made

If you are made bankrupt, it is very important that you cooperate with the Official Receiver or the trustee in charge of your bankruptcy.

There are two possible bases for applying to annul (cancel) a Bankruptcy Order. You can apply either because you feel that there are good reasons for saying the Bankruptcy Order should not have been made, or because you have paid or secured all of your debts (not just the amount you owed to the creditor who made you bankrupt). If you apply to annul on the first basis, the grounds (reasons) are largely the same as if you were disputing the Bankruptcy Petition before the Bankruptcy Order was made, and you will need to organise your evidence in the same way and the guidance set out above should be helpful. If you apply to annul on the second basis, you will need to give the court full disclosure of all your debts and provide evidence that they have all been paid or secured ahead of the Hearing. Applications on the second basis are particularly difficult. You should try to get specialist advice if you apply to annul on either basis.

You must act quickly if you wish to annul, because the bankruptcy costs will start to add up. You can ask the Official Receiver or trustee if they will hold off from working on the bankruptcy while you make an application to the court, but you must still cooperate with them. If your application does not succeed, you are likely to face a further costs Order. This will fall outside the bankruptcy and would mean that you had a new debt to pay.

The trustee may seek to sell your home. This is a difficult area of law, and you should seek specialist advice.

Sometimes, a challenge is made to the fees charged by the trustee. If you wish to make such a challenge, you should also seek specialist help, because this is a difficult area of law. A trustee's fees will often seem high, but a challenge will not necessarily succeed.

Glossary of terms

Addressing the court. This is usually by way of invitation by a judge who will invite a party or representative to make a speech or to respond to something the court has raised. Whenever an advocate or a party speaks to those hearing the case during the course of the hearing they will be described as addressing the court. Other individuals at a hearing are more likely just to give evidence through the medium of their witness statements or by answering questions about their evidence. An advocate's speech may be made both at the start and the end of a hearing. At the start they may be invited to outline for the court the basis of their client's case or claim. We will look at closing speeches below.

Adjourning. Putting a date back which the court has already fixed for a hearing to take place. A decision to adjourn can only be made by the court or tribunal and could in theory take place at any stage either in the prior stages, in the preparation for a hearing, or during the hearing itself. A party can ask for an adjournment for whatever reason but cannot force the decision on to the court.

Being minded or being of a mind. This expression is sometimes used by judges to indicate how their thinking is going and in what direction in relation to a particular issue. It is sometimes used by lawyers in discussing cases with their clients or with other lawyers.

Being without instructions. This refers to a lawyer or representative who cannot take any steps on behalf of their client as they have no instructions from the client to do so. If a representative in court is without instructions there is nothing they can do. Where they have placed themselves on the court record as representing a client they do need formally to inform the court if their instructions from that client cease, whether in writing in advance of a hearing or at the hearing itself.

Closing speech. A closing speech is given by a party's representative in a court or tribunal. The representative will be addressing the court. They will have prepared that speech before the hearing and will then need to adapt it to the way the evidence has gone. It will be a speech summing up the evidence and highlighting for the judge or jury the best analysis of that evidence in order to argue that their clients' case is the one which should succeed. We referred in chapter 11 on advocacy to the preparation of this final speech as preparing submissions. See below also for making submissions.

Cor (Coriam – 'cor-ee-am'). This Latin word will appear at the foot of a barrister's brief when they record the outcome of a hearing. When that brief is handed back to the adviser who has asked the barrister to attend they will see the word Cor, meaning 'in the presence of' and the name of the judge who heard the case.

Costs in the cause. In the main civil system, costs applications may be made prior to the completion of a hearing. If a judge is unwilling to commit to a costs order at an early stage, he or she may order that all costs will ultimately be borne by the party whom the trial judge orders to pay costs. The question of who pays the costs therefore is decided at the end of the case and earlier costs orders of 'costs in the cause' are added to that party's requirement to pay. As previously indicated, costs in the court system are complex but relevant, and people using the court system will need to be aware of their application, of which this is just one example.

Counsel. This simply refers to a barrister representative but is often used in the third person in the context of a court hearing (eg 'Counsel may wish to make an application to deal with this matter').

Ex parte ('ex-pah-tey'). This Latin expression refers to applications as well as hearings which a judge hears and where only one party is required to attend. A typical example will be an application heard by a judge in a matrimonial or childcare context with only one of the parties being present. Since the introduction of the Civil Procedure Rules (CPR) courts are meant to refer to 'without notice' applications or hearings and the phrase 'on the application of X' is more commonly used.

Executing. This word is used in a range of different contexts in court parlance. It means 'carrying out' or 'putting into effect'. It can be used to mean that a person with a judgment against them might have their goods seized (executing a writ or court order to seize goods). It is also used to describe the process of writing out a person's will (executing a will).

Finding for or against. This expression is sometimes used when a legal representative is discussing a point they are making in court. They may put the point on the basis that the judge may decide in their favour or not. This will be known as a finding. At the end of a case the judge will find for one party or another. A finding can also be made on part of an issue being tried. So the judge might find that the defendant owed the claimant some money but not the actual amount claimed.

First open date. When a court decides either to list a case or to adjourn a hearing they will usually refer to the first open date, meaning the first date when the court staff will be able to allocate that case to a judge for a hearing.

Judgment. At the end of a formal hearing the decision maker, if they are a judge, will always come to a decision known as a judgment. Note how this word is spelled in this context. They can 'hand this down' which means that the parties' representatives in a hearing are asked to come along at a later date and be handed it or have it read out to them by the judge or judges. Tribunals will often instead make a **decision** where they have heard an appeal against an administrative decision. Judges and tribunals can also make less final decisions such as **orders** or **directions.**

Inter alia ('inter-ay-lee-ah'). This means 'among other things' and will be used both in court and in court pleadings (see below) to make it clear that this item is one of a number. For example, a landlord may claim that the tenant has caused damage to his property and may refer to the fact that damage was caused, **inter alia**, to the furnishings and fittings.

Making submissions. This is what a representative or a litigant will do when summing up their case at the end of a trial. The submissions will refer to the evidence heard and state how it assists that party's claim. There will also be references to case-law which supports the party's position (see chapter 19).

My (learned) friend. A barrister in court will refer to his or her opponent (representing the other party in the case) who is not themselves a barrister as 'my friend'. When the barrister's opponent is also a barrister they will refer to that person as 'my learned friend'.

Obiter dictum ('oh-bit-er dict-um'). More Latin. This phrase refers to a part of a judgment which is not the main reasoning of the case decision, but is a reference to similar situations or to other cases which are relevant. A judge may decide in favour of one party, applying the law. He or she might then state how the law might apply in similar circumstances. This is not regarded as part of the judgment but is an 'aside' made in the context of giving the judgment.

Opening speech. This is made by a representative who will be leading off with their case in court, either because they are prosecuting a criminal case or because they are claiming against a defendant in a civil case. They will outline the facts briefly, refer to the issues which the judge has to decide on and sometimes, in a civil trial, ensure that the judge is aware of the history of any earlier hearings and has access to all the relevant documents.

Part heard. This is used of a civil case where the hearing has begun but has not been completed and will need to be completed at a later date.

Pleadings. These are the statements made by a claimant and a defendant on the relevant court forms relating to a civil claim. The claimant sets out the facts and the basis of the legal claim which they are bringing, and the way in which the defendant has caused them wrong. The claimant will also state what they are asking the court to do: award them compensation or another remedy. The defendant will write out the ways in which they might be disputing the claim and why. The pleading will form the basis of a civil claim and will be frequently referred to when witnesses are giving evidence in court. They are now usually referred to in the civil court system as 'a statement of case'.

Prima facie ('pry-ma-fay-see'). Latin. This literally means 'at first sight'. It is usually used in the context of looking to see if the evidence in a case will stand up to proof. Is it enough to show that there is a case? For example, if there is a prosecution for burglary, there would have to be some evidence that the accused person was at the premises at the relevant time and took the missing goods. This evidence may be by way of witnesses, security cameras or forensic evidence. If there is no prima facie evidence then there can be no case.

Reasons. This word has a stronger meaning in the context of giving out a decision or judgment at the end of a hearing than in everyday language. It is important for any court or tribunal to give reasons for their decisions so that they can be clearly seen to be properly addressing the case before them and have reached a properly deliberated judgment. A court will find in favour of one party or another and then will go on to give reasons why they have done so, taking into account the evidence heard and applying the relevant law.

Reserved judgment. Sometimes a judge or panel will indicate at the end of a case they have heard that they will not make a decision that day but at a later date and will therefore reserve their judgment which will then be sent out in writing once it is ready or is handed out or read out at a future hearing.

Skeleton arguments. These are an outline of the legal arguments which each party will be making to the judge or panel at the end of the hearing of a case. They are traditionally regarded as being drawn up by barristers. However, in any court or tribunal it will be a useful exercise to prepare to represent a client by drawing up a short document which summarises the law and any previous decided cases which are relevant and helpful to the client's case. The argument then runs through how the facts of the case are supported by the law referred to in favour of that particular party.

Statement of truth. Various documents used in the context of court proceedings will be required to be endorsed by a statement of truth. Some of these used to be known as Affidavits. Relevant documents include a witness statement, an expert's report or a pleading (now usually called 'a statement of case').

The statement of truth should use the following words at the end of a statement of case:

I believe that the facts stated in this document are true.

The statement of truth at the end of a witness statement should say:

I believe that the facts stated in this witness statement are true.

Those instructing [me]. Used by barristers in court to refer to solicitors or other legal advisers who will relay to the barrister what their client would like the barrister to achieve for them. Sometimes it can refer to the client themselves.

Witness statements. A witness statement is either factual as provided by a lay person or that containing an expert's opinion. It should be signed and dated. Prior to giving evidence in a court or tribunal the witness will swear on a holy book (eg the Bible or Koran) or affirm to the court that what they are about to say will be the truth.

Index